MAEVE'S TIMES

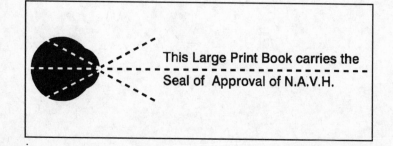

This Large Print Book carries the
Seal of Approval of N.A.V.H.

MAEVE'S TIMES

IN HER OWN WORDS

MAEVE BINCHY

Edited by Róisín Ingle
Introduction by Gordon Snell

THORNDIKE PRESS
A part of Gale, Cengage Learning

GALE
CENGAGE Learning·

Farmington Hills, Mich • San Francisco • New York • Waterville, Maine
Meriden, Conn • Mason, Ohio • Chicago

GALE
CENGAGE Learning®

LIBRARY OF CONGRESS CATALOGING-IN-PUBLICATION DATA

Binchy, Maeve.
[Essays. Selections]
   Maeve's times : in her own words / Maeve Binchy ; edited by Róisín Ingle ;
introduction by Gordon Snell. — Large print edition.
     pages cm. — (Thorndike Press large print basic)
   Selected essays as published in The Irish times over fifty years.
   ISBN 978-1-4104-7390-5 (hardback) — ISBN 1-4104-7390-2 (hardcover)
   1. Large type books. I. Ingle, Róisín editor of compilation. II. Irish times
(Dublin, Ireland : 1874) III. Title.
   PR6052.I7728A6 2014b
   824'.914—dc23
                                              2014035423

Published in 2014 by arrangement with Alfred A. Knopf, Inc., a division
of Random House LLC, a Penguin Random House Company

Printed in the United States of America
1 2 3 4 5 6 7 18 17 16 15 14

NOTE ON MAEVE BINCHY
AND *THE IRISH TIMES*

Maeve Binchy was appointed Women's Editor of *The Irish Times* in October 1968. As a young teacher she had loved both her job and her holiday travels, and had been a favourite contributor since her first travel letter, sent in by her father, was published a few years earlier. On her appointment the then News Editor, the late Donal Foley, declared, 'Won't she be great crack to work with? And she's a brilliant writer!' Both proved true over a career which lasted the best part of fifty years.

Maeve wrote for and edited the daily 'Women First' page until 1973, when she transferred to the London office as a columnist, feature writer and reporter, balancing the day job with her rapidly growing career as a writer of fiction and drama. When Maeve resigned from the staff of *The Irish Times* in the 1980s, she retained her close association with the paper as a regular contributor. Maeve and her husband, Gordon Snell, moved back to Ireland in the early eighties.

CONTENTS

11

INTRODUCTION

From her earliest childhood, Maeve loved stories — and wanted to be part of them. When her father started to read her some tale of two children wandering through a wood, she asked at once, 'Where was I?'

He would say patiently, 'You were sitting in a tree beside the path.' And with Maeve happily located, the story could go on.

When she grew up and became a story-teller herself, she made her readers feel that, like little Maeve in the tree, they were on the scene, among the action and the characters. She did the same in her journalism, writing with on-the-spot directness of the people and events she met with.

It was her father's enthusiasm that led to Maeve becoming a journalist in the first place. As a teacher she used her long holidays to travel all over the world, on cargo ships, cheap flights, trains and hitch-hiking. She worked in school and holiday camps, on a kibbutz, and as a tourist guide, in North America, the Middle East and Asia.

Her father sent some of her long, lively letters home to the newspapers, who published them as articles. That was the start of her career as a columnist — a job she kept doing happily even after she had become a celebrated novelist.

Whether she was observing a couple having an angry but icily polite disagreement, or feeling the panic — including her own — brought on by the trials of air travel, or watching the outlandish fantasies of the fashion industry, she had a unique eye and ear for the quirks, intensities and absurdities of human behaviour.

No wonder her readers were delighted with her — for she told it all with the eagerness and enthusiasm of someone who says: 'Just wait till I tell you what happened . . .' and goes on to tell an enthralling and often hilarious tale.

She brought the same directness to her many serious reports for the paper — on the bombs in London and other cities, the capsized ferry disaster, and the savage war in Cyprus.

Maeve followed the advice she often gave to aspiring writers — to write as you speak. Her view of the world and the people in it was the same in her writing as it was in her life: she was compassionate and perceptive, she treated everyone with the same considerate interest, and her humour was uproarious but never sneering or cruel.

Her capacity for friendship seemed limitless, and hundreds of people from all over the world, who never knew her, have written to say that they thought of her as a friend.

I can almost hear her say, 'That's enough of that! You make me sound like some kind of saint!' Indeed as a schoolgirl, sainthood was a role she considered aiming for, but decided against — partly on the grounds that it could involve martyrdom, but really because it just wasn't her style.

We must all be glad she took on the roles she did, as teacher, writer and friend to so many — and I above all feel specially lucky that we met, and spent so many happy and loving years together.

When I read these articles, stories and reports from *The Irish Times,* I hear her voice and feel she is back with us again, in all the vivacious joy she created around her. In these words, and in her many novels, short stories, plays and films, Maeve lives on — and always will.

Gordon Snell

■ ■ ■ ■

SIXTIES

■ ■ ■ ■

SCHOOL OUTING

29 October 1964

Oddly enough, the horror of a school outing is not the responsibility of looking after other people's children in alien surroundings, nor is it the noise and possibility of them getting out of hand. The real problem is wondering whether they are going to be bored. The outing is so eagerly anticipated, and so much discussed, that it has to be an anti-climax — unless there are a few unexpected delights, like a teacher getting stuck in a hedge, or half of the sixth years being left behind in a chip shop, or someone getting involved with a man.

Of course, the real disaster is collecting the money. How often have I collected 38 times 18s and spent it three times over before the day came when the man in CIÉ had to be paid?

Then there is the likelihood of someone getting sick; far from being able to minister to such unfortunates, I start to get sick myself, which undoubtedly heightens the awfulness for everyone involved. In all the years of hot bus journeys and twisty bends on the roads, and 12-year-olds eating four pounds of sweets in between bags of chips and bottles of Coca-Cola, no one has ever gotten sick, but I can never believe my luck will hold.

We went to Wales recently and to date this was by far the best outing. From the children's point of view it was going to a foreign country — there would be Customs and foot-and-mouth spray on the way home. There would be new, strange Woolworths to investigate, there was a chance to see both the mail boat and the ferry, since we went out by the former and came home by the latter. They could even send postcards to people saying 'spending a little while in Wales' without elaborating that the little while was five hours. There was also Caernarfon Castle, the *raison d'être* of the whole visit, but no one gave that much thought.

From a teacher's point of view, it also had everything to recommend it. It didn't leave at a ridiculous hour in the morning; in fact we only left Dún Laoghaire at eleven-thirty a.m. Once you got them on the boat there was really nothing that could happen to them except the obvious and if that did happen someone would be bound to notice and stop the ship. Exploring the boat took most of the first hour, settling on a place for the mammoth eating of sandwiches brought us up to about two o'clock. Then there was an hour of everyone rubbing themselves with Nivea cream. After this the Welsh coast was sighted and approved of, and we got on to land and into a bus in a matter of minutes.

The bus is a must. Firstly there is nothing whatsoever to do in Holyhead, and if you just bring them out to Bangor to swim, there is all that nightmare of counting them the whole time. Anyway, if they spend the day on a beach, someone is bound to say that they should have saved the 37s and gone to Dollymount. But the bus is very cunning indeed, and anyway, if you have a soul at all, you would want them to see Caernarfon and this is not really feasible without your own bus.

The bus driver was called Fred. He looked as if he might be offended if the children sang in the bus, so I hoped they wouldn't, but I didn't like to forbid it because that sort of singing is all part of the Outing anyway. However, they were quite sensitive about the whole thing, and every time he pointed out an RAF camp, or rock climbers on the mountains, they would pause respectfully in the middle of some terrible song about 'I'm the son of the Hickory Hollow tramp' and listen with interest.

There was enormous and unfeigned interest in the village with the longest name in the world. Pencils and notebooks were out and the bus had to stay beside the signpost until everyone copied down Llanfairpwllgwyngyllgogerychwyrndrobwllllantysiliogogogoch.

Fred, because he could not only spell it, but could also pronounce it, became the hero of the hour.

We only had an hour-and-a-quarter in Caernarfon, so my dissertation from the battlements had to be shorter than I would have liked. But I could see that the lure of the foreign Woolworths and the alien sweets would outweigh too much chat about Edward I and the Welsh Barons, and the one thing you do realise as a teacher is your limitations.

A horror story of the previous week — when apparently a Dublin boys' school had missed the boat home because the bus arrived back too late — so impressed me that I encouraged Fred to speed through the setting sun back to Holyhead; we may have had to forego a few slate quarries on the way, but not even a diamond mine would have seemed worth the risk of having to sleep in a bus with forty schoolgirls and face their parents the next day.

From motives of economy we had an enormous and unlady-like feed of fish and chips in a Holyhead café, then, fragrant with vinegar, we got onto the ferry. The children went out on deck, I went to the bar. Later a deputation came in with faces of doom.

'You're wanted on deck, Miss Binchy,' they announced to the whole bar, and everyone assumed it was probably by the police. I assumed, with even greater fear and certainty, that someone had been sick. In fact, it was only to settle an argument about the Wicklow mountains, which had just come purplishly into view.

For 37s each (only 18s 6d for everyone under 15) plus a sum of £11 for the hire of Fred and his bus, it was a marvellous day. The trouble is, it went so successfully that they are now talking confidently in terms of a trip to France.

JUST PLANE BORES

13 September 1968
The dangers of getting stuck with a bore in a plane considerably outweigh the other

hazards of plane travel. There is no comforting insurance policy against this, however, for what actuary could possibly relate the risks to any practical premium?

I often hear people saying that they sat beside a frightfully interesting chap on a plane, but I just don't believe it. The only people I sit beside are people who read the safety regulations with an intensity that could only come from certainty of disaster. One woman even asked my advice when she came to the bit about removing false teeth during a forced landing.

'Do you think I should take out my crown filling?' she asked me anxiously.

Sometimes, I must admit, I escape these relatively harmless people and I sit beside know-alls, people who wince when the engine sounds change, people who have known better lines, faster jets, classier meals and more certain likelihood of reaching one's destination.

I never met anyone remotely interesting in a plane but I have seen interesting people. I sat behind Kirk Douglas once, and I sat across the aisle from a couple who had the most terrible argument that ended in their throwing drinks at each other and me. I heard a girl complain to the hostess on a flight to New York that Aer Lingus must have lost all sense of shame to let men and women use the same toilets. I was once on a plane where I was the only passenger and sat in a Kafkaesque silence surrounded by empty seats. Risk of boredom at the hands of a passenger was minimal certainly, but it's not usually practical to fly solo, so most of us are stuck with the plane bores for all our flying years.

People have a habit of confiding terrible secrets in planes. They tell things that would in a less rarefied atmosphere remain much more wisely unsaid. A man who told me that he was smuggling 15 watches made me so nervous that I was the one blushing, stammering and hesitating at the airport, and was eventually and very reasonably searched after the performance, while the smuggler ticked his way unconcernedly to the airport bus.

The last time I was coming back from Israel my neighbour sobbed the whole way from Tel Aviv to London, choking out explanations about how badly she had behaved all the summer; she'd never broken the Sabbath she said until she went to Israel, she'd always eaten kosher until she went to Jerusalem. The irony of it. She wept, and I nearly wept with her, but of course when we got to London Airport she had recovered and I was the one who couldn't bear to meet her father's eye as he stood there with his long black beard, he who'd always kept the Sabbath and eaten kosher all his life.

If people are not telling you about their operations, their bank balances, the highly unsatisfactory state of their marriages or how they were cheated by hoteliers, travel agents and the entire population of whatever country you happen to be leaving, then they are inclined to interrogate you about the most intimate details of your life.

'How can a schoolteacher afford to go to Hong Kong for the summer holidays?' rasped a terrible Australian, who was going to be my neighbour for the next 20 hours.

There is no fully satisfactory answer to a question like that, and as I was already afraid that my bank manager could well be waiting on the tarmac in Dublin with the same words on his lips, I couldn't say anything convincing in reply. The Aussie became sour at my refusal to be frank and began a tirade against all Europeans, who were a miserable bankrupt lot altogether — he had no further fodder for this in my uncalled-for explorations.

Europeans always sneered at Australians, he went on, they thought Australians had

26

nothing but beer and going to the beach and sheep stations — he went on, and on, and on. Singapore, Calcutta, Beirut, Vienna — all came and went and we were still talking about the outback and the Aborigines. We were making maps on our plastic trays of food and letting the ice cream be Queensland and the salt be Perth. We nearly came to blows about the hors d'oeuvres. I said it should be Adelaide, he said it was Melbourne and since it was his continent, I let it be Melbourne. But the whole journey was exhausting and I thought longingly of the wonderful journey out which took five weeks, and there was an adventure every single day and nearly 600 people on the ship.

Shortly after this marathon flight I decided that the fault was certainly mine. No one else seemed to have such bad luck and when I read Helen Gurley Brown's book *Sex and the Single Girl* I knew it must be my fault. Planes, she said, are wonderful places for picking up Grade A men. The more international and exciting the flight, the better your chances would be. I had an unworthy suspicion that even the vibrant H. G. Brown would not have made much of old Waltzing Matilda and his White Australia policy, his wallabies and his test match. However, I decided to follow her instructions on the very next flight.

According to *Sex and the Single Girl,* you should get a seat fairly near the front of the plane (if that's how you get into the plane; presumably if it's one of the ones where you climb in through the tail, you should sit near the back). Then leave a great big handbag on the seat beside you. At the approach of other women or Grade Z men you leave the bag there, but when a Grade A man approaches you whip the bag from the seat and stare straight ahead.

Once the Grade A man is installed you must establish contact by fumbling over your safety belt and the intention is to entangle yourself and the man in a knot from which with much tinkling laughter you both extricate yourselves, and such splendid rapport having been made he offers you a refined cocktail once you are airborne, and things progress from there.

I'll say this for *S and the SG,* the beginning part works like a dream. A man like Marlon Brando sat down beside me; the belt business was a fiasco because he started to fumble with his belt at the same time, and whatever way we seemed to do it we had to call the air hostess to disentangle us from the muddle. She took so long that I thought she was going to send for an acetylene torch. Anyway calm was restored and we were airborne. All around us people were clicking cigarette lighters and ordering refined cocktails, but the false Marlon Brando was staring straight ahead. It turned out that he was absolutely terrified of flying; all that business about the safety belt was the last straw and he seemed on the verge of having a very loud and serious fit. Determined to avoid this at all costs, I bought him a Scotch, the worst possible thing I should have done apparently, but it calmed him and he went to sleep almost at once on my shoulder.

Now the journey from London to Gibraltar is very short, and although it is undoubtedly good for the morale to have a handsome man asleep in my arms — I smiled pityingly at all the people who passed by, who had no man at all — it did present grave problems when we got to the Rock. He just wouldn't wake up. One of the hostesses thought he was dead but the other said he was just unconscious so I had to stay around for what was going to be either a revival or an inquest. I missed my bus to Malaga, I had to deal with Marlon Brando's business partner who fortunately came to collect him, there was much face slapping, and 'wake up Pete old man'. Nobody believed me when I said he was afraid of flying but everyone agreed that to feed a highly strung man like Pete Scotch whiskey was a most foolish and suspect course of action.

So whenever I hear about the excitement and glamour of air travel I'm inclined to be a little cynical and I look forward to the day when we'll have either single rows of seats, or compulsory films that must be watched in silence by the whole plane load, or better still, the sort of club car, Pullman lounges that you see in American films, where you can talk to everyone. Until then, we'll just continue to belt ourselves in two by two or three by three and bore each other to death at altitudes of thousands of feet, flying hundreds of miles an hour all round the world.

BUT DOES ANYBODY CARE?

1 January 1969

Perhaps it matters to you that Hull is 226 miles from Brighton and that there are 40 poles (or perches) to the rood. I feel that if you had started out on the road to Hull you'd have a roadmap or the signposts anyway, and if for some extraordinary reason you were lying down on the ground measuring things in roods and perches, it would all be written on the measuring tape.

Anyone going back to Oxford this month *knows* that the Hilary Term starts on January 19th and no one else will be at a disadvantage by not knowing; and since neither the March nor September eclipses of the sun will be visible from Greenwich, why torment us by telling us about them?

I must say that I find it very disagreeable indeed to open my diary on New Year's Day and find pages of advice about poisoning, shock and wounds. Choking, in particular, is very loathsome.

Would anyone remember 'to dislodge obstruction, bend head and shoulders forward and in case of small child, hold upside down then thump between shoulder blades' — just because the eye happened to light on this one day when looking for a telephone number?

The advice is not all that practical, either. Severe Case of Cramp usually sets in when you are standing in a bus, and you can't very well 'take hold of foot and turn toes firmly upward until spasm has passed'. And in the case of poisoning by mouth, how on earth are most people to neutralise acid poisoning by administering *chalk*?

This year's diary seems loath to leave any

space at all for what I hope will be my own memorable activities, so full is it of ridiculous information. Sandwiched between the telephone number you should call in Upavon if you want the weather forecast and a useless page giving the equivalent American and Continental clothes sizings (but admitting sadly that it is always best to try on the article before buying it) there is a type of Bon Viveur guide to wine, compiled by the Wine and Food Society. Everything gets a mark from 0 to 7; 0 equals 'no good' and 7 'the best', it says simply. Apart from the interesting historical question it raises for the amateur — who must wonder whether it was drought or storms or strikes in the vineyard that made 1956 a poor starter — surely no one is going to take it seriously, and whip it out for consultation while the wine waiter hovers?

Then there is the page marked 'my car' with all kinds of spaces for numbers of boot key, of ignition key, of chassis and insurance policy. To my mind, the type of person who would fill all this in is also the type who keeps a leather-bound log book in the glove compartment with the same details lovingly inscribed. He probably calls the car 'she' and knows everything by heart anyway.

Yet into this whole field of bushels and

pecks, centigrade and Fahrenheit, Lammas Day being August 1st and the sun rising at 9.05 a.m. next Saturday, Queen Elizabeth the Queen Mother being born on August 4th, 1900, and Ramadan facing us on November 22nd, has come a new challenge — the Special Interest diary. Not only the schoolboy, the businessman and the lady are catered for now, but a whole range of unlikely diarists from the filmgoer to the gardener, the photographer, the motorcyclist, the electrical engineer and the handyman.

It certainly seems more reasonable to gear a diary to someone's job or hobby than to assume that everyone in the world is going to be interested in the Golden Number, the Dominical Letters and the Epact, whatever the Epact may be. Last year it was nought, and this year they forgot it, thankfully, in my particular diary.

Still, the specialised diaries have problems of their own. Would you rather carry around pages of advice about planting and pruning, or handy hints on slapping crows' feet away from your eyes? You'll have to make up your mind whether you are a lady first or a gardening enthusiast, or else buy two diaries. Perhaps they might organise detachable pages of information and you could make up personal diaries for your friends out of all of them: for the golfer — business-man — Catholic — music radio ham, for example. It has endless possibilities.

The main idea of a diary, in case you have lost sight of it, is to provide some open space. From years of catastrophe with the page-a-day ones, I've now settled for a week between two pages, so that Sunday is always on the top left-hand corner. In the excite-ment of all those empty pages you think that you can fill a page a day easily, but by Janu-ary 11th the whole thing has become im-practical. Pages glare at you in empty ac-cusation, two pages stick together and you completely forget to do something that you'd written in in red ink — there are pitfalls all the way with the page-a-day kind, unless you are aged 14 and have something to say to yourself.

What do people write in diaries anyway? I remember seeing a television programme quite a long time ago, about children's diaries, and the kind of things they put in them. Apparently there was a relentless litany of 'Got up, got dressed, went to school', broken only by the triumphant but shaky hand of the mumps or measles victim: 'Didn't get up, didn't go to school.' They seemed to be obsessed with what the teachers wore; whether or not they liked them was quite immaterial to the interest in professional garb. Very few children's diaries carried on in February. I can never quite regard mine as just an appointment book, and I feel a terrible urge to put in happenings and comments. I know it is both foolish and dangerous, particularly for someone who loses a diary so regularly.

But after I discovered that in my indiscreet days I entered for Saturday, July 27th, 1963: 'This was one of the best days in my life,' and now I can't remember why, I thought that whatever the risk, names and places must be brought back again.

Actually, if you do put a bit of your life into your diary you are much more likely to get it back when you lose it than if you just list letters to write and how you spent your money. I'm sure it's not the fact that I have written 'Large financial reward for finder' on mine that makes people post it to me or ring me and arrange a personal delivery, because no one except an unpleasant schoolboy ever accepted the reward. I even telephoned the police in Pearse Street once to say that I'd left it in a phone box in Westmoreland Street, and could they ever ask any Garda who was passing to look and see was it there? As if this was the most normal request for Gardaí in that area, they agreed and I collected it, red-faced, from the station next day.

I'd even thought of bringing my diary to the Income Tax Commission in support of an appeal if necessary, but it's probably just as well that it hasn't been, yet. Even though there is lots of evidence of legitimate spending that no one would have had the energy to fake, there are all the other things as well which might take from the seriousness of the situation.

So, like the man who made his money not out of the mustard eaten but by what people leave on their plates, diary publishers never really care whether or not we are faithful in our New Year's resolve to record the happenings of 1969. Until they invent diaries that come in shorter editions at more frequent intervals, they have nothing to worry about. While disclaiming any responsibility for errors, they can continue to blind us with information which we mentally note as certain to be useful while we leap through it, looking for the cheerful space about whom to notify in case of accident.

A Turkish Bath

12 May 1969

I didn't believe that anything could cost only £1 in The Dorchester, it is not the kind of place that you expect to get much change from a fiver even if you were buying a drink. But they were right, the Turkish bath is only £1 and if you lose all sense of proportion and decide to have a massage as well it comes to £2. The porter nodded understandingly and approvingly when I asked him for directions to the Place; he didn't quite say that he thought it an excellent idea on my part, but he certainly implied that it was a much wiser way of using The Dorchester than joining the ladies who were having morning coffee and sticky cakes in the lounge.

Down a carpeted stairs to a receptionist who takes your name and hands you to a further receptionist in a white coat. 'Do I pay now?' I asked ignorantly, but this was all brushed aside with embarrassment, and indeed it *was* foolish, I suppose, to think that they have to take the money from you on the way in. Few people would have the courage to leave by a back entrance minus their clothes just to avoid paying £1. I was shown to a cubicle, given a key to a great big chest and asked to deposit not only my valuables, but also my clothes in this, given a huge white towel that would have swamped Finn MacCool, a pair of rubber sandals that wouldn't have fitted Madame Butterfly and led towards the Room.

The Room looked like something from a film set. There were about two dozen armchairs dotted around, all covered with snow-white towels. There was an alarming notice that said SILENCE in huge letters, and there was one occupant that looked as if she were dead in one of the chairs. The assistant led me to a chair, and said that I should stay there for about ten minutes before going into the heat. As I was already wondering if my heart had stopped beating from the temperature we were in, I asked was this not the heat, but she said disapprovingly that this was just the warm room and went away.

I sat nervously and self-consciously in the towel-covered chair. There wasn't a move from the corpse in the other one, and just as I was going to call the assistant and report the first fatal casualty of the day, it moved and said languidly, 'You should have brought something to read you know, it would make you more relaxed, and you would sweat more.' The possibility of going back to the newsstand in the foyer garbed as I was did not recommend itself, so we called the assistant and asked for some reading matter that would help me to relax and sweat. She brought the *Daily Mirror*. .

In no time at all it was time to move from what was called euphemistically the warm room, towards the Heat. The Heat was a tiled room with slotted benches around it, a bit like what I think a men's lavatory might look like. Suddenly the warm room seemed cool as a mountain stream. The corpse hadn't come with me, so I prepared to meet new friends. There was again one occupant, the thinnest woman I have ever seen in my life, wrapped from armpit to knee, not in a nice clinical towel, but in a red rubber sheet. The notice SILENCE was there again, but I thought I would die if I didn't know why she was wearing the sheet, so I risked it. 'It's better for sweating,' she said definitively, 'much better.'

It turned out she liked talking, so we agreed to waive the rules until someone else came in. She went there every week, when she came up to London to do the shopping. Sometimes she stayed for three hours and didn't ever get around to the shopping, but it didn't matter because most things could be delivered, even these days. She was surprised I hadn't thought of bringing a rubber sheet. It was great for getting all the impurities out of the body; she looked reflectively up into the clouds of steam, as if she could see them wafting away. I looked nervously, too, wondering where they would land.

We were joined by two chubby American teenagers, who didn't want to have a Turkish bath at all, but their mother had been appalled at how thin everyone was in England, and since they were staying at the hotel she had sent them down to the Heat for the morning. Momma was at this moment probably eating spoonfuls of something fantastic in Fortnum & Masons, they grumbled. They wanted to be outside seeing London. One of them complained that she was taking creative writing at school, and she wanted to have something to write about when she got back.

'You could always write about this,' I said helpfully.

'Who'd wanna read about this?' she said reasonably.

It was all-change time again soon. A woman wearing a black bathing suit came in and called me by name to follow her. 'Good luck,' said the Yanks gloomily. We went into a place resembling a clean abattoir with trestle tables and many taps and drains. I thought in my stupidity that this was the massage, but in fact it was what is known as the rub down, and incidentally is included in the £1.

The rub down consisted of the woman in the bathing togs asking me to lie naked on a trestle table while she took what could only have been a pot scourer and scrubbed every inch of me. I was afraid to look at anywhere she rubbed twice in case seven layers of skin would have disappeared forever. Then she took what must have been a giant shaving brush and lather and washed it all over again. Then there was a hose of warm water, which was nice, but lastly I had to stand up and be hosed with cold water, which was not nice. I was led back to my cubicle and told that the masseuse would come for me shortly, but to have a little nap.

What seemed like two days later, when I woke from the deepest sleep I have ever known, the masseuse was there; on with the mad sandals and the huge towel, and off to a part of the building where there was a swimming pool surrounded by cubicles that looked like well-equipped stables. 'Swim about a little, but don't talk,' I was told, which seemed an unnecessary caution, since there was no one to talk to, but perhaps some people, a little unnerved by all that scouring and heat, *do* in fact talk to themselves.

The solitary silent and stark naked swim being over, and I can't think when I felt so foolish in my whole life, we went into one of the stables, and I had the best massage possible. I can't remember what the woman's name was, though I did write it down at the time, but you couldn't miss her. She had been there for years, apparently, and is very much in demand. I only got her by accident.

On questioning, I told her how much I earned, why I was in London, whether I was in love, the state of the Irish economy, what I thought of Enoch Powell, and advised her where to go on her holidays. She told me what she earned, the famous people she had massaged, a very exciting story about a film star, 'no names mentioned, of course', how the type of person had changed over the years in The Dorchester, and that I should have a massage every day, and never eat again in my life. We had a lovely time and I was very sorry when the hour was up.

Back to the cubicle again, yet another deep sleep, a cup of tea, three cigarettes, and I got dressed. Taking the money at the door seemed to be a severe embarrassment to the receptionist, but we managed it, and I left The Dorchester three hours after I had gone in, feeling better than I have ever felt in my life. All the cares and woes of the Ideal Homes Exhibition were long forgotten, I had lost three pounds in weight and only two in money. It's about the best value in London.

Life as a Waitress

30 June 1969
The worst thing about life as a waitress was the Out door; it was only rivalled by the In door. One small miscalculation with either and you were on the floor with a tray of broken everything. If it happened in the dining room, the Wing Commanders and the Flight Lieutenants were so mortified that they all looked away and pretended it hadn't happened. If the crash came in the kitchen, there was more help, but considerably more abuse as well. The head waiter would repeat for the hundredth time that these damn students were more trouble than help, and the evil man who brought the vegetables would remind everyone of the time some unfortunate from St Andrew's had got his foot caught in the dishwasher and the wash-

ing up had to be done by hand for three weeks.

I was there for eight weeks, eight years ago, and I earned £10 a week and my keep. My keep must have been worth another ten, because we all ate huge meals both before and after the meal we were serving, and lived in palatial rooms, where we demanded new releases for the record player every week. We were miles from the nearest town, which was good, as there was no chance of spending all the Big Money we earned, and there were a hundred ways, most of them respectable, of increasing one's wages.

The greatest problem after the doors was the Catering Manager, who had an unfortunate phrase: 'I'm not a church-going man myself, but I know what's what.'

This was invariably said when the occasion least called for it, and we were all puzzled by its significance. He said it to me when I arrived, and as I had done nothing yet except stammer that I would work very hard, it was rather a blow. He followed it up by warning me sternly that the men didn't *marry* the waitresses and said that I might laugh now, but many of my countrywomen were laughing on the other side of their faces at the expense of the National Health. It was not an auspicious start.

But I soon got quite good at it all. There were all kinds of new things to learn, like how to carry seven plates without spilling the gravy and not resting three of them on my chest. There was no little crook in my wrist to balance them like everyone else seemed to have, but I practised and found that if you put everything on top of each other regardless and gave them a quick wipe before putting them down it was the best. All the rest of the waitresses wore powder-blue nylon overalls, but there wasn't one that would fit me and allow me to appear in public. So I wore a dignified restrained navy dress of my own, and everyone thought I was the manageress, and made complaints about 50-year-old waitresses who had been there all their working lives. I accepted these complaints regally and did nothing about them.

It was very hard not to join in people's conversations. I was severely reprimanded for contradicting a student, who said he had landed beautifully that morning on the airstrip. When I told him very truthfully that everyone in two miles' radius had thrown themselves on the ground at his approach, there was consternation.

'You must know what's what,' said the Catering Manager disapprovingly. 'I hope I won't have to mention this again.'

There was a lot of dishonesty in the kitchen, which was as pointless as it was professional. Everyone was well paid and reasonably happy, but the stealing seemed to be a way of life. There were three dust-bins, but one of them wasn't a real dustbin. Every time we used a dozen bottles of tomato juice or a dozen anything, in fact, one bottle was put in the false dustbin and a mysterious man came every week and sold it all. We got about £1 14s each from the profits, and I was warned sternly that if I didn't like it I was to shut up about it, because there had been a bit of trouble one year over a student. He had behaved fool-ishly, and instead of giving the money to a charity like any normal well-heeled student should have done, he wrote a series of let-ters to everyone, including the Catering Manager, who had been very upset, and this was partly responsible for his strange at-titudes and limited vocabulary ever since.

I learned, among other things, that you must never send a knife or fork back because it is dirty. This only resulted in extreme indignation, plus class and racist remarks about it being far from clean forks that the clientèle were reared. The usual method of cleaning the offending fork was to rub it in the under-chef's hair. His oily head gave it an unparalleled shine, and the complainer ate his dinner, happy to have scored a point, with a piece of cutlery that shone with brilliance, oil and dandruff.

I hated the way we were told to recommend the food that was going off in the kitchen. At a briefing council before lunch we would be told that kidney stew wouldn't last another hour; it was to be proffered, suggested and even brought in error to anyone who looked as if they might eat it. It was a nightmare to ask those innocent boys, whose stomachs were already turning over at the thought of flying that afternoon, to eat something that we in the kitchen had rejected automatically. The pink blancmange was about the most revolting of all, and I think the only Reserved Sin I ever committed knowingly was to tell a weedy-looking Scot that blancmange was the best thing known to man for building muscles, and he would wolf it down obediently every day.

Sometimes I went for a flight in an aeroplane. The students and air people (the ones who never married the waitresses) were occasionally at their wits' end for entertainment, and when all else failed would fly me to Cambridge for afternoon tea. They thought it was very jolly of me to be a waitress, and hoped that our economy would recover sufficiently to let me get work at home soon. I made up terrible lying stories about having worked in Kilburn, but moving to the country to meet a nicer class of person, and they were delighted with me.

One of the respectable ways of earning more money was to work in the bar at night. I did this once with disastrous results. You got £3 for the four and a half hours, and, since my only other diversions were having my hair permed into what looked like a Brillo soap pad by the other waitresses, I thought the bar seemed a great plan. I must be the only person who ever lost over £5 by having to work there.

Firstly, I didn't understand about the tips. When people said 'have a drink yourself' I beamed with pleasure and gratitude, and refused every drink virtuously on the grounds that I was a bit busy. I never thought of putting two shillings into a glass jar on the shelf, which was what they meant me to do. Then I didn't know how to work the automatic stopper on the spirit bottles, and a whole bottle of Gordon's gin flowed down the sink. Worse still, I couldn't keep up with the washing of glasses and had to send a fevered message to the evil vegetable man, who charged me 30 shillings to help with the washing up.

There was a most attractive-looking Welshman whom I fancied greatly, and even though he wouldn't marry waitresses, the Catering Manager had said yet *again* when he saw me getting out of a helicopter with him, I had great hopes. However, I lost him completely the night I worked in the bar. He wanted to arrange some very complicated deal about drinking that night with 'the old man'. Whenever *he* bought a drink it was to be a small one, and if by any chance the old man bought one it was to be a large one. I totally misunderstood his intentions and thought simply that he wanted to get the 'old man' drunk for some fell purpose. Actually, of course, he just wanted to get drunk himself at the expense of the old man, and when I made the obvious mistake he became very sour. He came into the kitchen next day and fingered the meat cleaver thoughtfully. 'I thought you were clever,' he said, and I never saw him again.

There was a sex maniac in charge of the cooking; he was called Pio, and was like a stage Italian. In the middle of most confusing orders, when I would call, 'Pio, could you give me two liver and bacon and three cottage pies,' he would put on a vulpine smile and roar, 'I geev to you if you geev to me,' and everyone would laugh as I rushed out the In door and back in the Out door, in sheer fright.

But, still, I think I liked it. I liked John, the sad Irish waiter, and I liked Julie, who was described by everyone as a tramp, as they gave her cigarettes and leaned forward breathlessly to hear her latest adventures. I liked all the food, and the fact that I saved £73 in eight weeks, which I never did before or since. I learned a great deal about Life, and, more important, I learned never, no matter how great the temptation, to send back a dirty fork. Not every under-chef might have such hygienic hair as the one I knew.

BACK TO SCHOOL

21 August 1969
I have been so long on the other side of the classroom that I almost forget what going back to school was like for the pupils. To me it was always a hectic rush in from the dawn flight or the mailboat, and a total disbelief that the long hot summer had really become a matter of timetables, home-work, corrections, schedules and textbooks

once again. If I got through the first day without remembering that I had left my suitcase at Milan or that I had lost the address of some sinisterly handsome Yugoslav, it was a miracle. I never had the least sympathy for the unfortunates in front of me. All that came the second day of term when we had more or less settled in.

But then I didn't have to deal with four-year-olds. All my kids were jaded, yawning sophisticates of 14 and upwards. I had to divulge only the new and terrible text of Livy we would be attacking, and try to pretend that this one was better than the others because Hannibal would be sliding up and down the Alps instead of having endless parleys with everyone at the foot of the mountains. I had to tell them that Otto and Henry the Fowler were really swinging people once you got to know them, and to utter a few hollow remarks about clean sheets and new leaves and all being forgotten since last term. I could never have coped with four-year-olds.

I would see them arriving up to the school door, little hands clutched in the nervous hands of nervous parents. I would see the faces pucker up, the hostility, the forced cheer on everyone's part, and wonder yet again was there any possible way to make the First Day any less harrowing for everyone concerned. About 20 minutes before school began the first howl would be heard from a cloakroom. It may have been caused by some perfectly reasonable cause like not being able to change one's shoes or Mummy saying something idiotic like 'Don't cry now' to a perfectly happy child, but there it would come anyway, and like brucellosis it's catching. 'Why is he howling?' was the immediate thought that flashed around everyone's mind, 'this place must be howlworthy in some way,' and then everyone would start.

There was one mother that I really admired. She had about five children at the school, and from the time they were three years old, those children were used to the place. They would come in and deliver elder brothers and sisters, they would come and collect them again in the afternoons. They knew when others didn't know that school was not a place where one would be abandoned forever with a brand new school bag one day by a weeping mother. When this mother had a chance she left her three-year-old casually for an hour in the back of the tinies' classroom anyway, and said, 'Get on with your colouring book, I want to talk to the headmistress.' They were all so well adjusted it was almost frightening.

Then there was the mother I couldn't bear. She came in like Maria Callas one morning and asked to see all the lavatories. Then she asked to be introduced to all the other children by name, then she took her own frightened offspring out of a car, and with more pomp and ceremony than all the doings in Caernarfon she marched the unfortunate boy into the classroom.

'These are your new friends, Johnny,' she intoned as you might address the life convicts of Cell Block B. 'You are going to have a lovely time playing with them all'; she held the traditional handkerchief to her eyes and left under severe emotional strain. The kindergarten teacher said that it took Johnny six months to get over the shock of it all.

If mothers only realised that going to school is not the severe break for the child as it is for themselves, a great deal of unnecessary trouble could be spared. It is obviously a great milestone for a mother if the only child ceases to be under her feet for the whole day, and is plunged into a new environment for the very first time. But it is only hard for the child if all this tension is built up beforehand. I don't think it's a good thing for everyone from Grandmother to the milkman to say how big a day it is for the little darling to be going off to school. The little darling might be tempted to believe that it is. I don't think it's wise to make too much fuss about a new school uniform, since the trappings and paraphernalia can become an obsession. A five-year-old is not a good recipient of a long emotional lecture from both mother and father about how much they expect from this giant step.

What *is* a good idea for parents is to maintain a steady and informed interest in their children's work and play during school-days. This will be a hundred times more valuable than regarding the first day as something like a Royal Command Performance and then forgetting the whole thing for evermore. The happiest children I taught were the ones whose parents knew and cared what the actual school day was like. Not necessarily the busybodies, in fact not at all the busybodies now that I come to think of it. The children would often complain that their parents were fascinated by all their efforts when they were at the stage of making pot hooks, but lost interest once it came to conjugating verbs.

'Well what *can* we do?' said one gloomy mother to whom I mentioned this with my sledgehammer tact. 'Am I to spend the whole day with *Teach Yourself Physics* propped up on the eye-level grill, so that we can all speak the same jargon?'

Parents should try to remember their children's friends, their teachers, their activities. They should listen when the children talk. It is all a matter of sustained interest rather than initial histrionics. I remember sitting behind a child aged about nine and her mother on a bus. The child was talking enthusiastically about Miss O'Connor.

'That's the maths teacher?' yawned Mama.

'NO, I told you it's the history teacher,' said the child.

'I didn't know you were doing history,' said Mother. 'Will you really need another pair of shoes this term, you've had three this year already.'

I thought it was very depressing, not because we teachers want to be enshrined between pictures of popes and American presidents in every child's home, but because parents should care.

There are 20 books to be written on how parents and teachers can do so much for the children by cooperating in spirit as well as in crashingly boring PTA meetings. One of the first steps is to get to know each other. So next week, when you take your four-year-old's little hot hand and lead him up the steps of his new school, or encourage your 14-year-old to his new senior school, try to get to know the teachers. Forget all that amateur psychology about children reacting to new surroundings and remember all that good old-fashioned idea about your friendly local teacher being a real live human being. If bank managers are busy portraying themselves as normal decent souls, we teachers will have to start the same process. Only the trouble is that we don't have the money for all that advertising.

THINKING ABOUT UNDERWEAR DOWN UNDER

10 September 1969
At some stage in everyone's life someone said that you must always wear nice underthings in case you were knocked down by a bus and had to be taken to a casualty ward. I was so frightened by this that I bought new sets of everything and then defeated the whole object by staying well clear of buses. Still, there is a great deal of truth in the statement that you feel much better if everything is snow white and lace-covered

from the skin out. I have spoken long and loud before about how difficult this is for anyone who is not a Stock Size, because there is an international conspiracy that large ladies should wear gunmetal underwear decorated and relieved only by huge rolls of elastic and what they call slimming panels. But even so, there are people who can buy attractive underthings and don't, on the very dubious grounds that they aren't going to be seen.

I asked a few doctors who have seen women at their most defenceless to comment on our record as regards underwear, but they seem to be what we never really thought they were — totally unconcerned with it all. One said that the only thing he really objected to was nothing at all to do with underwear, it was drainpipe trousers. If you have something wrong with a knee or a calf you have to remove the pants entirely, causing enormous embarrassment to patient and further delay to doctor. Another said that people who come to be examined should realise that not only the part you consider to be affected may be looked at, but also a great deal more. He will never forget the mortification of someone who showed him a lily-white foot to be perused about a swollen ankle, but when he asked to see the other one for comparison it was almost covered in moss. He suggested a good bath as the solution, and was surprised that more people hadn't thought of this before.

I don't believe all this nonsense about not wearing nylon underwear because it doesn't absorb sweat. I think it is a lot worse to have all the fabrics that do absorb sweat, and have to be treated like precious fabrics from the Orient as a result. At least nylon knows the pace of modern life, it can be washed, it doesn't ask to be ironed, and it will be there winking at you in the morning ready to be worn again. It can be dyed a nice bright colour if the original white gets grey, and most of all it doesn't complain. It costs a bit less than all these prestige fabrics, and they actually manage to make it in a few nice colours and designs. No one who has seen nylon should ever be pitied if they end up on an operating table feeling foolish in long, hairy combinations that belonged to their eldest brother.

But the real joy of living when we do is, of course, the invention of tights. Years ago at the pantomime I saw a Principal Boy in these and thought they would be the end to all problems, and now eventually everyone has come around to agreeing with me. They are more expensive in that if one leg or the middle goes, you are economically minus two legs, but there are all kinds of cunning things you can do about this, like hacking off the good leg and wearing it in the old traditional way with the old traditional apparatus. It means that you must remember to buy all your pantyhose in the same colour, but that shouldn't be too much for any of us fashion-conscious people, should it?

The joy of being able to cross your legs without seven minutes' judicious edging to the front of your chair and back again, and much surreptitious feeling to make sure that acres of thigh are not visible, has to be known to be believed. The sheer delight of knowing that you need never again hunt for an Irish threepence to put in your suspender when the terrible little knob has worked its way down to the sole of your foot, is one worth having. The days you feel too fragile to wrestle with a corset, for want of a better term, are no longer with us since the invention of tights. If we could only get the makers to invent something which is both sheer and long-lasting, we could be said to have arrived in the perfect society. As it stands, one can often be in the lovely position of having to choose between something that looks like a stocking and lasts three days, or something that will last but looks like a surgical bandage.

Men are always being asked their views on women's underwear and they never say anything useful, so I just wouldn't give them all the chance here in the office. Men always profess to like blacks and scarlets and things, but like their wives to wear broderie anglaise from head to toe until they look as if they had just wandered off the film set of *Oklahoma*.

Women were loath to talk about the whole subject, which may or may not be healthy, but one great thread of uniformity ran through what everyone said. We are all in favour of wearing things that have a double purpose, like bra-slips, or panty-girdles or any other hyphenated garments that save effort in the mornings. Whereas we all used to wear one bra, one girdle, one slip, one pair of pants and two stockings (no one admitted to wearing vests), which was a total of six garments, now this *can* be cut down to a bra-slip and a pair of pantyhose, which is two. The national average is probably three or four. It is all more labour-saving and comfortable somehow, in these busy days.

On the topic of pretty underthings, everyone said that if all things were equal, which they aren't, they would indeed choose the attractive lacey flowered ones. But there is a big problem here. Anything that has any remedial nature manages to sacrifice beauty somewhere along the conveyor belt. The bra that holds you in or pads you out is not necessarily or at all the bra that has little rosebuds and pink lace. The girdles that look alluring could let you bulge alarmingly.

But is anyone ever satisfied with their own shape anyway? As someone put it, there is always one unanswerable question, in the words of the old song:
'Which would you rather
Or rather would you be
Legs to the oxter
Or stomach to the knee?'

THE NONSENSE OF ETIQUETTE

30 October 1969
The real immorality in life is to pretend that etiquette matters. It is the kind of pretence that brings a whole trail of neurosis and misery, as well as creating an artificial society of poseurs. The worst type of columnist is the one who orders her readers to follow the waiter under pain of death, rather than do the normal thing and let the unfor-

tunate man who brought her to the restaurant crash his way through the tables.

These etiquette fiends do not answer a great need in the country; they create it. I do not accept for one moment that anyone feels more secure and able to face life once they have been definitely forbidden to say 'pleased to meet you'. The happiness of knowing how to say 'How do you do?' is a very ephemeral joy, and the amount of security that a nervous, socially aspiring woman can get from a paperback book on how it's done, or a weekly nightmarish sermon in a magazine, seems very dubious.

Of course there are legions of people who will not agree. They will say that it is all very well for those who are born to it to scorn etiquette and social ease; that a duchess has the right and the aplomb to tear her meat apart with bare hands in a restaurant if she chooses. But this is only perpetuating the whole terrible conspiracy.

There is no such thing in Ireland as being born knowing how to eat oysters or how to address an abbot in speech and on the envelope, or whether you should hunt for a fishbone that is certain to kill you in ten seconds with a fork or with your fist. Nobody will need to know all these things. Telling people how this must or must not be done is going to conjure up a world of decision-making, where the wrong choice in a heavily charged moment is going to mean instant disgrace, and months of recrimination.

I don't know how to eat mussels. I am neither proud nor ashamed of this, and if ever I wanted to order them in a restaurant I would ask the waiter or a neighbour how to attack them only if I thought that what seemed the obvious way would reduce everyone to helpless laughter or nausea. If I were on my own eating them, I think I would try some way that managed to get them out of the shell and into my mouth without covering myself and the table with sauce. But what a world it would be if I felt I had to slink into bookshops, and look up 'Eating' under the letter M when I thought there was a chance they might be placed suddenly and viciously before me.

The only real rule in etiquette is to realise that times change, manners change and that there are no absolutes. And even if there were absolutes, what would it matter? What will happen to the hostess who serves to the right and takes away from the left, or whichever is the wrong thing to do? Does she really think it matters? Is there anyone in the world who could produce one single reason for it mattering except a whole lot of claptrap based on what someone somewhere decided had been the Only Way to do it since the court of Louis XIV?

When schools offer classes in etiquette, parents often bray with delight and think that here, at last, is something that will stand to their daughters in years to come. But my heart sinks when I hear of them, and I envisage some undoubtedly impeccable lady telling the girls how to word invitations for dinner parties, when the most probable type of entertainment they will have to organise is beer and spaghetti on a Saturday night. I know of one real and documented occasion when a nun told the pupils in the Confirmation class that one girl was not being asked to take the Temperance pledge because she would have many demanding occasions in her social life when she left school where she would have to drink, and all the parents crowed their approval of this wisdom. They should have been outraged that the nun had made a class distinction at the age of 12 between this child, who was of a better home and a lovelier family, and the rest.

I wonder if Emily Post's marathon guide to every possible situation that could rear its head to harass a human will help the situation or just make it worse.

Will everybody sit up in bed laughing themselves sick at the etiquette of gloves and napkin? Will they be depressed to think that in 1922 women went out in droves to buy this ludicrous tome, which eventually ran through 99 printings and sold four million copies? Most frightening of all, will any reader who pays £2 10s for the new edition, brought out, I assume, as a giant laugh at this stage, take one word of what Emily wrote seriously? More than any other book that has appeared recently, I would love to know its sales today. I would be fascinated to know who buys it and why I got it to review, but if I had seen it in someone's house I certainly would have bought it. At least two people I showed it to are ordering copies.

It is well over 600 pages of utter and complete nonsense, but it is compulsive reading. There is drama in every line, from the gentle warning not to refer to a bell as a 'tintinnabulary summons' or a cow's tail as 'bovine continuation', to the wording of engraved pew cards for weddings.

Emily Post was everyone's ideal woman in the twenties. Americans bought her book without question as soon as there was to be a wedding in the house. She was a Baltimore

Beauty herself, which of course gave her the right to speak; her wedding to Edwin M. Post Jnr in Tuxedo Park was one of the year's social events. As Edwin became more and more important in Wall Street, Emily became more and more obsessed with table settings and the duties of a chaperone.

It is easy to be wise after the event, and I know very little about either of them, but I do feel that it must have been quite predictable that the social event of 1892 should have ended in the Divorce Court of 1906.

Then Emily got down to business seriously, and told the world that if a wedding present had to be delayed through illness or disaster, a note should be written At Once to explain the delay and announce that the gift was on its way. She decided that people must have maids with low voices and that children in nice families should have visiting cards which they leave at parties bearing their name and Chez Maman instead of an address.

She goes completely berserk in the chapter about issuing invitations by telephone. Messages should always follow a prescribed form, apparently: 'Is this Lennox 0000? Would you please ask Mr and Mrs Smith if they will dine with Mrs Grantham Jones next Tuesday, the tenth, at eight o'clock?

Mrs Jones' number is Plaza one-two, ring two.'

I am afraid I cannot understand from the book how this message should be communicated. Is it from Mrs Jones' butler to Mrs Smith's butler? It would appear to be, because the answer is also in the third person. Even the most personal phone calls seem to have official starts, middles and ends, while the behaviour of engaged couples towards each other has to be seen to be believed.

There is a chapter on how to get people to talk to each other at meals. That is really called the Turning of the Table. I attacked it with enormous interest, thinking it was some form of spiritualism patronised by Good Society, but didn't it turn out to be a whole set of directions on which way your face was meant to be turned after the fish course! I am copying directly from the book at this stage: 'The turning of the table is accomplished by the hostess who merely turns from the gentleman (on her left probably) with whom she has been talking during the soup and fish course to the one on her right. As she turns, the lady to whom the "right" gentleman has been talking turns to the gentleman further on, and in a moment everyone at the table is talking to a new neighbour.'

But what in the name of God are they all going to say? Emily really falls down on this. What could you possibly say, out of the blue, to a man on your right when the starting gun has been fired by the hostess turning? Or perhaps you aren't meant to say anything. She has a stern chapter on people who talk too much. I find myself caught between fascination, horror and sheer disbelief. Could anyone have cared, I wonder, and then I remember that four million people went out, presumably sober, and bought the book, and it fills me with rage.

It is due to the Emily Posts, the Amy Vanderbilts and their successors that you have unfortunates writing urgently to magazines saying that they must know by return of post whether to call the bride and bridegroom at a wedding next Saturday 'The happy couple' or 'Mary and Jimmy', when they have to make a speech. No punishment is great enough for anyone who made them feel it mattered a damn.

SEVENTIES

THE WORLD'S GREATEST LIES ABOUT WOMEN

16 June 1970

1. Men like fat, cuddly women. They do, to laugh with and at, but not to fall in love with, behave extravagantly towards and join in matrimony with. If your role is that of sister, playmate and confidante, be as fat and cuddly as possible. If you hoped for anything more adventurous, get thin.

2. Men like women without make-up. They don't. They like extremely well and carefully made-up women whose skin has that expensive cultured look which comes from three hours at the dressing table. A woman who is really without make-up would frighten them to death. They regard blotches as ec-

zema, and uneven colouring as a sign of tertiary syphilis.

3. Men like women in midi-length clothes. Not in Ireland yet, they don't. A maxi was fine during the winter for a young second arts student, and only when worn over the briefest of midi skirts so that everyone got the best of both worlds. They are afraid that their girlfriend's midi might be mistaken for someone else's leftover skirt, or worse still for a foolish attempt to be ahead of fashion, which is considerably more sinister than being behind it.

4. Everyone looks better in summer than in winter. Completely untrue. Everyone has more courage in summer, that's all. In winter you wouldn't dare to show veiny legs that had undergone a half-hearted attempt at instant tanning, and wear sleeveless dresses that showed the most ageing part of the body — the flesh on the top of the arms. For all those who turn that mythical brown, thousands more go red, or

freckled, or that attractive shade of peel that can be a menace to anyone who sits beside you. Winter is safer, much.

5. Pregnant women are beautiful. They are, if they are sitting in a Chanel dress with a white collar framing an unworried face, thinking beautiful thoughts about a wonderful and miraculous event that is going to change everyone's lives. They are considerably less than beautiful if they are wearing their sister-in-law's maternity dress, elastic stockings, bemoaning the fact that they can't drink gin, and wondering how on earth they are going to afford another child.

6. It doesn't matter if you aren't beautiful. You are quite right, it doesn't matter a damn to anyone else, but it matters quite a lot to you.

BABY BLUE

24 December 1971
My first evening dress was baby blue, and it had a great panel of blue velvet down the

front, because my cousin who actually owned the dress was six inches thinner everywhere than I was. It had two short puff sleeves, and a belt which it was decided that I should not wear. It was made from some kind of good taffeta, and had, in its original condition, what was known as a good cut.

It was borrowed and altered in great haste, because a precocious classmate had decided to have a formal party. A formal party meant that the entire class turned up looking idiotic and she had to provide 23 idiotic men as well.

I was so excited when the blue evening dress arrived back from the dressmaker. It didn't matter, we all agreed, that the baby blue inset was a totally different colour from the baby blue dress. It gave it contrast and eye-appeal, a kind next-door neighbour said, and we were delighted with it. I telephoned the mother of the cousin and said it was going to be a great success. She was enormously gratified.

I got my hair permed on the day of the formal party, which now many years later I can agree was a great mistake. It would have been wiser to have had the perm six months previously and to allow it to grow out. However, there is nothing like the Aborigine look to give you confidence if you were once

a girl with straight hair, and my younger
sister who hadn't recognised me when I
came to the door said that I looked 40, and
I thought that was good too. It would have
been terrible to look 16, which was what we
all were.

I had bought new underwear in case the
taxi crashed on the way to the formal party
and I ended up on the operating table; and
I became very angry with another young
sister who said I looked better in my blue
knickers than I did in the dress. Cheap
jealousy, I thought, and with all that puppy
fat and navy school knicker plus awful
school belted tunic as her only covering,
how could she be expected to have any
judgment at all?

Against everyone's advice I invested in a
pair of diamante earrings, cost 1s 3d old
money in Woolworths; they had an inset of
baby blue also, and I thought that this was
the last word in coordination. I wore them
for three days before the event, and ignored
the fact that great ulcerous sores were forming on my earlobes. Practice, I thought,
would solve that.

The formal party started at nine p.m. I
was ready at six, and looked so beautiful
that I thought it would be unfair to the rest
of the girls. How could they compete? The

riot of baby blue had descended to the shoes as well, and in those days, shoe dyeing wasn't all it is these days. By seven p.m. my legs had turned blue up to the knee. It didn't matter, said my father kindly, unless, of course, they do the can-can these days. Panic set in, and I removed shoes, stockings and scrubbed my legs to their original purple, and the shoes to their off-white. To hell with coordination, I wasn't going to let people think I had painted myself with woad.

By eight p.m. I pitied my drab parents and my pathetic family, who were not glitter and stardust as I was. They were tolerant to the degree of not commenting on my swollen ears, which now couldn't take the diamante clips and luxuriated with the innovation of sticking-plaster painted blue. They told me that I looked lovely, and that I would be the belle of the ball. I knew it already, but it was nice to have it confirmed.

There is no use in dwelling on the formal party. Nobody danced with me at all, except in the Paul Jones, and nobody said I looked well. Everyone else had blouses and long skirts which cost a fraction of what the alterations on my cousin's evening dress had set me back. Everyone else looked normal, I looked like a mad blue balloon.

I decided I would burn it that night when I got home, in the garden in a bonfire. Then I thought that would wake my parents and make them distressed that I hadn't been the belle of the ball after all, so I set off down the road to burn it on the railway bank of Dalkey station. Then I remembered the bye-laws, and having to walk home in my under-wear, which the baby had rightly said looked better than the dress, so I decided to hell with it all, I would just tear it up tomorrow, at dawn.

But the next day, didn't a boy, a real live boy who had danced with me during one of the Paul Joneses, ring up and say that he was giving a formal party next week, and would I come? The social whirl was beginning, I thought, and in the grey light of morning the dress didn't look too bad on the back of a chair.

And there wasn't time to get a skirt and blouse and look normal like everyone else, and I checked around and not everybody had been invited to his formal party; in fact only three of us had. So I rang the mother of the cousin again, and she was embarrassingly gratified this time, and I decided to allow my ears to cure and not wear any earrings, and to let the perm grow out, and to avoid dyed shoes.

And a whole winter season of idiotic parties began, at which I formally decided I was the belle of the ball even though I hardly got danced with at all, and I know I am a stupid cow, but I still have the dress, and I am never going to give it away, set fire to it on the railway bank or use it as a duster.

Women Are Fools — Mary

7 May 1973
Mary's father died on her 21st birthday, when she had been celebrating not only the key of the door but an honours BA. She missed him in a mild guilty sort of way because she never knew him too well. All those years at boarding school, then at university, she hadn't brought friends home much because there was nothing to do, she thought, in the small country town, and her friends would be bored.

She had a sister years and years older who was a nun in America, and got leave to come over for the funeral, and two brothers, one who was courting, and one who was only a schoolboy.

She didn't know her mother too well when she was 21, but now at 29 she knows her only too well, and doesn't like what she knows. Or so she says.

The mother sold the house in the country town and came to Dublin. It would be handier, she said. Mary could live with her while doing the HDip. The courting son was married and living in Dublin in a year and the schoolboy son could go to a good school in Dublin. It was all a great idea said the mother, and Mary thought it would be cheaper certainly and it had been a bit lonely sometimes in Dublin on her own, and at least she would get good meals and have someone to talk to at weekends.

She forgot what it was like to be living at home again. A home where her mother always said, 'If your poor father were only here he would . . .', and he would always be doing or saying something so unlikely that Mary grew to resent the phrase, and the inevitable accusations that she didn't respect the memory of her father began.

Mary got a job easily enough teaching in Dublin. It was a large convent school, and it was in this that I met her, because our school had a debating competition with hers and her pupils beat mine, and annoyed as I was because I thought my kids were better, I liked their teachers, who seemed kind of interested in the whole idea of giving them self-confidence and not teaching them typical debating phrases off by heart. So we went and had a coffee after we put our various charges on buses and sent them home with dire warnings about not getting distracted by chip shops en route.

She told me that she didn't really like teaching, and wanted something abroad, that she found it difficult to find a sort of 'set' in Dublin now that she had left college. People were all scattered, and at school who on earth did you meet except the nuns, the other teachers, the children and the parents? I knew it only too well, but assured her that it sort of evolved. She was bored by her married friends, she said, they all seemed so complacent. I said mine weren't because they were all poor and didn't have much to be complacent about. We thought a bit about how to get a job for her abroad, and about how dreadful it was that the only kind of men you'd want to go out with were all married already.

Again I met her and this time she said she was going to start going to dances again; she told me a bit about her whining mother, who always went on about her missing her chances, and Mary wondered aloud even more whiningly to me and her mother where on God's name were the chances?

The first Chance came at a dance hall where Mary spent a really appalling night.

The dancers who weren't her pupils were elderly nurses in cardigans, she said; the men were either children or ageing, dribbling drunks. One man in the room seemed to be neither a drunk of 50 nor a child of 15; at the second last dance, he eyed Mary and they jived away until the national anthem.

She had nothing in common with him, but he took her home, and when he said that he'd give her a ring next week he actually did. And Mary was delighted that she had a fellow, although it has to be said she did talk about him as you would about a worn-out carpet sweeper that someone had given you when they had bought a new electrical thing. She was grateful but not totally satisfied with her lot.

Her mother wanted to know all about him, who his people were, and didn't like the sound of he works in Aer Lingus or Guinnesses or CIÉ or wherever it was, because his job was never defined there. So Mary didn't bring him home, they went to the pictures a lot, and necked in the back of his car out at Burma Road in the nice car park built just for that purpose, and he gave her a handbag for her birthday, and he didn't ask her home either which was a relief because Mary didn't feel bad about her not doing the same, and just as she was getting ready to buy him a cashmere sweater for his birthday some Good Friend managed to tell her that it wasn't his difficult mother he didn't want her to meet, it was his difficult wife.

We agreed over a lunch one day that it had been a horrible shock, a great relief that she hadn't been really interested in him and an even greater relief that Mary hadn't given in to all his frightful sexual demands. That was the biggest bonus of all.

Her next Chance came when I introduced her to a professional bachelor, professional in the sense of always being determined to remain a bachelor. We were sure he wasn't married, but I was equally sure he never would marry. It lasted about three months, dinner in little restaurants where you could dance, theatres.

I don't think he made any frightful sexual demands, if so they weren't mentioned, but she brought him home often, and he got very uneasy about the best china being brought out and Mary's mother saying that she would leave you young people alone and vanishing, so he asked me to help him unload her which was a lousy rotten thing to do and I said he was to do it himself, the weak fool, and the weak fool just stopped ringing her, and her heart was broken, because school was getting more and more boring and mother was more and more trying and Mary had really thought that This might be It.

She met a man in a pub shortly afterwards while waiting for a girlfriend. He invited them both to a party, and there was a lot of drink and messing, Mary said, but it was better than nothing, and he and his gang had parties nearly every weekend up in Rathmines, where they all lived in bedsitters or flats, and it was getting harder and harder for Mary to take a taxi out nine miles home afterwards, so she got into the habit of staying with her friend Brenda in town. Mother would be a bit sour, but at least not suspicious, and indeed at this stage she had nothing to be suspicious about because Mary *was* staying with Brenda and they would both have glasses of milk and discuss the talent at the party and wonder which one of the lads they should try and settle for.

And then she fell in love. Yes, that's what it was; she really found someone she loved much more than herself, and someone she couldn't live without. I didn't see her at all during this great period, but everyone who knew her said he was a total bastard, had got one of these funny divorces, because he had a load of money and a small luxurious flat that he actually called a 'pad' somewhere in Fashionable Dublin Four, and this was even further from Mary's home than ever, and so Brenda was being used as a very real excuse this time.

Brenda had a phone, and if Mary's mother rang, as she often did, Brenda would say, 'Hold on a minute, she's in the bath,' and then ring Mary at the pad and tell her to ring her mother quick, for God's sake.

I met them once and I agree he was very, very attractive and charming. He had a certain smoothness which I didn't like, but then put that down to prejudice because I had heard he was a smooth bastard from people who are kind of right about these things. But that night when I was eating a very quick meal before going to the theatre, and was by myself, they asked me to join them, and he did have something very warm about him; he seemed to be interested in her, and pleasantly interested in whatever I had to say too. He talked a bit about 'my little nipper' and explained that he was divorced, so there didn't seem to be any great deception or anything involved. Mary said her mother was going on a coach tour soon and that she and the guy would be having a party in his pad and I must come. The relevancy of the coach tour didn't strike me for the moment until I remembered that naturally her mother thought she was staying with Brenda four to five nights a week. He said it had been very, very nice to meet me, which I thought was a bit overdoing it; it might have been nice enough, but since I was shovelling food into my mouth and looking at my watch, it could hardly have been very, very nice. Still, people talk different ways.

And act different ways, too.

He never suggested marriage to Mary, though she was quite willing to go to England and get married there, or in the registry office here, but apparently whenever she brought it up he said that the Irish laws were funny, and even though he did have a Mexican divorce or whatever it was, there was always the possibility that one could be prosecuted for bigamy here. Not likely, he said, because the courts hate doing it, it makes them look ridiculous, but possible. He would, however, like Mary to move in with him.

And Mary loved him so much and her mother was still so unaware of his existence, and Brenda was leaving town to go to London, that there really were problems.

'Could you tell her the truth?' I asked foolishly, because really it was a foolish question.

All right, so Mary was 26, she was entitled to do whatever she liked; she certainly didn't love her mother enough to be deeply upset about hurting her. But then mothers are mothers and I can't believe that four years ago a woman in her fifties would like her daughter to move in with a divorced man. I couldn't believe for a moment that Mary's mother, who was practically a law unto herself, would countenance it for a minute.

Selfishly I thanked heaven that I lived in Dalkey and there was no fear that Mary could ask me to pretend I was living with her, because there is no way you could say Dalkey was nearer her work than her own house was. What did the man say? Oh well, he said, it was up to her to arrange things and she was so desperately afraid that she'd lose him, and he did so need someone to get his shirts cleaned, and cook his supper, she couldn't leave and there would have to be a way.

The way, when found, was so ludicrous and financially disastrous you will find it hard to believe.

Mary told her mother that she was going

to do an evening course and would have to take a room in town. She rented a bedsitter and paid £6 a week for it, brought in some of her things. She now had clothes and possessions in three houses, her mother's, her man's and her new totally unused and useless bedsitter. Every Tuesday, which was her half day, she would bring in some more things from the pad to the bedsitter and ask her mother to tea. Mother was getting older, sadder and sourer. She couldn't understand why Mary was paying £3 to her old home, £6 to a landlord, when she had a perfectly good home of her own, and, said the mother sinisterly, perfect freedom to entertain all her friends there. The house was now too big for Mother. Tuesdays took on the nature of a nightmare.

Then there were the weekends. Mother couldn't understand that Mary had suddenly joined An Óige and was going on winter and summer hikes, when she didn't seem to know a thing about the organisation nor anyone in it.

I don't know Mary very well, remember, but I think that the man loved her a lot. He certainly made her very happy and apart from all the deceptions at home and the effort and the covering up and trying not to meet people that might conceivably split on them, it was a good, happy relationship.

For nearly a year.

The man, it appeared, was a little mean. Mary was only taking home £22 a week from her teaching, and nine of that was gone on two other sets of accommodation already. He expected her to pay for half their housekeeping and he liked living well. He bought her nice presents of course, but Mary was getting into debt. He had pictures of his nippers all over the pad; and none of Mary. She thought that was a bit hard, but the price you pay for this kind of setup. He had to go to business dinners, and naturally couldn't bring her along. So she spent long evenings looking at television, wondering what time he would come home. And she couldn't ask her friends in because it wasn't her place. So she would go out to a coin box phone occasionally and ring her mother, pretending she was phoning from the hall of the place she was meant to be living in, and her mother would have some other complaint. And she often went to the cinema on her own.

Then the doubts began. Was it a simple magazine case of letting herself go, did he find her less attractive now, had she moved in too easily, why were there so many business dinners now and hardly any at all six months ago? Was there someone else?

It couldn't be that he was lonely for the children because his ex-wife had remarried and the children were living with her in Switzerland. He didn't even have to send her alimony because this time, she had married a near millionaire. He never spoke of her at all, or why they had separated. Mary had never asked.

The summer holidays were coming up, and to get over the guilt feelings about Mother, Mary decided to get herself further in debt and take the two of them to Majorca. She wrote every day to tell him how she loved and missed him. He didn't write at all, because her mother would probably ask who the letters were from. She admired his tact in not writing.

Eventually the 14 days were over, and for appearances Mary stayed the night in her mother's home, and then looked in at her false flat to make sure it hadn't been broken into, and happily trotted up to the pad.

He wouldn't be home for ages, so she could make a great dinner. There was washing up in the sink, two of everything; he must have had Freddy to a meal. There was new talcum, and perfume in the bathroom, but they weren't presents, they were half used. It couldn't have been Freddy, he doesn't use Blue Grass.

The door opened and the Man came in, finding Mary sadly looking at a white dressing-gown on the back of the door. He had been coming back to clear up the evidence. They looked at each other, according to her own tale, for five minutes without saying anything, and then he had to say something and mercifully for Mary he didn't say, 'I can explain everything.'

What he did say was, 'Well, I suppose it had to end sometime.'

She doesn't know why he took someone else in, she doesn't know who the other person is or was, or if they are still there. She just knew that life was over. She packed there and then, borrowing one of his suitcases, and saying, 'Is this record yours or mine?' He stood stonily, and she never spoke to him again. That was three years ago.

Then Mary became known in the current attractive jargon of our times as 'an easy lay'. She moved properly into what was her false flat and made it her real flat. She got drunk and told her mother all about the Man, her mother forbade her to come back again and told the priest, and Mary told her to keep to her lonely bitter ways, and hasn't seen her mother properly for three years except at frosty Christmas lunches.

She had a short affair, which by her standards now means a relationship that lasts a month or two, with the father of one of her pupils, and was sacked from the school. She got another job in a provincial town for a while, but didn't even need to be sacked from that one because her poker playing, drinking and sleeping with the commercial travellers at the hotel made her a town name in three months.

I met her at the races there a few weeks ago. I didn't know her at first, but we met in the bar where I had lost my purse and it had been retrieved by an honest barman. She looked a little lost, and offered me a drink. I had people searching other corners of the race course for my purse so had to refuse but asked her to ring me during the Easter holidays, which she did.

She is pregnant; she hasn't a clue in the world who the father might be. You name him, it could be that person. It's now too late for an abortion, she thinks, she doesn't even damn know. She supposes she'll have it, and get it adopted. Would I know where she could do that? I would.

She also had a sort of half idea of keeping it, would I know how she could get help to do that? I would. What did I think about it all?

Well, what on earth could I think, except that life is unfair as I think more and more these days, and wonder was it ever meant to be fair? It's unfair on Mary's child who isn't wanted, it's unfair on Mary's mother who has no husband, and a daughter a nun in America, and a married son, and an emigrated son, and a daughter who is going to be a Public Disgrace. And it's unfair on Mary because she had no strength, and she has this belief that a lot of women have that they don't control their own lives. That they are somehow blown along by fate.

And I said that perhaps a child would give her something to live for, and someone to love. But I knew when saying it that she would have loved it to be His child, the only man she ever cared about, not the child of a number of people who stopped the loneliness of the night for her by coming home to her flat.

And I also know that a teacher will not be able to rear a child alone, and that Mary's mother won't help. And I know that if Mary is going to carry on the way she is at the moment, she won't be much of a mother or a teacher anyway. And so I gave her the addresses that we have listed in our little green note book, and hoped that the professionals will help her, and I rang Ally and Cherish about her, and said that she would be contacting them, and they said certainly they would do all they could for her. And I know they will, but I don't know that Mary will do all she can for herself, because she has that kind of hopeless beaten look, which has nothing to do with being pregnant and unmarried, it was there before. It has a lot to do with expecting life to be beautiful and easy like it is for everyone else and bitterly disappointed when it isn't. And that's why we are all such fools.

WOMEN ARE FOOLS — LORRAINE

8 May 1973

Lorraine was at UCD with me in the late fifties and when everyone was wearing ten of those ridiculous stiff petticoats, Lorraine wore 20. She was in digs with a motherly kind of woman who liked her because Lorraine was obsessed with clothes and would lend Mrs whoever-she-was her good handbag in exchange for a blouse or one of her son's long sweaters, which were all the rage then too.

I didn't know her very well at this stage

and always thought of her as one of those who used to be back combing their hair in front of the mirror in the Ladies' Reading Room, as it was called.

When we went to dances in '86' or in the Four Courts where the Solicitors' Apprentices used to run a very great kind of hop, Lorraine always danced with this fellow called Martin who was good-looking and quiet and did Commerce. It was assumed, again in the language of the time, that they were doing a line.

The year we were all meant to be studying for our degree, I got to know Lorraine better because nobody was studying at all. We had all taken holiday jobs on the grounds that if we got away from the distractions and the barbecues at White Rock and all that sort of thing there would be more chance of getting some work done.

I was teaching in St Leonard's-on-Sea, and by chance Lorraine was there too, working in a library in nearby Hastings, so we used to meet a bit and talk. I was mainly worried in case I was teaching the pupils rubbish, and that I would fail my BA because I didn't know one word, line or fact of American history. Lorraine was worried because she was always giving out books to people who looked like professional book thieves and she was hoping that her hard-to-get policy with Martin was going to pay off.

We had hours and days of Martin as we sat on the beach, me with American history books, Lorraine with unopened old English tomes. It *had* been the right thing, hadn't it, to pretend that one wasn't available? It would make him more interested, wouldn't it? There was no danger he'd meet someone else at home, was there? Reassurances from me, struggling with names I had never heard of and battles I hadn't known had taken place. Positively the right thing.

In August when everyone really *was* studying, I heard that they were engaged and would be married immediately after graduation. It seemed the most remarkable and romantic thing in the world, a triumph for all that Angela MacNamara advice about not giving your favours too easily, and not being too easy to get. She was just 20, he was her first and only boyfriend.

The rest of us went on sourly to do our HDip. Martin got a job in the Civil Service. Lorraine got a hopeless kind of job as someone's personal secretary.

Then she was coyly pregnant, and they had to leave their flat and I used to meet them at the odd party and it was always whine, whine, whine about the price of houses, and the not knowing whether to knit things in pink or in blue, and we found them a bit of a drag. We who had so much else to live for, like trying to find a teaching job in Dublin and/or a boyfriend.

And again by chance they got a house next door to a great friend of mine, so I kept coming across her for years afterwards. My friend had advised her to knit everything in white; it would be safer, and she had been delighted with that idea and kept out of everyone's way knitting until the girl was born, and a boy was born a year later and another girl after that.

This brings us to about 1964 and Lorraine and Martin had a new whine: it was about family planning. They just couldn't afford any more children, and you just had to sneeze and Lorraine got pregnant, and they were both very good Catholics and really wasn't it all terribly unfair? They had discussed it with Father Peter who had been very understanding and said that they should see a good doctor about the rhythm method, and with Father Brian who hadn't been a bit understanding and said that God never brought a life into the world that He didn't want, and there was never a mouth that He couldn't feed. And we were all so helpful to Lorraine and Martin and said yes, isn't Father Brian right? Look at the thousands who die of starvation, God just didn't want those apparently. And they became bewildered and didn't talk about it so much, which was what we wanted.

Martin was doing all right in his job, he was promoted and went back to college to do a post-graduate degree as a sort of part-time release. Lorraine just learned a bit of dressmaking and they went to the odd dance and my friend minded their three babies for them and they seemed just like any other married couple with a little too much money and a little too high aspiration in life.

I got the shock of my life when I saw Lorraine extremely drunk at a party about four years ago. She was simply incapable of standing up, so with the loyalty of the American-style old alumnae, a few of us got her out of it and brought her to the nearest house and sobered her up, with coffee, lots of it. Nobody could find Martin at the party.

He wasn't there. He was minding the children but Lorraine had decided she was sick of everything and of him being so dull and not wanting to go anywhere and she was still attractive for God's sake and she had no one to talk to all day, and he at least had his friends in the office, and all he wanted to do was to look at the telly and make love. And he had got round some priest, who said that if the doctor said she should take the Pill, then it was all right, and now she was taking the Pill and she and Martin would go to hell when they died. And she felt such a hypocrite at Mass every Sunday and it wasn't fair. She hadn't been to Communion for two years and she sobbed after we had all said something soothing about 'If the priest says it's all right. . . .'

So Lorraine said that wasn't the point, *she* didn't believe it was all right, it was just that Martin was a glutton for sex, and he had told it all to the priest in some dishonest way, she knew that. And perhaps the priest was one of those who were leaving. Priests were getting married all round the place, and you didn't know who you were talking to these days, and the whole Church seemed to be very confused.

More important than the Church being confused, in the short term we thought, was how to get her home to Martin sober and without explanation. She said she didn't give a damn what he thought, he was a man who never thought about anything anyway.

Pure *Woman's Own,* we felt, as someone

with a car deposited her on her doorstep and weakly drove away before she got out her key.

And then I began seeing her everywhere, smartly dressed and laughing, and not drunk, but drinking, at press receptions that I had to go to because of work or coming out of smart bars that I wouldn't go into because of what they charge for drink, justifying it on the decor and the fact they give you peanuts. She was always being photographed at the races 'seen exchanging a joke', and I caught a glimpse of her in a sports car with a fellow who is known for describing in detail every encounter he ever has with a female.

The children were nine, eight and seven when I came across Martin in a country hotel with a woman who was not Lorraine. Two days of pretending not to see him, and rushing out of lounges as he came in, and eventually he said, 'I don't suppose you'll tell.' Which annoyed me to hell for two reasons.

The arrogant Edwardian assumption that the gent is allowed to have his little fling and little floozy and that everyone will stand by him, and the other assumption that I might be on the phone to Dublin already saying, 'Lorraine, dear, I think you ought to know. . . .' I was just sad, the way anyone would be sad, and for some reason all her religious confusions came back to me, and I knew with a kind of instinct that she was not being unfaithful to him in the literal sense but was trying desperately to have a good time and be part of what she thought was a glamorous world, a world she missed by marrying so young, a world that confused her because its values weren't the ones she had learned in a country town, a convent school, a motherly digs and one summer abroad working in a library in Hastings.

You know the way it works. I wasn't back in Dublin two days when I met her.

'I believe you ran into Martin on a business trip,' she said.

Dishonest, mistrustful clown, I thought, and agreed that I had been talking to him for a few minutes. Had I time for coffee, she wondered? Oh God, I might as well hear it now. I might as well start saying I didn't know who he was with, whether all men were sex fiends and brutes or not. It was now or sometime. Right, we'll go to Bewley's.

But I was all wrong, couldn't have been more wrong, in fact. She wanted a chat just. The children were all so well, she was on the committee of this and that and could we ever give a little publicity to their flag day, and now that everybody was interpreting Humanae Vitae so liberally and all these cardinals were saying it as well, she felt fine, and she went to Communion regularly. She was a member of a little group that did spiritual reading and met once a fortnight to discuss it with each other and a priest who knew a lot more than they did.

She had stopped running around. It was all so silly, really, these parties and night-clubs, people thought you were there for One Thing. And now that Martin was so busy and had to take so many business trips she spent much more time with the kids. Everything was going so well it was a pity that I had never married. Oh yes, I agreed, but I keep trying.

That pleased her. Martin wouldn't be at home next weekend either but when he was, they'd have a little dinner party and he could bring along some single men, and you'd never know. I wondered did Martin know any single men; but said it would be lovely, and she was right you know, you never did know. We parted very happily.

Martin's next affair was so public that the children even heard about it at school.

Now Martin's latest really was a tramp. It's hard to give that description to anyone, but this girl was the end. She went with anyone who could give her a good time, she didn't know the meaning of love and she didn't care about families or people. She was out for her pretty little self.

Lorraine eventually got one of those 'I think you ought to know' calls. It was only a matter of time, I suppose, but it was terrible the way it hit her.

She didn't start any of the devious tricks of winning him back. She didn't go and have a silly perm and wear glamorous nightgowns, she just decided that it was all over and assessed the whole situation over a lonely cup of instant coffee in the kitchen one morning. If he was having fun, well so would she.

She picked on the most unlikely man in the world. A quiet, rather inarticulate man who had a fairly happy home life, and she just set herself at him. He had vague connections with libraries and publishing so she played up all she knew about the pathetic little holiday job she had a hundred years ago it seems, and assumed an interest in all his work. It took six weeks, they tell me, before he gave in. Then they started hiring rooms for the afternoon in Dublin hotels, and she just felt she was getting back at Martin, and he felt desperately worried in case someone might tell his wife.

'Pure playboy' we decided at this stage, because you see no one was very fond of Lorraine, and no one could understand her motives. It went on for about a year. If anyone thought anything I suppose it was about how dreadful it must have been for the children. Mummy with a worried man, Daddy with an out-and-out chancer. But anyway none of us had enough courage or interest to say Stop.

And it stopped when the out-and-out chancer found someone else richer, freer and more fun. And Martin wanted a bit of home life and it just wasn't around. And about six months later the quiet, inarticulate man took a job about a thousand miles from here, to get out of the situation, and brought his fairly happy wife with him, and there they were. Mutually suspicious, and deeply unhappy.

To this day I don't know what Martin does with his life. I don't really care because I never got to know him, but I care a bit, I suppose, because I see what a failure he and Lorraine made of the whole thing, the whole business that was meant to be sickness and health, in good times and bad times. I just see what had happened to her at the age of 32.

She is probably the best-known easy lay in Dublin. You only have to be nice to her, if you are a man, and she will get a little drunk and a little emotional, and say that God was very unfair when He made the world, and go home to bed with you.

It didn't come home to me until a few months ago when a friend, a good friend of mine, said he had got himself stupidly involved with a very clinging woman, and she kept ringing him indiscreetly at his office. He was trying to get out of it, but she seemed so dependent and she seemed to have nothing to live for, and she was deeply religious, and guilty, and he wondered what the hell he should do.

I knew it was Lorraine because I had seen them talking in a pub one day and knew that this is a village, not a capital city, and that it was the latest of her 'involvements'. All right, what should I do, women are fools. Should I go out to her house and say this guy has a good job and a good wife and stop bothering him? Should I tell him to choke her off, and have her eventual breakdown on my neck? Should I ask Martin out to dinner and say, 'You're both young still, can't you make a new start?'

I did one thing. I had a party and asked a priest, and got him talking to Lorraine. I eavesdropped every few minutes and they seemed to be getting on fine. He was saying things like 'Your teenage children will need you now more than ever' and she was saying, 'I know, I know, but I feel so dishonest and neglectful, how can I ever re-establish something?' And I felt like some kind of Solomon. That evening anyway.

But she didn't stop her way of life. As I write she is involved with a boy, and I mean boy, of 22 who keeps ringing me and saying things like 'That brute of a husband ill-treats her and how do you get an annulment in this country?' And I don't know what to say.

And last week she rang me up and said that she would be very grateful if I could ask someone what that priest meant on television when he said that Marriage was dead when Love was dead, and could I tell her about all that old thing about annulment costing a lot of money. Was that true these days?

'Why don't you just go and live in England for a bit and get a divorce?' I asked, tough but practical.

'It has to be an annulment or nothing,' she said.

It appeared that God would sanction an annulment and just about everything else, but not a horrible secular thing like a divorce.

'Oh God, Lorraine,' I said, 'you are a fool.'
And I know she'll never speak to me again.

Women Are Fools — Sandy

9 May 1973

Sandy read Exodus when she was 18, about the same time as I did, but she read it in Yorkshire, and had married Johnny by the time she got to Israel. She believed that life was very commercial and rat race–ish in London and that in the orange groves and the purity of Israeli kibbutz life, they could really be both themselves and part of a greater movement. Johnny was easy going, he looked into the practicalities of the thing, and he decided that they would try it for a year or two anyway. He could always get a job in engineering again when they came back to London; it didn't seem like a New Life, but if Sandy was so determined, there could be nothing lost. They bought eight good books on teaching yourself Hebrew, they bored a lot of their friends with talk of going to a new land and a new life. They packed their two tiny children into a plane and went to the kibbutz.

I saw them the day they arrived, pale and

blonde and starry-eyed. They handed the two little boys over to the Children's House and were given a bungalow to live in. They were told, as I had been, that the kibbutz could make no promises, if they were going to stay forever it would have to be by a vote from all the members. But then they didn't have to spell it out so much for me, because I was going in September anyway, back to teaching. There were no problems in my case.

And indeed there seemed to be none in Sandy's either. That summer she became tanned and happy, she worked with me in the chicken house for a few weeks, we used to take day-old chicks and inject them against something, and we both cried the day that I choked one by mistake, because I held it too tightly, and Sandy was so soft that she buried it, instead of throwing it into the dustbin like the rest of them would have done.

Johnny was working on the dam, we had all learned passable Hebrew, but Johnny was better because nobody at his end spoke any English at all.

Their children were very happy. They were three and one, and the three-year-old was saying things in Hebrew to Sandy in one month, which excited her very much. She and Johnny were with them for five hours every day from two in the afternoon until seven, when they would put the baby to bed, and send little Tom to his tea. Nobody ever mentioned to any of us or to the children that we were any different to anyone else because we weren't Jewish. We never thought about it ourselves anyway.

And the long hot summer wore on and I was changed to making yoghurt from six a.m. until two instead of being in the chicken house, and Sandy was out picking grapes and got even browner and healthier, and she had a funny, happy smile, and a way of saying 'Shalom' to everyone with a grin that should have made us realise her happiness wasn't going to last. But then why should it? I mean, what was wrong with the setup? They were a young couple in love and idealistic, and getting on well with everyone. Sandy didn't look a fool at all. Compared to all her other friends, the working wives that she had left behind in London, she was in a paradise; no money worries, no health worries, near the sea, part of a commune.

They weren't my *best friends* there, but I missed them and thought about them a lot when I went home. No one is much good at letter writing on a kibbutz, and apart from a New Year's card I never heard from them. The following summer when I got off the bus for my three months visit, they were all there, as usual; nothing seemed to have changed. Miriam was still the cynical wit, David the fellow who got things done. Some of the older men and women with Polish names that I never got to know well threw their arms around me and said that I was one of the few summer visitors who ever returned. Sandy and Johnny were so good at Hebrew now that they could hardly bring themselves to talk in English, they said! They were terribly happy; a year and three months had gone by and no one had said anything about a vote. They were obviously there for life. Why didn't I go up to Tel Aviv for a month, marry someone and bring him back to the kibbutz? Life was so perfect.

And it was. No yoghurt making, no chickens, I was allowed to bring the kids for swims, if I could prove that I could shout, in Hebrew, all right and useful phrases like 'Come in at once' or 'Nobody out further than their waists'. Sandy's little boy Tommy was there and he literally couldn't speak a word of English. He was golden and had lots of friends.

One evening I was listening to the record player I had borrowed from a nice old

Hungarian, who said that he now knew all the records in the library, and I could have the player until they got a few new ones. There were a lot of crickets outside competing with the music, and the laughter of a very young army group of boys and girls of about 18 who had been billeted on the kibbutz for a month and we all found them a terrible nuisance.

Sandy knocked at the door, and she didn't seem happy at all and there was very little of that fey glow. 'I'm pregnant,' she said.

Now what is so bad about a happily married woman having a third baby, you might wonder? The words didn't strike the terror into me that they have when other people have said them. But then of course I remembered the kibbutz rule, two children and no more. There was every kind of birth control available free and medical help as well, as regards a choice. Anyone who miscalculated had to go to Tel Aviv and have an abortion, there were simply no exceptions. There was no shame about the abortion either in the community, people just laughed and said how stupid of you. But Sandy was really grey with worry. She would like another little Tommy or Frank. She didn't know after all if they were going to be allowed to stay there forever. Should she have the child and go? If she had the child, there was no way she could stay, we both knew that. We decided to ask David, he knew the answer to everything.

David asked us in for coffee, he asked his wife to go off somewhere for an hour and she good-humouredly agreed. He said that in fact there had been a vote about allowing Sandy and Johnny to stay and that out of 300 people 287 had said yes. So they didn't bother telling this to the two of them because they might go around wondering who the other 13 were and it might make them feel edgy. Go ahead and have the abortion, said David, there's no fear.

I went to Tel Aviv on the bus with her. We found the doctor.

'Silly girl,' he said kindly. 'Sit up in the chair here.'

'Now?' screamed Sandy and I together in horror. We thought you went to bed for a day or two and got injections and tranquilisers and pep talks and anaesthetics and days to recover.

'Now,' said the doctor.

A nurse came into the room. She was young and pretty, she was kind, she spoke English, which was a great help to me anyway. She said the doctor had done five that morning and would do another 11 before leaving. There was simply nothing to it. Sandy could go home to the kibbutz that night; there was just no problem. Her friend, who had had one done yesterday, was working again this afternoon. It's all a matter of coming in time, like Sandy had; please stop getting excited now.

Sandy begged me not to leave. She told the doctor I was her sister. So I held her hand throughout and looked out the window and thought perhaps life is tougher here, and maybe Sandy after a year here would be tougher, and I would selfishly wipe it all out of my mind, and perhaps I could be tough too. And in 20 minutes Sandy was lying, wrapped in a rug, in a sort of waiting room, and the nice nurse brought her a cup of tea as she was coming round from one of those anaesthetics you get to have your teeth out. And the nice nurse reminded us that we could only use the waiting room for an hour.

I got a taxi and brought Sandy to a hotel. I telephoned the kibbutz and told them a lie, said we had missed the bus and that we would be back tomorrow. I said to tell Johnny that Sandy was fine.

'Well of course she is,' said whoever answered the phone, but whoever it was did tell Johnny anyway.

All night we sat and smoked, and she told me about her life in England and her wealthy parents in Yorkshire who hadn't wanted her to marry Johnny but softened a bit when he got a good engineering job, and how she believed that only in Israel could you be really decent.

But now she had this awful feeling that it wasn't a decent thing to do to kill an unborn child, and she wondered for the fiftieth time would it have been a boy or a girl.

The doctor had said casually, 'It's not possible to know at this stage, Sandy, do stop worrying, will you?'

And we went off on the bumpy bus next morning, and I deposited her at her bungalow, and Johnny came back from the dam and thanked me for going with her and asked me with his eyes would she be all right, and I kept nodding, and trying to put it all out of my mind.

And the second long hot summer went on and though Sandy had lost what I fancifully thought had been the glow, she seemed fine. And we worked together one week at the potato-peeling machine, which was such a lousy job you only got it one week a year, and we had plenty of time to talk; she never mentioned the event again, and with great relief neither did I.

The way they work things on a kibbutz is often by rotating the horrible jobs with the good ones, so that even if you are a specialist like Johnny was and are needed on the dam you have to take your turn in the kitchen as well. There is no status, which is what Sandy loved about everything, and at the end of August when it was Johnny's turn to work in the kitchen, he was also in charge of the money, which had to be paid out to some delivery man who came once a week. Nobody in a kibbutz sees or touches money, their meals, drinks, clothes, accommodation, and cigarettes even, are all free. So Johnny got the £45 from the kibbutz secretary and left it on the window under a big jug of orange juice to wait until this man would come to be paid. In a kibbutz £45 in cash would probably be like a thousand, because it just isn't used or seen.

When the delivery man knocked at the door, the money wasn't there. Johnny was disturbed, but not greatly so; someone must have taken it away for safer keeping. But a huge search was mounted and no one could find it. There was no question of the delivery man having snatched it because he hadn't even come in the kitchen door.

Suddenly the whole atmosphere changed.

Suddenly there was suspicion. In the 28 years since the kibbutz had been in existence, nothing like this had ever happened before. Johnny was scarlet with horror and Sandy was white with concern. They begged to have their bungalow searched and poor Johnny tried to account for his movements like an Agatha Christie villain, saying, 'Well I moved from the window to the dishwashing machine and then I went to see how the fish were frying and then. . . .' The kibbutz secretary had given another £45 to the bemused delivery man, who thought that all kibbutz dwellers were mad anyway.

Sandy went around saying to everyone very reasonably but also very repetitively, 'What would we want with £45 anyway, supposing we were the kind of people who would steal?'

Everyone shrugged, some more sympathetically than others, but they all, we all, said it was a great mystery, all right, and money didn't fly off a window sill. I tried to tell her it would die down like rows did in a school or an office, but she was deeply disturbed and kept saying it was a plot. It was one of the 13 who didn't want them to stay. She went to David's house day and night to ask him who the 13 were, and he begged both Johnny and myself to keep her quiet, she was upsetting the even tenor of their ways. Then Sandy would come to *my* room at all hours and beg me to realise that they were under suspicion and that the kids would hear about it, and really hadn't they a right to know who the people were that didn't want them to stay. And why couldn't we call in the police, or the army or someone with a lie detector.

One evening about a week later, when it all had far from died down like in an office or a school, Sandy stood up during dinner and became hysterical. She shouted and cried and said that she wasn't a thief and her husband wasn't a thief, and everyone was treating them as if they were. She then said, as I dreaded, 'It's just because we're not Jewish, because we're different, that you've picked on us. We aren't the same as you, that's what it all boils down to. It's a question of race. We're different.'

David stood up too. He had a calm voice and was a leader in every possible sphere of their life in that community. He spoke very gently. 'Sandy, that's not so. You, yourself, said you felt the same as we did, you wanted to build a new land, you wanted to live near and on the land, and you wanted to share. The day you and Johnny asked to be members of our commune you said you weren't doing it for atonement about Hitler or anything. I asked you not to look at the numbers on people's arms from concentration camps because you just *might* begin to feel different. You assured me that you felt one of us and we made you members. The fact is that Johnny "lost" £45 and that never happened here before and so people are upset.'

Six hundred eyes stared at them both, for what seemed an hour. Sandy spat at David and left the room, Johnny followed. They spent two days telephoning London getting £100 which Sandy threw on the floor of the kibbutz secretary's office, and they packed one small grip bag and their two startled children on to the bus. They wouldn't say goodbye to anyone.

Terrible, unforgivable, tragic were the words people used as the bus went away in a shower of dust and hot smoke. Every single person was upset; it was too small and parochial for people to be above judgment and comment. They wondered aloud at Sandy's bitterness, had it been latent there all the time, at whether she believed Johnny might have taken the money. They wondered why she had been so keen to come in the first place, they wondered could the abortion have unhinged her, they asked

117

me to remember everything she had said to me. They really cared what was going to happen to her. Not so much about Johnny, he was sort of adaptable, they thought.

At dinner the night after they went, there was a terrible argument at one table with people screaming and shouting in Hebrew. I couldn't understand a word of it, so great and frightening was the intensity. An old man was being hustled out the door, a nice old man, he used to work in the chicken place with me one year and help me with holding them so they would feel comfortable. He was crying, and his whole face was distorted. It took me an hour to find out what had happened; he had suddenly put his hand into his pocket and taken out £45, and said something like, 'Now that the hypocritical Goi have gone, here's the money; I have no secrets, and I don't steal from my own.' Instead of being congratulated, as the old man thought he would be, he was turned on by everyone. His shouts about what the Goi had done to his wife and children and everyone he knew in Treblinka were ignored, his rage that the Christians, especially the English Christians, had stood by in 1948 and let seven Arab states attack the new pathetic Jewish homeland, went unheard. He was marched to David's house, where David was minding Malka, his quiet wife, sick with a kind of flu and a kind of depression over Sandy and Johnny's terrible exit.

David wasted no time. He tried to find out had they left the country. No, they were booked for the following morning, someone in the airlines told him eventually. He took a motorbike and went miles through the night to find their hotel; he didn't, but he was at Lod Airport before they arrived. That much we knew as we waited in the hot day. David will bring them back, it will all be made up, we told each other. The other poor man is sick, he will be taken away to hospital. Johnny and Sandy will understand; they will come back. We didn't really believe it.

David came back alone with a scar on his face. Sandy had hit him in the departure lounge with her handbag. She and Johnny and the two toddlers had got on the plane to London. They had said, David told a few people, that Treblinka hadn't been half hard enough for the old man.

It was a sad summer.

I wrote to them, and said I was often in London and that if ever they would like to meet me, we could talk about other things, not Israel. I heard nothing for two years, so after two letters I left it.

Two years later I got a letter from Johnny, he said he had just heard me on a radio programme and thought he'd like to meet me for a meal sometime I was in London. We arranged a place, and I asked, with some kind of unexpected sensitivity, first about the children. They were fine. I wouldn't know Tommy now, he was a little man; and Frank was a real character. I asked about his job and he about mine, we talked about the cost of holidays, and whether Snowdon would have been a good photographer anyway or had made it because of Margaret. When we started talking about the scampi we were eating I couldn't bear it any more.

'Where's Sandy?' I asked very quickly, hoping that the best he would say was that she was a bit depressed and didn't want to meet anyone with associations with the unhappy incidents. I thought the worst he might say was they had parted, because he seemed to be talking about the kids as if they were his sole responsibility. Nothing prepared me for his equally quick answer.

'She's in jail,' he said.

When they had got back to England her parents had been no help. They had told everyone that their crazy little daughter and son-in-law had done their stint out in the sun for the Israelis and had now seen sense and come home again. Sandy then turned against her mother. They had rented a flat in London and he got a job; Sandy seemed cheerful, for a while. They decided to have another child and somehow she wasn't getting pregnant. She went for an examination and was told that the abortion had done something which would not only prevent her having children, but might lead to a hysterectomy. Johnny was vague; I think he suspected that Sandy made it up, because he said pleadingly either you have a hysterectomy or you don't, isn't that right? I didn't know.

And then Sandy had lost all control. One day she had gone to Stamford Hill, Golders Green, and a couple of other areas where Jews lived in numbers. She had thrown stones in windows of jewellers, of places with Jewish names, of synagogues when she could find one. She had hired a motor scooter, and got away each time before she was caught. It was evening before the police came and found her with a bagful of stones on the pillion of the scooter, heading off again and laughing.

Of course he had got her psychiatric help. She was in a very nice place for a month, and convinced everyone, himself included, that it had been a wild aberration. She had seemed so ashamed of herself and asked everyone nervously was she going mad, and promised that she would make up the damage she had done so sincerely that she had fooled even the psychiatrist.

She was on the probation act or under it or whatever you are, and Johnny had to give up work for a couple of months and go cap in hand, he said, to her father for money to look after her. She read a lot, and wouldn't talk about it, and refused a psychoanalyst, and then six weeks later took a fire shovel and broke three windows again of Jewish shops, and said so coldly in court that she was perfectly sane, but just wanted to equal an old score, that this time the Law was a bit suspicious of her, and it was all at the time when people were beating up Pakistanis. Poor Johnny's face was more bewildered than when the £45 had disappeared.

She chose jail, and she said she would do it again when she came out. So they had better keep her there a long time. Her psychiatrist said she wasn't fit to be imprisoned.

He had begged everyone to let him state the facts and the history, but Sandy was so cold, so full of hate, so full of the Enoch Powell phraseology that really the Law had no option. She had been in prison now for

two months with four more, two if her behaviour was good, but she said that if they
were going to release her early she would
shout out more anti-Semitic things and be
kept in.

The psychiatrist, who was fuming because
she was in jail at all, said that he would get
her into a good place and they would cure
her, but Johnny didn't believe they ever
would. He wanted to know about the kibbutz, had I been back? I had. Did the
tomato scheme work? Did the dam still go
peculiar? Was the food any better? Had they
made a profit yet on the chickens? Did Ari
and Miriam get a divorce? Nothing about
himself and Sandy, it might have been a
book that he had read, and been interrupted
in. He wanted to know how the serial was
continuing.

'They are always asking do I see you,' I
said diffidently. 'They want news of you
terribly.'

'Well you'll have plenty to tell them this
year,' he said bitterly.

PAGEANTRY AND SPLENDOUR AT WESTMINSTER FOR THE ROYAL WEDDING

15 November 1973

The ushers were simply delighted to see me. 'Splendid,' they said, 'absolutely splendid. Let's have a little look. Oh, yes, seat number 17 this way. Super view, and just beside the telly, too. Super!' They could have been brothers of my dearest friend, instead of members of Mark Phillips' regiment examining the press ticket, which had cost £23.

Westminster Abbey was lit up like an operating theatre; the light from the chandeliers was only like candlelight compared to the television lights. Well, since 500 million people, including the Irish, were meant to be looking in, I suppose you had to have it bright enough to see something. There was plenty to see from the top of a scaffolding over the north transept. Grace Kelly staring into space, looking like she always looked, kind of immaculate. Rainier has aged a bit oddly and looks like Marlon Brando in *The Godfather*. Harold Wilson, all smiles and straightening his tie, his wife looking as if she were about to compose the final poem on the occasion. Jeremy Thorpe was all giggles and jauntiness, Heath looked like a waxwork.

Anthony Barber looked suitably pre-occupied, as well he might, with a State-of-Emergency going on outside the Abbey doors, and Whitelaw looked as if it was his first day off in two years. There were a lot of people whose faces I thought I knew, but it was no help asking for advice on either side. The man from the *Manchester Evening News* seemed to be writing an extended version of *War and Peace* in a notebook and on my right an agency reporter was transcribing a file of cuttings.

And then the royals started to arrive. We could see them on the television set — which was six inches from me — leaving Buckingham Palace in their chariots, and like characters stepping out of a film, they suddenly turned up a hundred feet below our seats. The Queen Mother looked the way she has ever looked — aged 56 and benign. The Queen looked thin and unhappy in a harsh blue outfit. Princess Margaret looked like a lighting devil with a cross face and an extraordinary hideous coat, which may have been some multicoloured fur. But then was there ever an animal or even a selection of animals that would have been given such a coat by Nature.

The Phillips' parents looked sick with nerves; nobody in the place was hating it as much as they were. Mother Phillips nearly tore her gloves to shreds, father Phillips let his invitation fall and it struck me as odd that the groom's parents should have had to carry an invitation at all. The son and heir stood smiling and resplendent in scarlet, dimpling and smiling, and you felt that if all else failed and he doesn't become a brigadier or something in six months, he will have a great living in toothpaste commercials.

The Dean of Westminster, who is a very civilised, cheerful sort of man, was sort of happy about it all, and so was the Archbishop of Canterbury. They beamed all round them and extracted a few return grins from the nervous-looking lot in the VIP seats. The choirboys looked suitably angelic and uncomfortable in their ruffs. One of them got his fingers caught behind his neck and had to have it released.

The trumpeters were noble and rallying, and the Beefeaters were traditionally beefy. Everything was as it should be in fact, as we waited for the bride.

About three seconds after the glass coach had left Buckingham Palace with Anne and her father we were all handed two pages of strictly embargoed details about the wedding dress: it would have threatened national security to have had it before, apparently. Journalists all around me were devouring it and rewriting the details of seed pearls and 1,000 threads of 20-denier silk to every inch of the garment. When she arrived at the door of the Abbey there was a bit of excitement about arranging the train and adjusting the tiara, and the bride looked as edgy as if it were the Badminton Horse Trials and she was waiting for the bell to gallop off.

Up at the altar all the royals looked out as eagerly and anxiously as if they thought the Duke of Edinburgh and his only daughter might have dropped off for a pint on the way. The Queen actually smiled when they got into sight and Mark gave a matinee-idol shy, rueful smile. Princess Margaret read her programme of the wedding service as if it were the latest Agatha Christie that she had promised to finish before lunchtime.

The Duke of Edinburgh went and sat beside his wife and mother-in-law and seemed to have a far greater control over his sword than did Prince Charles, who carried his as if it were an umbrella. I was waiting for half his relatives to have their legs amputated but there must have been some kind of plastic top on it because nobody seemed to be maimed or anything when they were leaving.

The service went as planned and the young voices were clear and loud, as everyone remarked approvingly afterwards, no coyness or nervous stutters. There were a lot of hymns, and I saw the Queen singing her head off, but gloomily, and the Phillips parents sang, too, nervously on their side.

Then off they galloped down the aisle and it was over. And do I mean over! There was no hooley in the palace or anything; the party had been on Monday night. The people who had got all dressed up went home, I suppose. The bridal couple had about nine hours of photographs, and all the people who had been camping on the street packed their spirit stoves into plastic bags and went off for lunch.

It was a superbly organised show, with all the actors playing their parts perfectly, timing and all. Everyone who had a role kept to it: the Duchess of Kent looked sweet and pure English girlhood; Princess Alexandra managed to give the odd vaguely tomboyish grin which she thinks is expected. The Duke of Edinburgh and Lord Snowdon looked as self-effacing as Mark Phillips is beginning to look already. The ushers saw us out,

thrilled that we had been able to get there
and hoping earnestly that we had a good
view of everything. The evening papers were
already on the streets with early photographs. 'The Snow White Princess!'
screamed one headline, as if the readers had
expected the bride to wear scarlet jodhpurs.

It was a very well-produced show, no one
could deny that, but then the actors are getting slightly above Equity rates.

HOW TO SPEAK PROPER

27 May 1974

I was particularly fond of the word
'antithesis' and used to drag it into all kinds
of conversations, until I noticed people smiling at the way I pronounced it. Apparently
there was something unusual about the 'th'
bit, which made me red with rage since the
English are totally unable to speak their own
language and insist on talking about the
Shar of Persiar, and having a good idear
about something, and wondering what's going to happen next in Eirer.

It was with a vicious joy that I discovered
that the BBC had a pronunciation unit no
less, a section which defined the correct way
to use words, where to lay the emphasis
and, most importantly, how to deal with

unfamiliar places and people's names. Armed with recent examples of their horrifying mispronunciations I went off to investigate it, sure that I would give them a few helpful hints and set them straight on it all. It wasn't only the infamous Droggheeda, and the multifarious pronunciations of Charlie Haughey's name at a time gone by, but it was words like 'Sinai' which I was certain they had got wrong.

Mrs Hazel Wright wouldn't give an inch on Sinai. Not a centimetre. Yes, she knew I'd been there, so had the hundreds of others who objected to it being pronounced Sign-e-eye. But still she had done her work and this was what had come of it. In Hebrew and many Arabic languages the A and the I were both lone vowels, in rapid speech it was pronounced Sign-e-eye. Look at the file, look at the research. But since you could never be doctrinaire about language, it was quite possible that this pronunciation might change. They were not pedants, they didn't want to impose a pronunciation, in a few months they might agree that common usage had sanctioned it and then it would be Sign-Eye, as I wanted.

They were not stuffy in the pronunciation unit, she said firmly. And indeed stuffy they are not. They have a huge metal filing index with over 100,000 entries. As soon as a word is queried or thought worth querying, a little card is filled out on it, with the whole history of the investigations and a summary of the findings. Sometimes, of course, a place or a person comes into the news so rapidly that they don't have time to find out how it should be pronounced. But they usually have it right in a few hours. 'Like some Northern Ireland names,' I said, thinking of the time that poor Henry Kelly had been going to bed in Belfast satisfied that he covered the main stories of the day. He turned on the two a.m. news and heard that there had been great trouble in Collisland, a place of which he had never heard. Frantic, he checked around and was told to go back to sleep; they meant Coal island and he had done the story hours earlier.

Mrs Wright agreed. Scottish, Welsh and Irish names were difficult to pronounce to a southern English ear and voice. If they had to be pronounced without recourse to any advice people usually tried to say them as they were written, which, she agreed, was not only unwise but which had too many bad precedents. 'When you think that the English have a name like Featherstonehaugh and are capable of pronouncing it in at least five ways including Fanshaw and Feesonhay it's ridiculous that we should expect others to go by spelling alone. But we don't really, you know. We go to great trouble to try and get it right, and sometimes it's not as easy as you think.'

In the case of an Irish place name the following procedure is used. Firstly they go to their enormous index to see is it included. A great many names are there already. Asked to pick one at random, I chose 'Magherafelt'. There were four pages of notes on it, beginning with the report of a BBC overseas reporter who said that when he was there during the war, local people had called it Maarafelt, and going on to various contradictions of this all dated and documented. There were reasons for accepting or rejecting the Macherafelt pronunciation, and an eventual conclusion as to how it should be uttered. Suppose the name did not appear in the index? Mrs Wright and her assistants would telephone the Irish Embassy in London. There was a girl in the library there, Dympna Coughlan, who went to great trouble to tell them how it was pronounced. If she didn't know or gave a couple of alternatives they would ring their man in Dublin or Belfast or wherever and ask him to enquire around a bit and see what was the accepted usage; sometimes they rang Brigid Kilfeather in RTÉ who would help them. I wouldn't believe all the trouble they had had with Seán Mac Stíofáin's name. Honestly, everyone they asked gave them a different variation.

Were the biggest files on Irish names then? Not at all. You had to remember how many countries they were dealing with, especially through the Overseas Service at Bush House. Actually if I wanted to see the biggest file it was on the word 'Nyasaland'. It went on for over 16 pages, coming up with the final conclusion that it should be pronounced Nee not Nye. The biggest problem was that they had to remember they were speaking in English and since English people didn't call Paris 'Paree' they had to concentrate on what would be the accepted English pronunciation of the word. They weren't monitors or spies in the pronunciation unit. They didn't listen to broadcasts and ring up a speaker and pounce on him for saying the word incorrectly. They don't have time for one thing, and that's not their job for another. It's funny that an organisation like the BBC which was for so many years considered rightly or wrongly the great authority on how to talk nicely should in fact have just a small section where people apply if they want to know how to pronounce a difficult word. Certainly Mrs Wright, who is an honours graduate in modern languages and who has phonetic training, is very capable of dealing with anything that occurs, and many things that don't occur. Every morning they send around a list of words which they think might be needed during the day, like 'Ma'alot' in Israel or 'Potchefestroom' in South Africa.

It all began, this care and emphasis on pronunciation, as long ago as 1926, when an advisory committee on spoken English was set up under the chairmanship of the then poet laureate Robert Bridges, and it went on gently, I would imagine, discussing things in an academic way until 1939 when the war meant an end to all such committees. Shaw was on the team with them and gave a lot of good and memorable advice, although he is once meant to have said that it would have been a hell of a lot better if they had a few London taxi drivers and less lords and ladies on it. The woman who had done all the donkey work on the committee was Miss Elizabeth Miller, whose name is still a legend in the BBC. She took over the pronunciation business for the whole Corporation. Hers are the main body of the notes in the files and Mrs Wright pays tribute to the way she worked almost unsung and quite obviously had to fight long battles over almost every word for many years. Miss Miller retired two years ago but the standards she set in policy still remain, and are strenuously supported by those who have come after her.

I found some of the items in the pronunciation handbook utterly comic, like the paragraph that deals with local educated usage, which is established 'by consulting the vicar of the parish, the town hall, or the police'. How could you seriously ask the police or the vicar how to pronounce a place? 'I don't agree with you at all,' said Hazel Wright, 'you can't ask the first person you meet or take a name out of a phone book to define how a place is pronounced. Vicars and policemen have often been a long time in the area, they meet a lot of people by the nature of their work, they get a good average idea of how the majority of the people pronounce the place and that's what we need.' It is interesting to note that the BBC these days is more anxious to avoid being patronising than to sound posh. For example, they don't try too hard to get local accent or pronunciation and emphasis in case it looks as if they are trying unsuccessfully to take off the accents of the people who are strangers to them. The British say *post* office. In Ireland we accent the second word; a reporter in Ireland would not conform to this because it would look odd and sound odder.

They try too not to be too accurate. This came up over the recent football match. There is no adjective 'Argentinian'. In fact, the word you should use is 'Argentine' to describe the team. But the pronunciation unit did not recommend this as it sounded a little too hair-splitting and liable to be misunderstood by the majority of the audience. If I thought that the BBC pronunciation unit was rather over-documented, said Hazel Wright, I should have a look at the way the French go about it. Almost every day she receives their documentation and it is incredibly detailed and indeed much more dictatorial. It is also extraordinarily charming since every manifesto about the wrong pronunciation of consonants before vowels ends with a little quote from the famous. I examined a few. 'I've been speaking prose for forty years and didn't know it' Molière. Or: 'A knowledge of words is a knowledge of things' Plato. The French do things with style, thinks Mrs Wright. Who wouldn't like to do things with more style if there were more of them, and more time?

She doesn't want to order people what to say but to be able to give exhaustive reasons for any particular pronunciation she suggests. Her rooms are surrounded with reference books as well as files. The phone hardly stopped ringing with people wanting to know how to pronounce things.

'Life would be very simple for us if we didn't have news,' she says. 'You see we could get the correct pronunciation of any word correctly in a day or two, but somehow that isn't the way a radio and television service works. It has to know at once or not at all.'

WHO SENT THIS POSTCARD?

2 September 1974

It arrived the other day. A nice postcard of Paris. On the back was this message: 'Everything arranged this end. Have finished the book finally. Paris as lovely as it always was. Hope everything fine with you now. Love John.'

This is the greatest mystery that has ever occurred in my life. What has he arranged at his end, for God's sake? Is it a hotel room, a bank robbery, an interview with the President? Who is he? I checked the Johns I know. The ones in *The Irish Times* are still working away at their desks and are arranging nothing in Paris.

I know a travel agent called John, who told me gloomily that he couldn't afford to go to Paris to arrange anything. I rang a John who works in the hotel business and had a ridiculous shouted conversation with him about bed nights and tourist receipts, but he hasn't been to Paris for five years and doesn't think he'll ever see it again. Then what could the book be, is it one he has written or just one he has read? I suppose I can watch the book lists for a year or two in case John Somebody published something, but suppose he was just wading through *War and Peace*? I'm delighted Paris is as lovely as it always was, but is there an implication that we once saw it together? I was never in that city with anyone called John, never. There were no moonlight walks by the Seine holding the hand of a John. He must mean that it was as lovely as he separately and I separately had always found it. Why shouldn't everything be fine with me? Now or any other time. What wasn't fine? It's terrible to try and think of the things that haven't been fine, you just become very neurotic. Could he be somebody I met when I fell down all those stairs and had to be taken breathing oxygen to a hospital?

That was the last time that things weren't fine. Or was he around when I lost my diary with every address, phone number and piece of information I will need for the rest of my life?

Oh to hell with him; anyone who has the arrogance to sign himself John and expect to be recognised doesn't deserve a moment's thought. But why can't I sleep worrying about what he has arranged at his end. And what damn book has he finished? And why did he spell my name right if I don't know him, and why couldn't he have sent a postcard to somebody else?

HOLIDAY ROMANCE

6 November 1974

If you go to the Club Méditerranée on your own, you have to share a hut or a bungalow with someone else. One time, when I was in Turkey, I shared with a girl called Francine. She was very, very beautiful; she examined all my clothes with a lack of interest, went through the three pieces of make-up I had with disappointment, asked me rather humiliatingly did Irish women not care about being chic, and finally, deciding that I would be no threat to her, became my best friend for three weeks.

Francine was an air hostess. She was recovering from a serious operation, the details of which I tried to shut out but it seemed to be bits of stomach being untied from where they were and tied to other bits. She was also recovering from a broken heart, had borrowed £200 from a friend for clothes and was going to have a marvellous time, and return to Paris looking magnificent and possibly with a new remedy for the broken heart in tow.

We had an unspoken arrangement about not meeting during the day. Because Francine would spend the morning on the beach miles away from everyone, sunbathing nude. She would have three green figs for her lunch, which was insanity since the food was included in the price and was magnificent. She would spend the afternoon in the 'Hammam,' or Turkish bath, and emerge after about three hours looking lovely.

Dinner time was when she would cast around for men to hunt. For the first week there was little interesting to catch. She would discuss the conquests flatly when we went to bed. 'No, the Italian lawyer was very boring. I wish I could have found him suitable, because he is from a very wealthy family, but no.' And a most handsome lounge lizardish sort of person who paid her constant attention was dismissed petulantly. 'You see, he is a great nuisance. Other men do not come and talk to me while he is there, and he is a very stupid and very vain little man.'

I left her to go off and do a strenuous six-day excursion in the valley of Goreme. It meant crawling through rock-hewn churches, climbing what looked like the face of the Eiger. Filthy and out of breath, I would return to our central Turkish base each evening for a quick wash and a night of cheap wine, wondering vaguely how Francine was making out with the checklist of possibles she had drawn up. There seemed nobody likely for me to bring back to her on the outing. They were all filthy as I was, and seemed to have no interest in anything except rock-hewn churches, which I guessed might not be Francine's secret passion.

In fact, they were a pretty dull lot, the men on that trip, and the dullest of all was a surgeon with a pipe which made him totally inarticulate in any language. He had a difficult 18-year-old son behaving like a 12-year-old, full of sulks and shoulder shrugging and boredom which drove us all mad. The surgeon said to me once that he couldn't continue talking with me unless I would learn to pronounce the French word 'suspendu' correctly, because it made his teeth water to hear the way I did say it. That kind of thing can either be a challenge or a pain in the face. It was a pain in the face. On our return to the main camp, Francine looked even more beautiful but a bit cheesed off on the quest for the grail. Men there had been in plenty presenting themselves, but they were all of inferior intelligence. Since Francine was not exactly Einstein, this seemed odd but interesting. I wondered hesitantly should she go out and look for friends during the day instead of waiting until dinner time. I had found some play-mates of my own out in fishing boats and at barbecues. No, said Francine purposefully, that would not do at all. You would meet a rough sort of person that way. And how could you judge their manners and their style if you didn't meet them at dinner?

The next night I introduced her to Christian, the sour doctor. I thought it would be a conversation of ten seconds' duration, and was surprised to see them half an hour later chatting away. That night she sat with him at dinner and was very, very late back to our bungalow. She turned on the lights, handed me a cigarette and, clasping my hand, said, 'You are a genius; he's perfect, just perfect.'

To be woken from sleep to such enthusiasm is startling, but the more I thought of the strange doctor and the magnificent-looking romance-seeking Francine, the more I began to think it was one of those dreams where you imagine that your younger brother is married to Catherine the Great and you wonder what to do about it.

It was no dream. The 24-year-old Francine and the 50ish Christian were inseparable for the rest of the holiday. She would wake me every night to tell me the details, which were very, very boring, and mainly involved her strategy in not giving him all he would naturally as a man want, because it was wiser to wait until they were married.

One night, despairing to be woken to the same story, I said that perhaps he might not want all that men might naturally want on account of sharing a bungalow with his 18-year-old son, and she said I had a lot to learn. The son, who was called Claude, became even more painful as time went on, and was sitting shrugging and yawning every time I was dragged to join them all for a drink. He was interested in no subject and one day in desperation I asked him what he would like best to happen that afternoon.

He said, 'I would like that stupid girl to leave my father alone and find some cowboy to divert her. My father is very easily swayed.'

Oh drama, drama. I couldn't bear to leave them not knowing what was going to happen though I didn't really like any of them enough to be on anyone's side.

But the months went by and the time I could afford to go to Paris came eventually. I wrote to Francine and said it would be nice to meet for lunch. On the way to the restaurant I expected she would have difficulty in remembering what Christian's name was. He seemed to be such an unlikely life partner. But there he was, the two of them smiling, and a bit of diamond flashing. They had just become engaged; would I come to their wedding? They insisted on giving me a ticket as a present, because I had introduced them, remember? Well, I was polite for a bit. They would have met anyway; it wasn't fair to take a ticket. And then, of course, I gave in as we had all known I would.

It was an extraordinary wedding. The town hall one day, a church the next, two great feasts, lots of congratulation, everybody on both sides of the family assuring me of the good work I had done. If ever there was a couple so right for each other it was Christian and Francine. The sour Claude had become less shruggy. He said it was better for his father not to have a lonely old age. I swore to become a deep and intimate friend of the whole family, and we exchanged Christmas cards for about three years as an assurance that this is what indeed I was.

Then I had a party, a party all of my own in Paris. It sounds very grand, and in fact I thought I would never get a chance to write about it. It was in fact 12 people invited to my hotel bedroom to have some duty-free Irish whiskey, which I had smuggled in. I invited Christian and Francine among the guests. Maybe you know already what was going to happen, but I hadn't a clue, and it staggered me for weeks. Francine arrived, but with her glum stepson Claude, less glum and deeply protective to the extent of embracing his stepmother in the most unacceptable manner, as the French would say.

Francine dragged me aside, telling me that I looked a bit better than before but not much. I should have my eyebrows done professionally and perhaps red hair what with being Irish. 'Where's Christian?' I squeaked, knowing I was going to hear something strange.

'Oh well, you know it was never very wise, when there is such an age difference and everything. He has gone to live in Switzerland. He is a very famous surgeon there now in a clinic, he is very happy. This man is interested really only in his work. You do understand and I would die in Switzerland. All those dull, clean, plain people. I would die outside Paris. He knows that, he writes from time to time. He did a very famous operation and it was in the papers.'

I'm really not able for all this sort of thing at all you know, despite my pretensions, and my voice was like some kind of puppet by the time I managed to get out the words, 'And what about Claude?'

'Oh, isn't he marvellous? You are a genius, he is just perfect. Everybody would have such a happy holiday romance if they only went on a holiday with you. I can never thank you enough.'

I Was a Winter Sport

21 November 1974

I knew that I would probably fall, but I didn't expect to fall coming out of the railway station. Crowds of elegant Germans in posh ski wear tramped over me, a few British looked embarrassed and then looked away, an Italian man bent down and told me that it happened to the best of us and went away without picking me up. When the station was empty three porters got me to my feet and begged me not to take the next train home. Madame would be skiing like a bird, they assured me, and like a fool I believed them, and slid and crawled my way to the hotel.

It was full of sweat and heat, and pipes gurgling, and basements with people throwing skis around like darts, and radiant faces talking about the south piste, and worried brows discussing ski bindings. There was registration for the nursery school and a lot of hot rum, and a view from the bedroom like the best Christmas card ever and a very deep, slightly bruised sleep.

Next day, hot chocolate, plenty of buns to keep up the strength, into the ski pants that looked great in Dublin and cost a week's salary. Beside everything else on the patio they looked like fancy dress. On with about four sweaters, in case I got frostbite and a jar of cream rubbed into my face in case there was sunstroke going around as well. Left, right, left, right, and we marched to the foothills of a crag.

The ski instructor was called Mike, and nobody fell in love with him. In three languages he told us how to put on our skis, which were waiting in battered splendour on the snow. A man fell over just bending down to pick them up, and I was so sympathetic that I rushed to help him up and fell on top of him, which was a bad start, since Mike said in three languages again that there would be time for that sort of thing later, could we concentrate on getting the skis on now please. We extricated ourselves, and a nice 12-year-old tied on both our skis for us.

It was the most awkward thing I have ever done. Each foot seemed to weigh a ton and to be 20 feet long. It was impossible to point oneself anywhere without doing damage to someone else and one woman became quite hysterical because she found herself sliding sideways with gathering speed and couldn't stop. Mike had to go and head her off before she went into a wall at a hundred miles an hour and that caused a lot of alarm in those of us who stood rooted to the ground. Skiing sideways was a new horror we hadn't thought of.

He put us in two circles like a Paul Jones and we were asked to walk around to get used to the feel of the things. The space between each walker increased to huge distances because everybody seemed to be sticking a ski into the bottom of the person in front, and you couldn't turn around to protest because you fell over at once if you moved in any direction except purposefully forward. So there were great oaths in many languages, as we marched gloomily around the churned-up snow dragging these fiend-ish appendages.

Just when I was wondering would it be time for the après ski to begin, Mike said that it was now nine-thirty a.m. and that we should all have the feel of the skis, so would we please follow him and we would learn walking on a slope. A small gradient, he explained, in case the nursery school be-came frightened by the word 'slope'.

It looked like the wrong face of the Eiger when we had to climb it, and the scene began to be like one of those dreams where you try to move but find yourself constantly in the same place. Worse really, because in those dreams you are at least vertical, there is no sense of constantly hitting the ground. The Falling Man and The Hysterical Woman and a Twitchy Swede and I spent most of our time clutching each other and dragging each other down again. About ten of the group seemed to have mastered it and were scaling the small gradient as if they had been born to such things.

'Cheats,' said The Falling Man. 'I've read about those kind, they know all about skiing. They only join nursery classes to look good and improve their egos.'

'I think I'm going sideways again,' screamed The Hysterical Woman, and we all plunged out to rescue her, knocking her to the ground in the effort.

'The rarified air is doing nothing for my heart, he is beating too rapidly,' said The Twitching Swede. So The Falling Man gave him a nip of brandy, thinking that this might slow it down.

Mike skied back to us in a show-off way from the front of the group. He rolled his eyes to heaven. 'Drinking is bad,' he said in many languages.

We were all sitting in the snow drinking The Falling Man's brandy at this stage, and if ever spirits are said to be medicinal it was in this case. Mike thought, however, it was loose living. 'I will take that,' he said like a school prefect and confiscated The Falling Man's flask. We watched it disappearing like you would a life raft, but were too mute with fear to do anything except agree. Drinking was bad, we admitted humbly and repentantly.

Mike dragged us all to our feet, and pushed us towards the ascent again. It was a sorry progress. The Swedish heart was beating much too rapidly, hysteria was coming on strong with The Nervous Lady, The Falling Man and myself dragged ourselves painfully towards the summit, and Mike whizzed around us like a butterfly telling us always first in German, then in Italian and finally in English that we mustn't lift our feet so high, and finally we made it to the group who were on top of the hill. 'Now comes the interesting part,' said Mike.

Great, I thought, about to take off my skis and run back to the hotel, it's time for lunch. Not at all. The interesting part was apparently the exercises. The limbering up, the bending and stretching. The kind of thing in fact that I used to tell terrible lies in school to avoid, and here I was on a glass mountain abroad, at great cost, trapped and unable to get out of them. It went on until my body cried out with the agony of it all, and I wondered what would happen if I said I felt faint.

I tried it. 'You are out of condition,' said Mike. 'Keep bending, it will make you less faint and more fit.'

I don't remember coming back to the hotel, but I gather we stumped and spiked our way down, falling, and knocking down others, and the good ones in the group were beginning to be released from the rest of us and to have two beginners' classes: one for good beginners and one for bad beginners. I went to bed immediately, and didn't wake until the next morning, which was roughly 18 hours' sleep.

We kept it up for three days, the bad beginners. We were joined by a fifth bad beginner who was an elderly Brazilian learning to ski secretly so that he could accompany his young wife on her winter sporting holidays. The third day he agreed that he didn't mind if she made off with every ski instructor in Europe. He wasn't going to join the game. We assured him that if they were all like the dreaded Mike, he would have no competition at all, she'd only be screaming to get back to him and to Rio.

This cheered him so greatly he decided to hire a sleigh one day and take us on a tour. So we climbed in with rugs and flasks and great goodwill and roared past the good beginners and Mike, who were walking around in circles practising an elementary turn, and we had a beautiful day in a forest where there was no cracking ice, and you could walk in powdery snow without falling at all. The next day we advised the Brazilian to write to his wife saying he was passing through a posh ski resort but the snow didn't seem to be good. We advised this because he was becoming morose and guilty and wondering what she was thinking; he was the kind of man who sends telegrams rather than letters, and that night he had one back from her saying she loved him, so he took us all to a great log cabin and we kept drinking her health all night.

And The Falling Man taught us to play canasta, so we sat all day out on the terrace and got great suntans playing cards. And the Swede, who had stopped twitching, said that his heart felt much better and he had gone and discovered a very cheap place where they had schnitzel and salad so we wouldn't get fat. The Hysterical Woman had become as calm as the Mona Lisa. She asked us to take pictures of her in various ski poses, and we did, and in return she gave us a great recipe for cheesecake, and we went to the kitchen of the hotel and tried it one day when everyone else was out doing elementary bends and falling and breaking their limbs. I told them all about proportional representation, which is a great party piece for foreigners, and wrote down how it worked, with explanations of quotas, first counts, eliminations, distribution and transfers. They loved it and said that the whole trip had been worthwhile for this alone.

And then the week was up, and we avoided Mike's eye and went to the station, where nobody fell and the porters remembered me and said that it was always the same, people came nervously but they left being able to ski like birds.

KEEPING FAITH WITH MY DEAR, DEAR DUBLIN

5 February 1975

A friend of mine who emigrated some years ago used to drive me mad when she came back to Dublin for holidays. Firstly her accent had changed and had overtones of Chelsea, then she was using phrases that the natives do not know, like 'Isn't that a pretty little house?' 'That was naughty of you to buy me a large drink.' Having lived perfectly happy for 20 years in Dublin, she suddenly saw all its faults and filth on her return. The streets had become covered with litter, she would say how terrible to see children begging, all the lovely buildings were being knocked down, wasn't it odd that you found Irishmen always drinking in pubs without their wives, and wasn't it amazing to see so many people outside churches on Sundays?

I determined that I would never behave

like a returned emigrant and at least nobody has detected the slightest change in the way I speak — only, I suppose, surprise that I still speak so much after exposure to the more taciturn British. But I am making the same kind of mistakes, the little tell-tale things that show you have been living in another world, and it's worrying.

Like the phone, I can't believe that you have to pay fourpence. I simply can't take it in, and it looks absurd to come back from a telephone in my own home town saying, 'It doesn't work and I did put the tuppence in.' I had forgotten you couldn't get beer in a restaurant, which is idiotic since I spent at least two years shouting in the paper that the licensing laws should be changed.

The minimum fare on the bus startled me so much that I thought the conductor didn't understand I only wanted to go four stops. My first gin and tonic of the weekend nearly knocked me out after the pathetic drop in the bottom of the glass that goes as an English measure. I had brought people home grand cheap little velvet jumpers you can get in Marks and Spencers and thought they would be ecstatic with them. The ecstasy was dimmed by the fact that you can buy the same ones here and everyone had already bought half a dozen.

At least half a dozen men I know have nice long, clean hair when they used to tell me that they hated their sons having the same thing not two years ago; at least 20 women who used to have a great line in chat about their deep freeze and their au pairs have joined some kind of helpful thrusting organisations and are helping and thrusting all round the place. People ask me did I hear about things like us having a new President, and Ireland beating England at the international, and I begin to wonder where they think I am and who I work for.

Nobody at all speaks about doom, nobody has mentioned that we should be hoarding food, or putting money into building societies or taking it out of building societies. Things seem to be as dear, if not dearer, than in London, salaries don't seem to have jumped accordingly and yet everyone thinks we'll be fine once the warm weather comes.

Food seems to be extraordinarily expensive, and so do clothes, but nowhere do I hear great cries about how hard it is to live, to manage to eat, to dress or to get by. They ask me is Britain breaking up, which is a bit difficult to answer because I have no idea, they don't seem to be worried about Ireland breaking up and think that it will all be grand once the fine weather comes.

Nobody mercifully has had one conversation about the drop in share prices or the rise in them or whatever, which is great because even though the people I meet in England don't have any shares either they always seem a bit worried about other people's and the consequent ill-health of the nation if they go below a certain figure.

Out in Killiney I saw people walking Afghan hounds which, I feel, must be a sign of prosperity, but I am assured that it's just the same person with the same hound that I keep seeing. A few people who should have done it years ago are talking about medical check-ups, and cholesterol, and increasing their subscription to the voluntary health, but that is probably a sign of nothing except that we are all getting older and more worn out. I took two taxis and both taxi drivers knew me but didn't know I had been away, they just thought I had got mean about taking taxis. You can get telephone messages in pubs, and leave your suitcase in restaurants again, which is lovely, and you can meet 20 people in the space of a morning just by walking about, which is lovelier still. You can't say a word about anyone because either they or their best friend are sitting at the next table.

I hear the most outrageous and utterly

unfounded stories about people that nobody has checked out but everybody accepts and then forgets. Half my friends disappeared suddenly out of Dublin to go to the Merriman School, which I get a feeling seems to be occurring every six weeks. I can't even talk about films like *The Front Page* because they're here already. I thought they were joking me when I had to pay 7p to post a letter. England nearly rose in rebellion when it went up to 4 1/2p not long ago.

It's wonderful to be able to go and see everyone again without undertaking mammoth journeys across a huge city, and even better when everyone will agree to come into Bowes pub to see me, instead of having to arrange rendezvous places halfway between me and them, as you would in London. You can cash a cheque in lots of places without hunting for your credit card, and I got over the fact that cigarettes were so much dearer because the woman in the shop was so nice and told me that they were ruining my health, she remembered when I had rosy cheeks and wasn't bent double whooping and wheezing over the counter.

I can take up any conversation where I left it off a month or two ago. I didn't have to explain about the IRA to anyone and

everyone kept asking me when I was going
back.

The Couple Who Behaved
Perfectly

7 January 1976
She had a lot of very good skirts and some
really expensive soft twinsets. She knew how
to knot a scarf around her throat so that it
didn't look like a bandage. She would read
the *Daily Mail* at breakfast while he read the
Daily Telegraph; their dog waited obediently
out in the hall since animals were welcome
but not in the dining room. She had nice
bright awake eyes and looked as if she might
want to have a chat as they ate scrambled
eggs and toast, but in her circle she had
probably learned early that men aren't com-
municative at that hour. So she would look
out the window a bit at the seagulls over
the harbour, and at the life of the village
getting under way, and say nothing.

Every morning he said the same thing
when the last cup of coffee had been drained
and his mouth carefully wiped for danger of
a last lurking crumb. With a rattle of the
newspaper, and with the air of a man who
has put up with ladies being late and slow
and unpredictable all his life he would say,

'Right, if you're ready, we might as well push off, what?'

She had always been ready at least ten minutes ahead of him. But a bright little smile would come on cue and she would say, 'Yes. Why not, I'm ready now, I think.'

And smiling at the waitress with the friendly but not familiar smile that those who are at ease in country houses or good hotels always have, they would walk from the dining room, pick up the dog's lead and stroll down the street to their car. It was very like them, their car — good, expensive, well-kept but not showy.

I used to wonder what they talked about as they settled in and fastened their seat belts. Would they have planned their sight-seeing the night before, or would he say, 'I thought we might go and look at that headland that Charles and Antonia told us about, what?'

Or were they in fact not real at all? Were they part of a gang of jewel thieves and once in the car would he say, 'Great stuff, Tiger Lil, we had them fooled again this morning, let's get to Diamond Harry's place and get hold of last night's haul.'

There seemed to be no way of knowing at all.

Or there wasn't until one night when the

hotel dining room was more crowded than usual and we all had to push our tables slightly closer together. They were in the habit of exchanging a few sentences over the evening meal so this was a marvellous opportunity to hear what they actually said.

She always wore something dark and understated for dinner, if understated means that it wasn't covered with jewels or cut to the navel. He would wear a dark suit and tie, the tweedy morning look wouldn't have been at all suitable. They had a sherry each before their meal and he would spend a considerable amount of time discussing with the wine waiter the half bottle of the wine they had nightly. Whatever it was she would sip, and think and sip again and say, 'Lovely, really very good.'

That much I had noticed when they were far away. I had thought that if he had ordered methylated spirits with the same formality she would have sipped it and given the same reply.

From close up he looked slightly younger and she slightly more tired than I had thought. They debated whether to have whitebait or the pâté with very logical reasoning, like having had pâté at lunch but not really knowing whether a whole plate of whitebait might not be too heavy a starter. I felt sure that they were not a real married couple on a holiday at all. They had to be a pair of actors brought in from a professional company to lend the hotel some style and character. Nobody could invent and mean dialogue like theirs unless it had been intended for the stage.

'I think the tide is coming in again, dear, do you?'

'No, actually, I think it's going out.'

'But it seems to be further into the harbour than it was at lunchtime.'

'Oh really? It probably came in further and then started to go out. Tides do, you know.'

'I don't want to disagree with you, dear, but it's further in now than it was when I was dressing, it's up higher on the pier.'

'Yes, I'm sure it may be, dear, but that doesn't mean that it can't be going out now, does it?'

'But you haven't even looked, dear.'

'Then how can you expect me to make any judgment at all, dear?'

It was riveting stuff.

When the wine ritual was over, and the main course eaten, they had their usual microscopic piece of Stilton. And here the pattern changed.

'I think we might have two vintage ports,'

he said to the wine waiter without consult-ing her.

'How splendid, port!' she said politely, in tones that you knew meant she would have said How Splendid if he'd ordered a glass of arsenic.

When the port arrived, he raised his glass and said in the same studied tones, 'It hasn't worked at all, of course.'

'I'm not sure what you mean,' she said.

'The holiday, the getting away, the behav-ing normally. It hasn't worked, it's just as bad as being at home.'

By this stage I was so interested I was practically sitting in their laps all the while, pretending to read, of course, the greatest cover an eavesdropper can ever have. But they were far too honourable to have sus-pected that anyone would be so unsporting as to listen to someone else's private conver-sation, so I was safe.

'I don't know,' she said, considering. 'It has been very pleasant really. We have been lucky with the weather, and we've been most comfortable here. No, I've enjoyed it, dear, a lot actually. I'm sorry if you haven't.'

'I'm not talking about the holiday,' he said, and there were no dears or whats in his conversation now, he was quite different to his normal self.

'I don't want to disagree with you, but you just said this very minute that the holiday hadn't worked for you. . . .'

'Please don't try and throw words at me to prevent me finishing what I'm trying to say. I said that it's all been a waste of money and time and we might as well never have come. I can't think why I allowed myself be talked into it at all. I knew from the moment that you suggested it that it was insane . . . and that we can't . . . can't . . .' He ran out of fluency.

'Dearest, you're not going to say "we can't go on like this", are you? It would be too much. I think I'd get a fit of hysterics.'

He grinned. 'I was going to say it, and I tried to change half way but couldn't think of anything else that began with "we can't",' he said, and again they looked like a happy couple exchanging a pleasantry.

There was a bit of a pause.

I decided that he was having an affair with someone else, and wanted a divorce, and that she had said let's have a quiet week away from everything and make no hasty decisions, and then we'll sit down and talk about it in a civilised manner. I was very sorry for her, because she looked nice and kind, and probably loved doing the flowers and taking healthy walks with that nice brushed dog, and gardening, and hanging up hunting prints so that they got the light. And now when he left her she would have a very lonely time, and she was undoubtedly very dependent on him and devoted to him, which passes for love with a lot of people.

I was sorry too that the nice week in the beautiful countryside and in the village with the magical little harbour hadn't worked for her.

The pause ended.

'You're not making it easy for me, you know,' he said, twisting his glass of port around in his fingers. 'You could make it much easier, you know, if you'd only allow us to talk about things. I don't think all this coolness is healthy, I really don't. Why don't you cry or show some emotion like women do?'

'My dear, I've said over and over again I haven't the least idea what other women do. They never discuss it with me, and indeed if I knew I don't suppose for a moment that I would want to copy it, just to fit in with some kind of convention. You should be very grateful that I am being so calm, it should surely help you.'

I don't know, I thought to myself, I think he hates it. Men like him would expect a woman to cling and weep, not just let him go without discussing it, but then why had she insisted on coming on a holiday with him? It was very confusing.

'After 15 years nobody has a right to be so calm,' he said. 'I seriously do think you are having some kind of depression or nervous trouble. Why don't you let me make an appointment for you to see someone? Old Harris has all the best contacts, and you could talk to somebody very sympathetic, somebody who's the best in his field, what? It wouldn't be like going to a psychiatrist because you were, you know, not quite . . . it would be more like having a discussion with somebody trained who could tell us why you want to do this.'

'Dear, listen to me just one last time, I've told you and I am not telling you again. I am leaving. On the first of next month I am going. The house will be perfect, the decorators are finished already. I am not taking any of the jewellery or furs, they will be put into storage. I want to take Nelson, but if you want him very much then he must stay with you. I will let you have evidence of adultery immediately I have left, and the divorce action will be undefended. I will ask for no alimony, I want nothing at all, least of all a scene.'

'But, for God's sake, why? And who are

you going to? I'll know sooner or later when I get this evidence of adultery, as you call it. You can't have had time to have any adultery. It's ridiculous.'

'Could you keep your voice down, please, dear? There will be no discussion whatsoever. I really didn't expect to have to say this so often. You have always behaved perfectly to me, and I think that I am behaving perfectly to you now. You looked very tired and overworked, so after I gave you my news I was concerned that you might become ill. That's why I suggested that we have this holiday, insisted on it, as you describe it. I was right, you look ever so much better now, all the rest and the good food and the change. I knew it would do you good.'

And then wiping away any crumbs of cheese, she stood up and said, 'Right, if you're ready we might as well push off, what? And perhaps we could take Nelson for a walk around the harbour before we go to bed.'

A SNATCH AT SOME HAPPINESS

5 February 1976
She had been married for 10 months and she found it odd that this sense of doom lay

like a big heavy meal on her chest. She couldn't explain all that to the doctor, of course, because she had already told him she felt a bit off when she went three months before to find out if she were pregnant. He had examined her blood pressure, her heart and taken a blood test, and he told her she was as fit as a fiddle.

And there was no reason she should feel a sense of doom. Andy was kind to her and he said he loved her often which she liked hearing, and she believed. The girls at work were envious of her because she was always rushing out at lunch hour to buy their evening meal, and they thought that was a lovely secure thing to be doing. They had a flat which got lots of sunlight, and had a bit of a garden. They often had people in for spaghetti on a Friday or a Saturday. They were saving £48 a month between them; putting it into a building society so that they would be able to get a deposit on a house when the Time Came.

She thought a lot about the Time Coming, and was very disappointed each month to realise that there was little hope of the excitement of wondering, hoping, getting tests done and discovering that she was pregnant. In her mind she never thought much beyond the pregnancy and the birth.

She never thought about what it would be like to have a child around the place, she just thought about having a child.

It was Andy's mother who started to make things seem more urgent. Six months married and not a sign of anything yet, was the kind of throwaway line she could manage to include into every conversation. She was a grandmother five times over, it wasn't any of her damn business whether there was a sign of anything or not. How dare people be so personal and offensive, they wouldn't dream of telling you that you had a poor sense of dress, or bad teeth, but they felt they could comment on the most intimate side of your life, with a kind of coarse ribaldry that they would never use in any other context.

Then it was the man she worked for. He was wondering, he had said to his wife the night before, if his nice secretary had been looking a bit pale recently. Now he was a married man, and he had four children, and she must have no hesitation in telling him if she thought there was a little one on the way. Women needed rest at the beginning and he would only be too glad to let her have a few days off if she needed them. His eyes seemed piggy to her rather than kind, and she thought again how appalling it was that this man who never even addressed her by her first name should feel free to comment on the possibility of a life growing or not growing in her body.

It was when her sister came back from America and oohed and aahed over the flat, over Andy and over the wedding pictures and presents that the weight on her chest got very heavy indeed. Her sister had a way of looking at her with an upwards downwards glance, a look that said starkly, Is she? Isn't she? Her sister managed to say at every meal that one of the greatest regrets in her own successful life had been that she had never had children. She used to talk about it to Andy at night sometimes. Would he like a child? Of course he would, eventually. Maybe three; an only child would be spoiled and lonely, and two might dislike each other and that would be bad luck on them. Three seemed a safer number. He spoke about it in the same way he spoke of maybe bringing all his golf clubs to Spain for a fortnight and staying in Marbella, playing 36 holes a day. As a nice but unlikely event.

And one weekend when she was shopping she saw two very pregnant women at the supermarket shelves, and they seemed smug and complacent, and knowing it all, and having it all, and she realised that what they had was the ultimate recognition of their role. And she felt very cheated and stood for a long time with her wire basket empty thinking that it had always been the same, at school she had never won the prizes, been on the first teams, been chosen to speak in debates. Even though she had been just as good as those who had got these things.

Not long after that she saw a baby in a pram outside a shop. It looked very small and very peaceful. It had a little red face but not a cross little face, its hand was under its little chin and it wore a furry bonnet. She put out her own hand and touched its face; it opened its eyes and smiled.

Minutes later an untidy-looking girl rushed out and started putting parcels on to the pram. She explained that the baby was a girl and she was four weeks old. Yes, she had a lovely smile but some people said those things weren't smiles at all, it only meant the baby had wind. She was no trouble, she slept for hours and hours, and she was great fun to play with. Her name was Amanda, and she was never going to let her be called Mandy, it must be the whole name.

So she went home and thought about Amanda who was great fun to play with and who, of course, had a smile, not wind, and wondered about her sleeping there peacefully in a pram, and decided that the pram would be nice near the window where the sunlight could come in. And that Amanda would like a row of coloured beads on her pram, not a lot of untidy parcels. And she thought about Amanda's hair for a long time and wondered if she had dark strands or blonde strands under that furry bonnet, and wondered did her toes have the same grip as her fingers, which was something someone had once told her about a baby.

The next day she left work as usual at lunchtime but, instead of going into the supermarket to buy the things for dinner for Andy and herself, she just went up to a pram where there was a sleeping baby, bigger than Amanda, no furry bonnet but a little pink hat. As if she had been doing it all her life, she kicked the brake free underneath the pram and wheeled it away. She didn't look around to see was anyone watching her, she didn't look into the shop to see would the mother come out, she just pushed the pram home and she went by different ways, she chose lanes and alleys through the city, not the main streets, she didn't feel like talking to anyone about Amanda yet. She just walked deliberately down lane after lane smiling into the pram.

She stopped at a chemist, bought a bottle, a tin of baby milk powder, a packet of disposable nappies, a tin of baby talcum powder, a shampoo that said it wouldn't hurt a baby's eyes. The man in the chemist said that the baby was a fine little fellow and she looked at him coldly and said it was a girl and her name was Amanda. The chemist man said apologetically that it was hard to tell when they were that wrapped up.

And then she went home and parked the pram by the window where the early afternoon sunlight came in on the pram, and touched the pink knitted bonnet. And the baby didn't wake up for a while so she didn't think it needed to be changed but she left the nappies nearby just in case, and she made up the bottle as it said you should on the side of the tin. And the sun went down so that the light was a bit pink like the bonnet.

And then Andy's key turned in the lock and everything changed. It seemed to be a series of questions and Oh my Gods, and whys and telephone calls to the police, and the police arriving in a car with a woman who had a scarlet face from crying, and her husband who was shouting, and a doctor, and an injection, and a bit of sleep. And there were days of people saying no action would be taken, and people asking her had she had infertility tests, and had she considered adoption, and did Andy refuse to let her have a child.

And all the time she was very calm because there was very little to say. She left her job, even though they told her she was always welcome back and her boss said that she was a woman born to be a mother and one day she would have a little one of her own. And the doctor told her that there was nothing wrong with either herself or Andy and, of course, they would probably have a baby in time. And they told her she was very lucky that the Law was so kind that no action was being taken, and she went to see a kind, wise man twice a week and told him about her childhood, and he gave her tablets which took some of the pain and the feeling of having a heavy meal off her chest.

VANITY OF VANITY, ALL IS VANITY

23 February 1976
No it is *not* my first Communion picture, it was taken on a cold Tuesday morning last November. I got it taken because I'm such an honest poor old thing that I didn't want

to be using a picture that was four years old.

Normally, I'd just look at the photographer with a desperate intensity and hope it would all be over quickly and I could get on with my life, but this time I'd been reading a surfeit of these articles about women who decline and go to pieces in their mid-thirties, so I decided I would go to a hairdresser and have a lovely memento of myself looking at my best. I also had a sneaking, ageing hope that someone I don't know at all might fancy me from afar and cut out the picture and put it over his lonely fireplace.

The hairdresser was very excited when I told her that I wanted to look nice for a photograph. 'Is it for a pen friend?' she asked interestedly. 'We get a lot of requests for pen-friend photography.'

When I told her it was for a newspaper she brought the whole salon around to discuss it. Kiss curls, wigs, streaks, colouring, perms and plaits were discussed and eventually she did it like a mad magician all coming up to a conical point, and they all said it was very slimming, and I went home in horror and washed it all out with a hungry detergent.

I had also read that if you wore something

soft and flattering around the neck it did marvels for you. I contemplated soft flattering things like an angora scarf. But somehow it looked like one of those halters people wear when they have been in a car accident. And I tried a necklace and it looked like one of these before and after things, where so and so used to wear cheap shoddy trinkets until we taught her how to dress, so I just put on a blouse backwards because the back of it looked soft and flattering and I pinned it all together at the back where no one would see.

Then I went off to a photographer.

Liam White is a professional photographer who earns his living taking pictures of things and people. Over 10 cups of coffee in his house I told him that I would like something soft and gentle that would let readers know what a lovely mind and heart I had, and that if it wouldn't cost a fortune I'd like the lines under my eyes touched up a bit.

Liam White said that touching pictures up did cost a fortune and, if I was being honest at showing myself at my real age, wouldn't it be a bit hypocritical having the eyes touched up? I said that if it was expensive we'd better leave it. And I sat and smiled at him soppily for about 15 minutes and never felt so foolish in my whole life.

Then he sent me the pictures and I was delighted with them, and I thought I would buy lots of big heavy silver frames and put the pictures in them and give them to people for their pianos with my name scrawled across the bottom left. And for a mad moment I thought that maybe a restaurant might like one, with a kind of a message like 'Thanks for all the lovely portions of No. 67 and the bottles of number 154.'

And then it appeared in the paper and people keep writing in and telling me that I am a disappointment to them, and why produce this old photograph taken during my teens, and since when have I become so vain that I have taken to having pictures retouched. A man who said he had always mildly fancied me from afar was now totally turned off and would fancy Nell McCafferty instead.

Well, to hell with the begrudgers. I don't see any of you lot who write in showing me your own photographs. That's the way I look when I'm nice and clean and tidy and that's the picture I'm going to use. And the only reason I'm making any fuss about it all is that if readers only knew how the men in this paper react when having their photographs taken there would be less fuss about my poor effort. I've been up in the photographers' department while fellow journalists have been recorded on celluloid or whatever it is. I've seen all the worried looking in mirrors, the careful tousling of the hair so that it will look natural, the wondering whether we look better with glasses or without them. Is the finger better on the left side of the chin or the right side? Do we look more urgent if we are on a telephone or not? Men have been known to tear up old pictures they don't like in case it might ever be used by accident, even in an obituary.

And then I knew a man who had all his teeth cleaned and filed and polished for a television appearance and who was most dissatisfied with his smile when he saw it on the screen. He actually wrote in to the head of engineering and wanted to know if they could improve their lighting techniques so that his teeth would look more brilliant during the next appearance.

And I once interviewed a man about a nice healthy manly outdoor sport and asked a photographer to take his picture. The healthy outdoor manly man behaved like Maria Callas over the whole thing and refused to let a line be printed until he had seen proofs of the picture, and even then he wanted it done all over again to the point where I told him that I had forgotten what I had interviewed him about now, and he wrote six distressed letters about me to people of importance and made my life miserable.

And I took a nice holiday snap of about six of us once sharing a joke and looking happy. One of the men looked a bit fat because of the way he was sitting. (In fact, without being too sensitive about it, he had a great beer belly for all to see.) When the snap was being handed around to recall happy, sunny days his face clouded over in rage. Could he have a look at the negative, he asked all in an icy calm voice.

Unsuspectingly, I handed it to him and he tore it up with the print so that nobody could ever again think of him with a paunch.

At a wedding recently there was more fuss getting combs for the bridegroom and best man in case they might look dishevelled than there was arranging the bride for the loveliest day of her life. It looked like a scene from some American comedy where everybody was in some kind of drag. And a man who is normally very well balanced and normal showed me 36 contact proofs of pictures to choose the best one. What was it wanted for? An old boys' school annual actually. The fact that the people who knew him knew what he looked like and the others didn't matter was something he couldn't grasp.

So I'm not going to become upset when people ring up with abuse, and write me these patronising letters. I know that I am young and simple and pleasant looking and that the day I got that picture taken I was all of these things plus very clean and tidy and wearing a blouse backwards.

A Nice, Traditional, Normal Sort of Patrick's Day

22 March 1976

I've spent years with people asking me what a normal St Patrick's Day is like in Ireland, but I've no way of knowing. I've never had a normal St Patrick's Day in my life. When I was about eight I remember a St Patrick's Day with us all wearing shamrock coming from Mass, and two great discoveries that I made. One that St Patrick's Day didn't count as Lent and I could eat sweets, which was an unexpected ecstasy. I also remember asking my mother as we walked back from the church how were children born, and she told me casually. I felt enormously sorry for her having such delusions about it all and confided to my father that she seemed to have got things very confused. He said that he didn't know but there was probably some truth in what she had said. I abandoned the whole idea of it being in any way accurate for about a year.

Then there was a St Patrick's Day at school when I was in my religious maniac stage and I insisted on coming in and helping the boarders to sing the Mass in case I was needed there more than in the parish church. And a nice nun allowed me to check that all the statues of the national saints were properly garlanded with flowers and I went home happy that up there Patrick was having a good day and didn't feel foolish in front of Peter or Francis or any of the other lads.

And there was a time at college when we had a St Patrick's night barbecue on the beach and we all had to bring a pound of sausages and a bottle of wine, and I didn't drink in those times and brought a bottle of orange for myself as well, which fell and broke as we were going down the cliffs and people said thank God it hadn't been the wine. I remember sitting there parched and singing 'Lazy River' which was having one of its ninetieth revivals at the time, and there was an awful incident where somebody went off with my best friend's boyfriend and she cried and cried, and we decided to punish this other girl, and somebody actually cut off her ponytail, which was an appalling thing to do when you think back on it.

There was a time when I was teaching that I actually forgot about St Patrick's Day and went into the school as usual. The town seemed unusually quiet and the bus unusually late, but since I was marking children's exercise books at the last minute as usual, this didn't occur to me as anything odd. In the school I felt that punctuality had reached a new low and was prepared to speak to the headmistress about it. It was only when I couldn't find her that I realised what day it was, and as I went gloomily to the dog show, I thought back on life and younger days of giving up sweets and decorating statues and I realised that growing up meant less deep feelings.

But the following year there were plenty of deep feelings. Some distant and pleasant American cousins announced they were coming to Ireland. Letter followed letter about all the fun they were going to have, all the great scenes they were going to join, the fantastic welcome they were going to get. Mystified, we reread the letters again and again. Could they be talking about the place we all knew?

They were coming so far and making such an effort we would have to do something. My mother refused to dye the potatoes green. Utterly. But, we kept wailing, they write about looking forward to the green potatoes, it wouldn't hurt us to make them green just once. My father refused to call himself O'Binchy for the occasion, and hang a harp outside the gate. I was beginning to think of dressing up in some kind of uniform to go out on the tarmac at Dublin Airport piping a melancholy tune. It was all solved for us by their plane being delayed. They didn't get here until the next day.

They had a great time at New York Airport, they said, lots of green beer and songs and entertainment. But they were of course heart-broken that they had missed what they kept calling The Real Thing.

And I spent a St Patrick's Day once in a hotel by the sea where I had gone to think about things and have a rest. And it was such a beautiful day I decided to go and walk along the beach to a deserted place and contemplate a swim. The sun was beating down, there wasn't a soul about, so I went into the sea alone and naked and swam about thinking about things and delighted with myself. From nowhere came an elderly couple who parked themselves beside my clothes. Suspicious that they might be about to steal everything I owned, I scrutinised them from the water. Not at all, they were people I knew slightly from Dublin who had heard from the hotelier that I was there. Kindly, they thought they would come along and have a chat with me in case I was lonely and all by myself. I contemplated the problem out in the sea. I was too sophisticated to say, 'You must turn your backs now because I have nothing on.' I wasn't sophisticated enough to walk out stark naked.

But then I couldn't stay in the sea forever. A hopeless kind of shouting match took place. 'I don't seem to have any bathing togs on,' I shouted idiotically.

'What?' they shouted.

'I didn't know I was going to meet anyone, I haven't any clothes on,' I screamed.

'What? Do you want your clothes? We'll mind your clothes,' they shouted.

'Perhaps if you went along the beach I'll join you later,' I yelled.

'Not at all, we'll wait here, glad to have a rest,' they called.

I had to do it. Yelling and screeching to alert them of what would be emerging from the water, I raced out of the sea and dived on my coat. Neither of them raised an eye-brow.

'It must have been cold,' said the 80-year-old husband.

'You should have brought a towel anyway,' said the 75-year-old wife, disapproving at my lack of care about my health. Stunned, I walked back to the hotel with them and played poker with them all afternoon.

There was a St Patrick's Day when I had to interview a famous person because he couldn't find any other free time, and I went to his hotel room as arranged. He thought I was part of the hotel staff and said to me wearily, 'I suppose you'd better send up a bottle of whiskey or something, I have some idiot woman from some paper coming to do an interview and I suppose she drinks like a fish like all of them.'

And two years ago I was in a hotel in Morocco with two girlfriends and we spent our National Feast day having a row with the hotel manager about the price of every-thing, and the fact that we had veal for breakfast, lunch and dinner. In between bouts of the row we would go out and sit in the boiling sun and say that it was all grand because everyone would be being drowned and bored at home and perhaps we were better here than there.

And last year I was standing amazed in New York at what looked like a million people dancing and skipping down Fifth Avenue, and the whole city went mad for 12 hours, and I wondered were there any words at all to try and describe it, or would people think I was just exaggerating as usual.

So what about last Wednesday?

With a history of abnormal St Patrick's Days, I waited its dawning with some interest. It began with a flight from Dublin to London. British Airways gave the passengers shamrocks, which was nice, and distracted me until the plane was off the ground.

I had also remembered the number of the seat which has room for long legs and that was good. I can't tell it to you actually, because it's a bit of special information you pick up from long, harrowing travel and nobody should be allowed to have it too easily.

And when I got to London there was a message for me on the board, which is something I love because it looks so important in front of all the other passengers. Actually it was only from a friend who had passed through the night before and who knows I love getting messages. It said 'Happy St Patrick's Day' but I nodded over it wisely for a bit, hoping that people would think it was about some major management decision that I would have to make in the next hour.

And all had changed utterly in London since I left.

Harold Wilson had gone, Princess Margaret's marriage had gone. Some lovely mustard seed that I had planted on my window sill had gone mad and only grown in one corner of its cheap little plastic tray, where it looked like all the seeds had jumped on top of each other instead of growing in nice normal lines.

But it was a normal working day, with people going about their work and forgetting about St Patrick, which was sad. I went to a businessy sort of lunch where the chairman did say at the end of it, 'and now not forgetting what day it is I ask you all to stand and drink a toast. . . .' so I thought this was great. But the toast was to the company which had been 25 years in business and not to poor St Patrick who has been in business for a hell of a lot longer.

And on the bus I met a man wearing a shamrock, too, and he and I had a great chat about St Patrick and what a shame it was that he wasn't more highly thought of everywhere.

And then the man went on and said that the real rot set in when some scholar in Ireland had done a bit of investigation and decided that there might be more than one St Patrick, but since the scholar was my uncle I kept quiet on that point.

And in the evening Córas Tráchtála had a little party where they invited mainly foreign people who had done business with Ireland or helped Irish exports or something.

And amid the roar of conversation and goodwill three different people said to me that it must be lonely to be over in London and not having a nice, normal St Patrick's Day at home.

THE DAY WE NEARLY WROTE A SEX BOOK

4 October 1976

I was nearly the co-author of a best-selling pornographic book, and sometimes when I stand in the rain waiting for a non-existent bus and unable to afford the taxis that come by empty and warm and comfortable, I think that it was very feeble of me not to have gone ahead with the project. I don't even have the moral comfort of knowing that I refused riches for all kinds of pure and upright reasons, it was just sheer cowardice that stopped me in the end — that and the laziness and inertia of all my friends.

A few years ago, struck by yet another blow like an increase in the price of fags or drink or huge telephone bills or something, ten of us sat grumbling in a pub on a Saturday night. The usual remedies to the taxing economic situation were discussed and dismissed. Making gin in the bath. Yes fine, but how did you do it? And it would mean you couldn't wash, you might be very drunk, but very dirty as a result. And there was a thought that people had gone blind or mad from it during prohibition.

And there was rolling your own cigarettes. Fine, but it took so long, and all the tobacco kept falling out, and it didn't taste as nice, and somebody had burned all their eyelashes off by forgetting to put any tobacco at all into the paper and just lighting the outside.

Phones? Well you could stop using them, and there was the widely held belief that if you started making suspicious conversations down them they would be tapped, and when your phone is tapped apparently it can't be cut off even if you never pay your bill at all.

But what we were really after was some big quick money, and we hit on the idea of writing a porn book between us. With ten of us, that would only be 3,000 words each, which is nothing. A 30,000-word novel full of sex, it would have to make us a fortune, and it wouldn't take us a week to write. So carried away with the sheer brilliance of it, we wrote out an outline plan. It was going to be the story of an innocent young American girl who came to Ireland to see the land of her ancestors. She was choosing Ireland because she was fed up with all the immorality in the United States and wanted to be somewhere good and pure. Our boon was going to be the tale of her disillusionment.

We were each 'to do a chapter on the kind of thing we knew best'. A sudden silence fell on the group at that stage. What did we mean 'the thing we knew best'? A great unwillingness to admit that we knew 'anything best' came over us and there was a lot of shuffling and the outline plan looked as if it were to be abandoned at birth. Then somebody bought a round of drinks and the price of them shocked us into action again. Why didn't we each describe the kind of ordinary life we knew best, and do a chapter of that, adding all kinds of torrid sexual overtones to it, so that it would be a book of merit as well as hardcore porn? That suited everyone and we divided it up happily.

There was an American in our midst and he was to write chapter one, 'Magnolia Leaves America'. He was to write about the filth and perversion that was making life unbearable for her there. He asked anxiously how deeply did he have to go into the filth and perversion, because he had lived in a small town, and probably didn't know in detail the great degrees of all that went on in big cities. Nonsense, we told him, all small towns in America are much, much worse than Peyton Place, use your imagination.

Chapter two, 'Magnolia Arrives in Ireland', was to be written by the man who had once worked in a summer job in Aer Lingus. He could do all the steamy scenes aboard the plane. He too started backtracking a bit and said that he had worked on the ground and he wasn't sure that he would have all the sex scenes aboard the plane absolutely accurate. That didn't matter at all, we told him firmly, he must draw on his background of working in an airline, otherwise he couldn't be in on it at all. Hastily and greedily he agreed that there must be something wildly sexual going on on most flights and he'd check it all out.

Because I was writing about tourism in those days I was asked to write chapter three, 'Magnolia Checks into Her Hotel'. Very easy chapter that, they said, hotels are full of vice and corruption, and I knew a lot of hotel managers, I'd do the thing in an hour. I bleated that most of the hotel managers I met used to talk to me more about getting tourists and getting better grading with Bord Fáilte than about the lust and licentiousness of their staff and clients, but I was assured that I had got an easy number and if I didn't take it I'd be given something more difficult, so I took it.

'Magnolia Looks for a Job' was to be done by a girl who worked in an insurance office, and she was told that she was lucky too because nobody else would have the access she did to what went on behind filing cabinets. She said that in her office the worst thing that ever went on behind a filing cabinet was that she went there alone sometimes to eat a chocolate biscuit so that the other girls wouldn't tell her she was greedy, and we said she's got to liven it up a bit.

Chapter five, 'Magnolia Has a Night Out', was to be written by a sort of glamorous man who always says I was at this place last night or the other place and the joint was swinging. He looked a little troubled when we said this was to be the most porno-graphic chapter of all to retain the readers' corrupt interest. 'Why do I have to write the most important chapter?' he whinged. 'Because you are a very good writer and you know all the joints that swing,' we said firmly and he was a bit pleased though still troubled and agreed to do it.

Chapter six, 'Magnolia Goes to the Dáil', was to be written by a reporter who some-times does Dáil reporting. He said that you don't get much training for lusty arousing kind of descriptive pieces when you are just taking down what the TDs are saying but we said nonsense. He didn't have to make Magnolia go through the whole business of getting elected, just have her as a simple-minded tourist coming in and asking to visit the Irish Parliament the way people do, and then sort of go on with the usual. 'But I think the usual kind of thing is that they come in and sit in the gallery and then go home,' he said in a nit-picking way and was advised he'd better make it a hell of a lot racier than that.

Chapter seven, 'Magnolia Takes Up Sport', was to be written by a journalist who works on the sports pages of a newspaper. 'What sport?' he asked. Any sport, we said.

Anything at all from watching greyhound racing to playing squash. His brief was so nice and vague that we all felt he was getting off too lightly, but he kept saying that we didn't understand how difficult his wife would prove if ever any of this was made public and we all said nonsense that we'd all get into appalling trouble with someone if it did, we would have a great pseudonym, and just divide the half million quid or whatever we earned into ten parts. We'd use a post office box number for all the correspondence about it, and all the dealings about the film rights and everything.

'Magnolia on Stage' would be chapter eight and an actress was going to write that. She was the most cheerful about it and said she'd have all kinds of terrible things happening. to Magnolia in her dressing room, and in the wings, but particularly at the party on the first night of the play. So that was very trouble-free and we all thought deep silent thoughts about the private life of the actress which we had assumed to be blameless and even rather dull up to this.

Chapter nine, 'Magnolia in High Finance', was the lot of a man who had always claimed that he had made a bit of money on stocks and shares in his time. He was appalled at his task. 'Have you ever seen the stock exchange?' he begged. 'You couldn't write anything vaguely pornographic about it, it's ridiculous.'

We advised him to think of the money he'd be losing by opting out and he said he'd rack his brains.

The final chapter, 'Magnolia Leaves Again', was to be written by a teacher because she had absolutely refused to write anything whatsoever concerning the school she taught in. We told her that the nuns were unlikely to be buying cellophane-wrapped porn and would never read it, and the book would be banned in Ireland anyway. But she said no, the nuns found out everything you did, and she wasn't going to be sacked and pronounced unhireable for the rest of her life, no matter how many millions she earned from the film rights of the book. Grudgingly she said she'd do the bit where Magnolia was sitting alone in her flat with the door barred against rapists and perverts and would write the big crisis part about Magnolia saying that wicked though the United States were they were like cloisters compared to Ireland. The book would end with her getting on a boat to America, not wanting to risk the horrors of chapter one and whatever had happened to her on the plane. And everyone went home happy with their instructions and promising to meet with the completed chapter next Saturday.

The only pornographic book I had at home was *Fanny Hill* and I read it again and again but there was nothing about hotels in it, so I rang a friend in London and asked her to send me something particularly foul from some seedy bookshop, and she kept asking me had I gone mad and said she wouldn't dream of doing it for me until she knew why. I said it was a secret and I was sworn not to tell anyone and she said that everyone seemed to be going off their heads in Dublin. By a great stroke of good luck I was sent to London for two days myself and I went into a terrible shop where I was the only woman and a small evil man kept asking me not to finger the books unless I was going to buy them. I humbly told him that I wanted something about sex in hotels and he became more benign and said he'd see what he could do. I stood for what seemed like a fortnight in the shop until he came back with a book called *Hot Honeymoon Hotel* which cost £2. I was too embarrassed to check it with him so I paid him and ran. It was an amazing book certainly, but it was mainly photographs, that kind with so many limbs in them it's like a puzzle in a child's book and you'd have to colour them in to see which arm or leg belonged to whom. It made me very uneasy, and I kept thinking how awful it would be if I dropped dead on the street while I had it in my handbag and people would think that this was my normal reading matter.

Anyway I copied down a few useful phrases out of it in a sort of code for myself and I left the book in a litter bin at Heathrow Airport where someone must have got a nice surprise later on, and came home to write the chapter. It took me about 14 hours to write and I kept wondering who would want to read it, but then the memory of *Hot Honeymoon Hotel* and its price tag of £2 came back and I persevered. Ten nice neat pages of typing with 300 words each on them. I put it in an envelope on the Saturday and wondered had the other nine found it as difficult as I had or were they all deep down much more experienced and sophisticated. Almost everybody was there, and I was waiting for someone to call the meeting to order. Nobody had envelopes or typescripts on the table or anything. I supposed like myself they were keeping them out of sight.

The chat went on, and on, and on, and nobody mentioned putting all the chapters together and sort of editing out any discrepancies. And finally I couldn't bear it any more and said, 'Well, did we all find the porn-writing difficult?' And somebody looked at me blankly and said 'porn-writing?' That was the damn sportswriter who had all the sports in the world to choose from. I knew his fear of his wife was too great, I knew it and the girl in the insurance company said, 'It was all a joke, wasn't it?' A bit nervously and hopefully I thought. And the man who had worked for a bit in Aer Lingus gave a sigh of pure relief and said, 'Oh yes, of course it was a joke.' And the others all ratted, so I ratted too and said naturally I was only joking, and went up to the ladies and tore up 'Magnolia Checks into Her Hotel' into little pieces and burned it in an ashtray and gave up my chance of being a millionaire.

A WEEK OF SELF-IMPROVEMENT

11 October 1976
During the weekend I made the mistake of reading one of those magazines written by a new brand of unreal woman. These are the dames who are on their third and finally happy marriage, who behave like an angelic drama mum to his children, her children

and their children, who earn £9,000 a year in some dynamic career, run a boutique and a charity shop in their spare time, give dinner parties, look magnificent, travel all over the world with pigskin luggage and 21-year-old male admirers, and still find time in their bionic hearts to advise the rest of us how to live our lives.

One of these hard-faced Hannahs suggested that I and the other million fools who would be hanging on her words should try a week of self-improvement. We would be astonished, she pontificated, at how much more alive we would feel. No, we were to make no excuses, everyone had a lunch hour, hadn't they? We were to forswear lunch and start improving ourselves instead. We would thank her later.

Monday: *Learn a new skill: yoga? calligraphy? a language?*

Well determined and all as I was to test this dame's theory, the lotus position was something that I didn't see fitting happily into my life. Slow, beautiful handwriting was for monks in the eighth century, not for journalists in the twentieth. Fast, accurate typewriting would be a much more intelligent thing to do. But since I taught myself to type despairingly eight years ago and worked out a great hit and miss system which involves five fingers out of the 10 that I have, and means that it's mainly readable, I don't think I'd learn anything from someone who tried to force me to do hard things like use all the fingers and not look at the keys. It had better be a language. So on Monday, yet again I took up Italian. I love it, of course, the only trouble is that I'm never able to remember a word of it, or create a sentence in it. But there was no excuse.

The Inner London Education Authority has provided classes in a place off Fleet Street which is actually 54 paces from my office. They have lunchtime Italian classes on a Monday. It would be nice and familiar anyway, I thought, all that *'Ecco il Maestro'* and *'Come sta? Bene grazie, e Lei?'* In fact I was really looking forward to the familiar business of getting as far as lesson four in yet another instant and painless way to master the language. There were 12 of us in the class. We sized each other up as playmates for the year; I thought they looked very good value. We all told each other eagerly that our ambition was to be able to sit in the middle of a huge Italian group, exchanging jokes and shouting and realising that everyone else wasn't fighting just because they were shouting.

The teacher came in, she was splendid.

She looked about 80, and was full of extravagant gestures, and delighted to meet us all. She was actually so nice and beaming and full of charm that she looked like a stage Italian mama sent over by Central Casting. And we all thundered out *'Ecco la classe, ecco il libro, ecco il maestro',* terribly happily with her, and this time — perhaps this time — I might stick to it. She was so damn nice, and she believed that we were all doing splendidly. I mingled with my classmates afterwards, because the awful article had said I would make friends of my own age and different sexes when learning a new skill. But they were harder working than I, and they kept talking about putting the definite pronoun before words like studenta and porta, and weren't at all into asking me to marry them or have a brief and brittle affair. But perhaps that will come later, I thought happily and put a few definite pronouns in with the best.

Tuesday: *Brighten yourself up, have a facial.*

The Italian class had been such a success that I ploughed ahead with all the rest of the advice. Indeed brightening myself up would be a fine thought, I decided, having examined myself in a magnifying mirror for the first time since I was a teenager, and it wasn't a joyous experience.

'Do you want the full facial, the mini facial, the city skin breather, or just a cleanse and make-up?' asked the voice from the big store.

'How much is the full?' I asked humbly.

'Well it would depend, Madam, it could be as little as £4 depending on what you want done.'

But I wanted them to tell me what I wanted done; I dithered for a while.

'Of course if you wanted eyelashes tinted, facial hair removed, unsightly blemishes covered up, skin peeling, and vapour masks, it would all add up,' the voice said.

This made my crumbling brain come to a decision. 'I'll have the mini facial,' I said firmly and went along at lunchtime to have it.

It was horror from the word go. I longed for the self-improvement of *'ecco il maestro'*. Instead I had 'Good heavens, we do need a little work here, don't we? Did you say you only booked for the mini facial? Ah, well, we'll see what we can do.'

I spent an hour and £2.80 fighting off offers to tear off my eyebrows, refusing to pay another 60p to have my face hoovered with some electric vacuum cleaner that had come in that week from America, and denying utterly that I wanted my ears pierced, even though there had been some mistake and a piercing girl came into the cubicle with what she called sleepers saying that cubicle eight had ordered them.

The beautician was nice but single-minded. She saw a course of treatments for my face, she saw them every week, the full not the mini variety. She saw herself selling me creams to plump out tissues and to beat back lines, she saw a rich heavy night cream, and a light nongreasy day cream. She saw much more than just Brightening Myself Up, which was what I saw. I regard it as the major achievement of the week that I was grown up enough not to see any of these things with her, and be able to leave with the lying promise that I would think about what she said. I didn't look any brighter at all, and I will *never* think about what she said. It's too dispiriting.

Wednesday: *Help other people, it will make you feel good inside.*

It seemed an odd if not selfish reason to help other people, but maybe these hard, brittle women phrase things oddly. Perhaps it was just a ploy to get us out there doing something instead of just talking about it. I rang an old people's home and asked could I help them serve lunch, they said they'd be delighted and off I went.

I was in the room where they served the wheelchair lunch, which meant gathering everyone together and assembling them around the table. You had to tie bibs around people, long plastic ones which practically covered the whole chair. I thought this was very undignified and said that I was sorry to the old man that I was tying into his bib first.

'Not at all,' he said. 'I'd much prefer a pinny, the old hands aren't what they used to be, and all this convenience food, you know, it slips off the fork. Much prefer to be well covered up.'

They were having soup, and then bacon casserole and mash, and then stewed apricots and custard.

'Why aren't you wearing a uniform?' asked one old lady to me as I was passing her food.

'They didn't have one to fit me,' I said.

'People are getting much fatter nowadays,' she said thoughtfully and not in any way insultingly. 'I suppose it's the lack of exercise, and so much food available and everything since the last war.'

She told me about her son who was married to a very fat selfish woman, which was odd since fat people are meant to be jolly, but her daughter-in-law was sour and selfish, and she had three sour fat grandchildren. It was a sad thing to end up having been responsible for three sour grandchildren.

'Perhaps they'll get thinner,' I said hopefully.

'But will they get less sour?' she wondered, and there was no answer to that.

I was helping to clean up, and an old man told me not to, that only people who couldn't speak English cleaned up. I thought this was a wrong theory, but he said it was very sensible, people who could speak English talked to the guests, the others who would like to talk to them but couldn't cleaned up.

So I went to talk to him and he told me he was 91 and very happy. He had been so lucky to get into this home, because there were three television sets, and three sitting rooms, so you could watch whatever channel you liked, and that this was the kind of thing that really made a home successful, and he got £2 of his pension into his hand every week, and was saving it up to buy a nice West Indian nurse a Christmas present, because she had been great to him, and she kept promising to take him back to Trinidad with her, even though they both knew it was a joke.

And then they were all having a little doze,

and they would have afternoon tea at four when other helpers would come in and serve it to them at their chairs. I don't think it really made me feel good inside but it made me a lot less afraid of being old.

Thursday: *Brighten up your office, we work better in bright surroundings.*

This was actually taken out of my hands because the office was full to the gills of workmen brightening it up for me. The London Editor had cunningly arranged that the Conservative Party Conference should be taking place in Brighton, as far away as possible from 85 Fleet Street while this chaos was going on, so I had to deal with it alone.

Well, deal with it? It was a matter of getting down on all fours and crawling under my own desk to be able to sit at it. Then I was trapped in a corner, while Alf and Bert walked backwards and forwards across it foot in typewriter and bottom on telephone, both cheerfully apologising and saying they hoped they weren't disturbing me. Every time the phone rang they both took out pneumatic drills, and made exaggerated dentist noises about a foot from my ear, and anyone who telephoned me on Thursday may well be justified in thinking that I had gone mad.

I managed a few calls by putting my head and the phone in a drawer. But when I got it out again, Alf had piled four chairs on my desk, and Bert had moved the filing cabinet over to block the door. They had both left in search of some electricians and so I missed the coffee trolley when it passed the door and I missed going out to a nice wine and cheese reception, but at least there were no drills going and nobody pacing backwards and forwards on my desk so I got a bit of work done.

And then they came back and they told me that this job was going to take a bit longer than I thought and than they thought and they started drilling again. And I picked up the potted plant that was going to brighten up my office for me and I left silently with it under my arm and went to a library not far away and read three books that I had to review.

I felt a bit guilty because it was a Christian Science Reading Room and I apologised for not reading anything about Christian Science but the woman said it didn't matter, I could read whatever I liked, so I hid the titles from her and read away until it got dark.

Friday: *Shake yourself out of your old routine. Do something you would never nor-*

mally do.

The trouble here is that I don't have an old routine. Nearly every day I do something that I wouldn't normally do, there's no normal. But I'm still not glittering and action-packed like these new women that upset me so much.

I must try to think of something really unusual to do at lunchtime.

I've seen all the lunchtime plays that I want to, and then that couldn't be called unusual. I've never been up to the top of the post office tower, but it's a dull day and would I see anything? There is a lunchtime cookery class I believe somewhere, but then that's too like Monday and learning a new skill. Eventually I thought of something. I'd take a walk. I would go and explore parts of the city I had never seen. This would be helpful about opening my mind and broadening my horizons, not to mention flattening my feet.

I set off happily and marched down towards the City, to the stockbrokers and the banks and the money houses, looking fearfully upwards in case I'd be hit by falling bodies of speculators. But nothing like that happened. I just got a bit weary plodding on through these caverns of streets, when suddenly a door opened, and two men, locked in what looked like a very un-Londonish embrace, hurtled out. Still groping each other, they fell on to the ground and rolled lovingly towards the traffic. Taxis and buses were now practically standing up on their hind legs to avoid them, and there was an enormous amount of excitement. So near me were they that they actually knocked my handbag out of my hand, so I had to join them more or less in order to get it back.

I was extremely embarrassed by the whole thing, kneeling beside them on the edge of the footpath saying, 'Excuse me . . . I'm sorry . . . you seem to have . . .'

Then I made the appalling discovery that they were not murmuring endearments to each other at all, they actually were trying to kill each other.

'I'll get you,' one was panting.

'Lying bastard,' the other was huffing.

I grabbed my bag and explained to all the onlookers that it was really mine, one of those long, boring explanations that make you seem guilty when you are really innocent. 'You see I don't know either of them,' I explained to a stunned crowd. 'You see, I was just passing by and they kind of knocked my handbag . . . it is mine, you see, it has all my things in it. . . .'

Nobody believed me; they were as amazed by me and my speech as they were by the men pounding each other in the gutter.

There are policemen when you need them, and two approached, the crowd was waved on. I moved off too and the two men were stood up, dusted down, and forced to give some explanation of their behaviour. I took a taxi back to the office, which cost 90p, and decided that if I had been asked to explain my part in the whole business and had said that it was all part of a week of self-improvement, well you might never have heard from me again.

VIOLET

25 June 1977

Violet rang yesterday with the bad news that she is coming to London for a week. When I think of the 164 people I would love to be coming to London for a week, I wonder why it has to be Violet. She's not a friend, she has no friends, she has contacts. It's me in London, and Hilary in Galway, and Helen in Cork, and Ruth in Paris, and Sheila in Belfast. Sheila had to take a week off to recover last autumn.

Violet's visits are very upsetting. If she was really horrible, it would be possible to say that you didn't want to see her ever again, to say that life was too short, and put down the phone. But she is only accidentally horrible, and that's why we all get sucked into these appalling arrangements, and end up hating her and hating ourselves as a result.

I was wondering if you could book me a hotel. Nothing too fancy, something rather quiet and nice.

Oh, that's going to be easy for a start. In London, in July, in Jubilee Year? If I knew how to find something rather quiet and nice, I could set up in business immediately and make a fortune. But I am not going to ask her to stay. I'm not. I'm not. It would be an abuse of hospitality. When she went to stay with Helen in Cork, Helen had scrubbed the house from top to bottom and Violet still managed to imply that she would get scurvy from it. She actually bought some spray thing and cleaned Helen's windows. She came to a meal here once and said, 'Aren't cleaning ladies unreliable?' which left me in a rage for two months, because it was an innocent remark designed to wound and hurt.

So a hotel it has to be, three hours of phoning and cajoling, and asking people do they know anywhere, and then taking the stick afterwards because it'll turn out to be full of foreigners, far from taxis or have a shower that doesn't work.

And I wonder if you could book me a couple of seats for some good shows. I mean, you're there on the spot, you'd know how it works.

I won't. I'll give her the name of a friend in a theatre-booking agency, and shift the lot on to him. I don't care if she has to pay 30 pence more a ticket, I'm not going to have anything like last time. 'Well, I suppose it was interesting. But very shouty, don't you think, and rather vulgar. I'm not prim and proper, and I think you should call a spade a spade, but honestly what was the point of it all? I suppose when you live here, you see things differently.'

And there was the harmless musical I had suggested. 'Well, I'm sure the children would have loved it. Very colourful and everything. But not quite what one comes to London to see.'

I'll want to pick your brains about shopping. I'm going to buy a complete summer wardrobe when I'm there.

If you want to know all the latest places, I don't even know the earliest places. I will not spend five minutes going into boutiques with idiotic names, and trying to recall what colour people are wearing this season. I don't know what shape of toe shoes have, and there are many other things I want to know before that piece of info. Violet's last visit gave me nightmares. 'I think you must have made a mistake in the name, I looked through everything, and honestly they were all a year old. Nothing new at all. And between ourselves just a little bit tatty, no cut, nor any style. You must have mixed it up with somewhere else or it must have changed hands.'

I had been told authoritatively that it was the smartest and most expensive shop in London. This year I'll be honest, I'll tell her I know only Marks and Spencers and food shops and off-licences, and newsagents. She'll think I have gone mad, but better to have her think that.

I thought I'd telephone Barbara and we could all meet for a meal, I'm sure she'd have us out to the house like last time. I'm dying to see what they've done with it now.

I'm surprised it hasn't had swastikas painted all over it by now. Barbara's fascist husband deserves them more than most. I'll never forget the evening there during Violet's last visit. I went to the bathroom so often to avoid jumping at him and hitting him that they all thought I had some intestinal disease. Barbara herself had been all right, but muted, and we had lots of nice chat about how he wouldn't let a Trade Unionist Commie under his roof, wanted military service for all the layabouts who wouldn't work even if there was work, and said that their launderette smelled of curry these days, because of all those blacks who would be much happier at home anyway, better weather and nice simple village life for them.

A meal with Barbara and her husband — oh that would be a lovely thing.

And I'm dying to catch up on all the gossip. There's lots to tell you from here . . . but not over the phone.

Violet, you're wrong. You could say anything over the phone. If half the Special Branch and the whole of Dublin were listening in, you could tell it all, and we'd be deafened with the clicks of everyone hanging up.

'Frank and Mary, you remember them, oh you must know them, well they spent a fortune on a tumble dryer, a fortune, which is ridiculous, Frank sends all his shirts to the laundry and Mary, well we all know how Mary looks, there's no need to be unkind. I can't imagine why their ordinary spin dryer wouldn't have done them. We went to this new place for dinner the other night. Everyone goes there now, it was full of people one knows. Who? Well, that actress was there, or is she an actress? She's on television maybe, very attractive in a brassy sort of way. She was there. I can't understand how you don't know David Frost. I mean, he lives mainly in London, doesn't he? I'd have thought you'd have met him by now. My sister-in-law's friend met him at a party a few years ago, and she'd only been in London a few months. Still, as you say, it's a big place.'

And I have one tiny favour to ask you. You know that ponyskin coat Gerald gave me for the last baby? Well, it needs to be cleaned, and there's a marvellous place in London, but — and this is the problem — it takes two weeks, so if I could give you the ticket and a cheque then the next time you're coming over . . .

Not again, not again. Finding somewhere in some street that not even taxi drivers have heard of, carrying it draped in tissue and polythene over my arm, trying to remember not to leave it in some pub, or I'll spend next year's salary replacing it. Dealing with security people about it, explaining to the Customs that it isn't mine, it wouldn't fit me, I wouldn't wear it if it did, that it was bought in Dublin, that I'm not a ponyskin smuggler from way back. I had to do all that with some sequinned thing she had once, and what was worse, everyone told me that it could have been cleaned perfectly well in Dublin. I'm not going to do it. I'm allergic to fur, I'm against animals being made into coats, my memory has crumbled. I'd lose it. Get someone else, Violet, get someone else. Remember what happened to poor Hilary. She was months getting hand-knit sweaters to her from Connemara and then bringing them back to women to reknit them because the shoulders weren't right.

Listen, this is very confidential. I was thinking of getting a sort of check-up while I'm there. It seems a waste to be in London where you can have all these cervical smears and breast examinations just by going to a Family Planning place. Could you ring up and make an appointment for me, I'm sure you'd know how to do all that, and it's much less messy than having it done here.

What do I do? 'Hello, is that the Family Planning? There's a tourist coming over for a week. She'd like a medical examination, please. No, I don't think she wants any advice about family planning, I think she has that under control. It's just the free medical she'd like. Yes, she could have it done in Ireland. Yes, they do have proper medical services there. No, it wouldn't cost her anything, but she doesn't like hanging about. I'm not sure why; it might be that it interferes with bridge or golf or shopping, depending on what day it is, I suppose. No, I don't think for a moment that she would regard this as an abuse of your services.'

What I don't want is to be any trouble to you. I know you lead such a busy life.

How can she manage to make a busy life sound something kind of underground and sordid? I get the feeling that she thinks I do several shifts a week as a Madam in a brothel, and this is why I am too tired to know about boutiques and posh dry-cleaning. Last time she was in Paris, she thought that Ruth was 'rushing about too much'. It was said with overtones that Ruth might have been rushing from one playboy's pad to another. Ruth, in fact, had been driven to such hysteria by Violet's relentless journey to jewellers and furriers that she had invented a heavy social life and gone to see six films by herself in a row, just to get out of the shopping expeditions. I could leave London for a week, but apart from being defeatist, cowardly and unkind it wouldn't really make anything any better. There would be a dozen horrors waiting for me on my return, parcels delivered to my house or left in the office to readdress and post; tickets, dockets, vouchers, goods to be exchanged. No, it's better to stay and face it and tell her, in controlled tones, what can and cannot be done.

In rational moments I tell myself that she is not evil, that she must be lonely running around from contact to contact exhausting us all, buying hundreds of pounds' worth of clothes, sending excited postcards to her rather glum husband and her neighbours. And I wonder why her visit fills me with such dread, when I know she can't be trying to put me down or upset me continually. That she only does these things by accident. But then, I can hear her voice saying, 'You must show me what you bought in Australia' and I'll take out the boomerang and the didgeridoo, and the huge bottle-opener shaped like a kangaroo. Violet will laugh indulgently and say, 'What funny rubbishy things, but show me what you really bought.'

ANNA'S ABORTION

9 July 1977
Anna loved Michael. She was sure of it. Michael was sure of it. Anna knew that she should take the pill, she used to take it two

218

years ago when she loved Stephen, but this time . . . well it made you fat, it was embarrassing asking the family doctor for it, it might give you varicose veins, and who knows what it could be doing to your insides.

Anna was very organised. She used to put little crosses in her diary when she expected her period; it didn't happen on May 1st, but Anna had read lots of magazine articles, so she wasn't worried at all. Anxiety could delay it, and she had loads of anxiety.

Her father wasn't well at all. He was only 60 but he was behaving like a man of 90. He was thinking of giving up his large business, he was complaining of pains and aches. Life at home, when she went there every month or so, was far from great; that made her anxious.

Michael made her anxious too, sometimes. He kept saying he liked his independence but if ever he could settle down with anyone, it would be her; he begged her not to rush him. Anna thought that was very honest. She never rushed him at all. Then on May 28th–May 29th this year, a long sunny weekend, Anna realised she had missed her second period, and she couldn't put it down to anxiety any more. So she did what she had once heard that people did, she took a sample of urine and brought it to Holles Street Hospital with a fee attached to it, and called the next day for a result.

Anna knew that they didn't normally give out results to patients, so she pretended that a doctor had asked her to leave the specimen in, because he was on holiday, and there had been no problem. No problem until the report said 'positive', and then there was every problem.

Her family would die. Yes, she knew that lots of girls had told their parents, and the parents had surprised them by taking it all very well. Her parents were different, they wouldn't surprise her at all. They had been appalled when a cousin had got married in a hurry four years ago. They would take nothing well. Her mother would say she was putting nails in her father's coffin. There was no question of telling the family.

She had also heard that fellows took this kind of thing well too, that they did all kinds of cliché things. They rose to responsibilities, they loved the idea of fatherhood, they found that this cemented relationships, they said they were pleased and proud. Michael wouldn't feel anything like that, he would flee from responsibilities, he would hate and deny the idea of parenthood. He would feel that this had cracked the idea of a relationship wide open.

So Anna decided that she would have an abortion. On Wednesday, June 1st, she rang a friend of hers in London — a girl she met maybe once a year, but who was nonetheless a friend. She told her the tale, she listened to the ten minutes' abuse about how could she have been so silly, and wasn't she 26 years of age, and didn't she know that these things could have happened.

Eventually the friend, whose name was Marianne, said she thought that abortion was wrong and that there might be an argument for it being called murder.

Anna said she had faced that argument and had rejected it, and what she wanted was not so much moralising as just the name of a doctor, an ordinary GP, and an introduction, because she didn't want to go through the time-wasting business of establishing an address in London and pretending to be on somebody's panel.

The doctor's name and address was found quite simply. It was Marianne's doctor, who had done three things for Marianne in seven years, two prescriptions for antibiotics and one ear syringe.

Marianne rang him and said a friend of hers who was pregnant wanted to visit him, and it would be a great favour if he could see her and discuss termination of pregnancy. Dr Smith said fine, tell her to come to surgery.

So on Monday, June 6th, Anna queued up with all the other patients, and when it was her turn, Dr Smith gave her a quick examination, confirmed that she was pregnant, and asked her to sit down and discuss it for a few minutes. This surprised Anna because she thought English doctors just wheeled you in and out.

Dr Smith said, 'Why do you want a termination?'

Anna said, 'You wouldn't have time to hear the whole story, the waiting room is full of people.'

Dr Smith said, 'You had to wait until I talked to other people; they'll wait until I talk to you.'

So Anna told him the bones of the story. She said that she could never support a child on her own, she couldn't give a child the love and attention it should have, that Michael would feel trapped, and wouldn't want any part of it.

She explained about her parents who lived in a small country town, and how they would be disgraced if the baby was acknowledged, and how she couldn't really hide it from them even if she wanted it, which she didn't.

Dr Smith listened to her, and produced a form which he had to fill in in order to get her a termination of pregnancy. He explained that it was very difficult to get an abortion, or termination as he kept calling it, on the National Health if you were not a resident in some area paying a regular contribution in the form of a stamp. People didn't like doing terminations, he said kindly, not that there was anything terrible about it. It was just that it was sort of anti-medicine, in a way. It had nothing to do with creation or curing, or healing; it seemed to have something a little bit to do with destroying.

Anna was upset to hear this. She didn't like the word 'destroy'. She thought that since it was permitted by law, people did it all the time.

Not all the time, Dr Smith thought. In fact, he knew several London hospitals which restricted terminations to four a week, even though the demand might be much higher.

'So where do the others go?' asked Anna.

'That's why we are filling in this form,' said Dr Smith. 'Presumably you have enough money?'

'Presumably,' said Anna coldly.

'I don't make any money out of it,' said Dr Smith, equally coldly.

He telephoned a gynaecologist, Mr Brown, and made an appointment for the next day at three p.m. 'Be there at two-thirty,' he said. 'You will have to discuss the arrangements with his secretary and she will tell you how much it costs. You'll have to pay tomorrow afternoon, and in cash, not in a cheque. I think it will be £150 to £170. That will include everything — nursing home, anaesthetist, operation, meals, the lot.'

Anna wondered aloud why it had to be in cash. She thought abortions were legal in Britain; it smelled of the back street and the charlatan to pay somebody in five-pound notes.

'It's certainly not back-street,' said Dr Smith. 'It's Wimpole Street, off Harley Street. It's not a charlatan either, he is a highly respected surgeon. There's nothing dirty or shoddy about it, he'll send you to the Welbeck or the Wellington or the Harley Street, or any of the best places. It's all legal; these are first-class nursing homes. You won't think that they are anything but luxury and highly professional when you go there. Only a very small number of the patients are there for terminations, other people are having appendix or gallbladders done.'

Anna was still worried about having to pay in cash.

Dr Smith had no explanation. 'It's just the way they do it. These men find that people are seldom grateful for their surgery and care, and that often they don't pay afterwards. So they insist on keeping everything businesslike, that's all.'

Next day at two-thirty, Anna went to Mr Brown's consulting rooms in Wimpole Street. His secretary looked like Jane Fonda and spoke like a deb, on a bad day. 'Let's be practical,' she said nauseatingly.

'Here's the damage, would you like to pay me now?' It was £173.50. 'You get a super lunch,' said the awful deb, consolingly.

'It's a bit dear for lunch,' said Anna.

'It's not only for lunch,' said the awful deb wisely.

Mr Brown was very elegant-looking. He had well-manicured hands, Anna noticed. He had that kind of half-grey hair that only wealthy people had; poorer people were grey at random, rich people were grey at the edges. It was all to do with expensive barbers.

Mr Brown examined her again. Not that

he didn't trust the word of her eminent GP, he said winsomely, but one had to be sure for oneself.

He confirmed that she was indeed seven to eight weeks pregnant; how wise of her to come in such good time, so many women are very silly about all this. She didn't have any doubts, no? Good, good.

Anna sat there wondering how much he earned. She knew a little about property and salaries. He must have to pay out at least £7,000 a year for the rooms and secretary. He probably took home at least another seven thousand to support the wife in the pearls with the Irish wolfhound, in the picture on the desk. He was probably taxed on an estimated £20,000. He probably earned a conservative £30,000.

He asked her to be at the nursing home, fasting, at nine next morning. Just bring overnight things, nothing to worry about. Simple at this early stage, she'd have forgotten about it in July. But why not get herself fixed up with some kind of protection while she was in Britain; they didn't have such things in Éire, did they?

Anna went back to Marianne's flat, and looked at telly, and refused to talk about it. Marianne was relieved. Marianne thought it was killing, and she wanted to put it out of

226

her mind forever, but she didn't want to hurt Anna.

Next morning, Wednesday, June 8th, Anna arrived by taxi at a nursing home in Putney. It was a lovely Georgian house, or three Georgian houses knocked into one. It had thick pile carpets and tasteful pictures, and recent magazines in the waiting room. At nine-fifteen a.m. she was in a bed in a bright sunny room.

It was a room for two. The other girl was a little drowsy; she had her pre-med, the injection to make her sleepy. She said her name was Sandra, she was Australian, and that her brother-in-law was coming to see her at lunchtime. She said that this was her second termination, and there was nothing to it. Anna wished she looked more cheerful, but then Sandra was very sleepy, so she decided to forget it.

Someone came and listened to her chest. A bossy Irish nurse gave her a hospital gown instead of her own nice nightdress, which she had bought for the occasion.

'Keep that for when you're back home again,' the nurse said. 'You don't want it ruined on you.'

That alarmed Anna, but she was determined to keep her mouth shut, and not to ask questions or tell tales herself. She thought the only way to go through this was with some kind of appearance of dignity.

Then she got her pre-med, and she felt drowsy and she thought about Michael for a bit. She had told him she was going to London for a week to stay with Marianne and that had pleased him. He had said it would cheer her up, she had seemed moody of late. She wondered if Michael would have liked a son or a daughter, and if they would have made good, laughing parents for a child. Her own parents had always been very gloomy; Michael's had been so old that they were like grandparents. By the time they brought the trolley in to take her to the theatre, she wondered should she have told Michael and given him a choice. But it was too late now.

In the theatre, she smiled up at Mr Brown, and he smiled down at her.

'You get your money's worth in terms of civility,' she said.

'The Irish have a great charm,' he said. And then she was asleep.

She remembers them helping her back into bed, but she went to sleep very quickly again.

She woke and they were doing an examination.

'All fine,' said the bossy Irish nurse. 'What

would you like for lunch?'

Anna said she'd like something light, and she got an omelette and salad and sauté potatoes, with a crème caramel and a silver pot of coffee. Sandra was awake and eating steak and beans to build her strength up. 'It wasn't bad now, was it?' she asked cheerfully.

For the first time, Anna thought about it. She felt no pain, no discomfort, nothing. It was like coming around from the anaesthetic when you had a tooth out. No, she agreed, it wasn't bad.

Sandra's brother-in-law came in, and had a whispered conversation with her. It seemed mainly hostile; it seemed to be all about some lie Sandra had told a friend of his, he couldn't understand why girls told lies. Men didn't tell lies.

When he had gone, Sandra explained that she had been having an affair with her brother-in-law's boss, and she had got pregnant. Her brother-in-law was so anxious to keep his boss's respect that he had paid for the abortion. But he had made Sandra swear to keep it secret. People were so stupid about things, Sandra thought.

Nobody came to see Anna, and the day seemed long. She had afternoon tea, and she had grilled sole for dinner. She paid an

229

extra £3 to have a television in the room, and she and Sandra looked at a few programmes because it was better than talking.

The Irish nurse came in to know if they wanted her to order taxis in the morning. They would get another examination at seven-thirty and then they should be packed and on their way.

Their beds would be taken again by nine-fifteen tomorrow.

'You sound very disapproving of it,' said Anna suddenly.

'No, I'm not,' said the nurse. 'It's not my business to approve or disapprove. I just think someone who's educated like you are should have been able to avoid it.'

'If we all avoided it, how would you earn a living?' asked Anna furiously.

'Somewhere where we didn't behave as if we were working in a posh execution yard,' said the nurse.

'I bet you don't tell them at home that this is where you're working,' said Anna.

'I'd tell them sooner than you'd tell them where you're visiting,' said the nurse.

Anna apologised; she said she was upset, she didn't mean to shout.

'That's all right,' said the nurse. 'I'm upset a lot of the time, I only shout some of the time.'

And she gave them sleeping tablets, and the two girls fell asleep.

Next morning it was all flurry. They were woken at seven, asked to wash in readiness for Mr Brown. He came in and behind screens gave each of them a quick examination and quick smile. All was fine, absolutely fine.

And so on Thursday, June 9th, at nine o'clock Anna went to Marianne's flat just before Marianne left for work. She said she'd like to stay the day, but would go home that night. Marianne felt guilty that she hadn't done more. 'Stay and we'll have dinner together, anyway,' she urged.

But when she got back from work Anna was gone, leaving a nice thank-you note. Anna went back to work next morning. She didn't want to sit at home thinking about it. They were surprised to see her in the office, but she said that London was so tiring she couldn't stick it any more.

That's all a month ago; she still sees Michael a few nights a week. He still thinks that an involvement of any more permanent nature would change everything and take away the magic. And Anna agrees; it would be awful to take away the magic.

IDIOTIC QUEUES

15 November 1978

All over London there were long, idiotic queues outside bakeries and even in supermarkets because of the bread strike. The English are mad about queuing, mad about it. At the slightest hint of there being more than three people anywhere, a queue will form. I think it reminds them of the camaraderie during the war when it really was necessary to stand in great long lines for food, any food. Because the queues you see nowadays are senseless. There's not a serious shortage of bread at all and, even if there were, aren't there other things, not necessarily cake, which people could eat?

The bread strike is, as people say, crumbling. In as much as anyone can understand what was happening it seems that at least a third of the workforce has passed pickets, and most shops have at least some bread every day. But the happy lines of queues are talking in blockade terms and have put on their siege mentality again.

'I've heard they have some in Islington,' says an old man. 'Now I have to get one for the lady in number six, and one for the sisters in number eight and one for my next-door neighbour, but if you like I'll try and get you one, too.'

It's a sort of game of triumphing over desperate odds and beating the system and ganging together. I'm hopeless altogether at it, because even though I like a 400-calorie hunk of bread and butter as much as the next glutton, I can't believe that you'd have to queue for it. Anyway, there's grand Indian bread, little packets of six flat oval things and they're lovely if you heat them up. At 30p a packet they're a bit dearer ounce for ounce than ordinary bread, but not that much.

I suggested to a queue fanatic that she buy this instead of standing on her old legs for an hour in the November winds. No. That wouldn't do at all. Indian bread would taste of curry and have a foreign smell. No it didn't, I said. It was like that flat Greek bread, it was exactly the same as our bread but it just had no yeast or baking powder in it. Her face fell in disappointment. She had been looking forward to the queuing, it would be a happy communal event. People would establish a common bond through groaning about workers who are never satisfied these days.

And in the little shops which sell sandwiches and plastic cups of coffee to workers at this end of town, which is office worker land, the bread hunt is on.

'Chubbies sandwich bar has real bread,' said an over-excited girl in the lift. 'I'm going up to get four cheese sandwiches, then I'll take the cheese out and we'll have proper bread at home.'

Some offices were even doing a shift system, with office workers replacing each other in the queues when lunch-hour was over for the one who had been standing there.

'What do you think is the best way to hoard bread?' I heard a woman asking someone quite seriously. 'I never understood what was so wrong with Mrs Thatcher hoarding things that time. People made such a silly fuss about it all but I think she was quite right. It's only sensible to stockpile if these Marxists are going to stop us getting our daily bread.'

Her friend suggested that she remove everything from her fridge and hoard it there. Another eavesdropper suggested to me that he'd like to tell her where to hoard it.

BATHROOM JOGGERS

9 December 1978

It is well known, of course, that joggers are mad, but when they jog in the torrents of rain you'd wonder should they be put away. All along the road this morning you could see them when the driving rain cleared a bit, steaming and glowing and giving themselves pneumonia as well as coronary arrest. Sometimes one jogs onto a bus, which is particularly bad news. I hate to see someone breathing unnaturally, like people do at the Olympic Games. I hate to see a grown man in a pair of pyjamas that he calls a tracksuit unable to gasp out his destination, and most of all I hate the aura of virtue that comes off him with the steam.

So it is with some pleasure that I see a new Christmas gift launched today by the Campari Sports Equipment Company for a mere £70. It's a sort of a home jogger which takes the offensive sight of public jogging off the streets. The 'Fun-Run', as it is misleadingly called, looks like a bathroom scales, and you keep running on it like mad and it clocks up how many miles you've gone, all the while you never have to leave your bathroom. It comes complete with heart-stopping charts and graphs showing you that you are past your prime if you are over 25 anyway, but with proper racing on old 'Fun Run' you might stagger along living some passable kind of life even after that age. It also gives you 14 danger signals to look out for if you jog. I'm glad they've got around to admitting that jogging had, in fact, some built-in hazards, though I think nobody admitted it until joggers started to drop dead like flies in parks all over the world.

Anyway, these danger signals include extreme fatigue, it says, and your fingernails turning purple. So Campari suggest that you should do warming-up exercises before you start hurtling off on the machine — things like limbering up your back and shoulder muscles apparently. And they stress you shouldn't do it if you feel exhausted. Naturally they don't want to be deafened with the clump of falling bathroom joggers keeling over dead on their 'Fun-Runs'. I was a bit disappointed when I asked what a 'Fun-Run' looked like. I thought it would be like that long rubber moving pavement that the bionic woman trains on when she has to do something a bit demanding, but no, it's just exactly like a scales except, instead of telling your weight, it tells you how far you've run.

The more your silly old knees keep coming up, the more theoretical three-feet steps you have taken. And an alternative Christmas jogging present if you can't manage a 'Fun-Run' would be the Runner's Diary. It's a huge thing like those impressive padded diaries with all the hours written in which executives have on their desks for women graduates to fill in for them. Anyway, the Runner's Diary is seething with information about running being the road to understanding and contentment and health. It has dreadful diets for each day of the year, calorie charts, spaces to put in how much you ran, which are good spaces, and how much you ate, which are bad spaces, and advice about breathing from the stomach rather than the chest and moving your legs from the hips not the knees.

It's altogether a very unsettling and unpleasant diary, which is obviously going to sell enormously well and delight the jogging recipients before their fingernails turn purple.

HAPPY HYPOCHONDRIA

28 May 1979
I am a very nervous person about my own

health; when I get a headache I wonder if it is meningitis, when I have a twinge in my stomach I wonder has my liver finally packed it in. If I get the smallest cut I watch the tiny drops of blood in horror in case I have haemophilia and will bleed to death there and then.

For years and years I tried to disguise this terror, and put a big brave face on it. I would try desperately to be casual when they were taking blood pressure, searching in the face of whoever was wrapping the terrible bit of canvas around my arm for some sign that I was finished. 'I suppose that's nice and normal,' I would say in what I thought was a healthy, uncaring voice, but inside my heart would be thumping in great booms of terror and my eyes were wild for reassurance.

I used to read magazines in doctors' waiting rooms until the words became a red blur of misery in front of me. Everyone else looked so uncaring about their bodies as they sat there genuinely absorbed in some out-of-date colour supplement, while I'd be afraid to glance at the horoscopes in case Gemini was missing, or it would say that I should make the most of the short bit of time I had left.

If ever I got a spot I thought it was a

harbinger of a skin disease that would peel back all the covering on me and expose veins and muscles. A piece of grit in my eye and I was wondering about Moshe Dayan and whether he left the patch on or took it off at night.

But all the time I hid this hypochondria from the world, because I thought grown-ups were meant to be brave and uncaring about themselves and their illnesses. The impassive faces around me in terrifying places like an outpatient ward, this must be the norm.

But now I've changed. Now I admit I'm terrified, and it's much, much better. You have to persuade people that you're not joking, because some of these hard-boiled medics actually think it's unlikely that you could be weeping with nerves inwardly. They think it's a fairly pleasant thing to come up against the medical profession and that we should be pleased rather than fearful.

I began to Come Out as a Bad Patient with the dentist. A gentle softspoken Englishman who had never as he said himself met my type of person before. I explained to him that I was probably more nervous of dentists than anything in the world except flying, and could he show me his hands to ensure that he had no hidden weapons on them. He did this and I relaxed a fraction.

We had a depressing discussion about my teeth and I managed to jump out from under his arms and nearly knocked both of us on the floor.

'Why did you do that?' he said sadly, putting on his glasses again.

'I thought you were going to pounce,' I said. 'I'm very nervous.'

He said he'd have to look at them.

'Could you look at them without instruments?' I asked.

He couldn't. He needed a mirror and a pickaxe. He promised me that he couldn't take out teeth suddenly with a mirror and a pickaxe so I'd be safe.

Since then life with this dentist has been easy. He explains everything, he shows me his hands and lets me examine the pockets in his white coat. He doesn't say 'Aha' any more because it terrifies me. He explains why it wouldn't be a good idea to have a card with me at all times saying 'I am a nervous person. In case of an accident, if I am unconscious, please remove all my teeth so that I won't ever have to worry about fillings and injections again.' He says that is not the act of a nervous person, it's the act of an insane person and I mustn't do it.

240

Now that he knows I'm nervous and self-dramatising, the whole relationship is on an honest basis. It's the same with the doctor. I told him that I was possibly the most nervous person he would ever meet in his whole career.

'Nonsense,' he said, 'a nice big cheerful person like you, nervous. Ridiculous.'

I argued this with him logically. Indeed I was very nice and very big and cheerful but that didn't mean I couldn't be nervous as well. The things weren't mutually exclusive. Why should he accept that a small, horrible, depressed person was nervous and I wasn't? It floored him.

'You don't look nervous,' he came back with a bit weakly.

So I was very glad that I had told him. Now I remind him each time I see him that I'm nervous in case he's forgotten.

'I know,' he said the last time, shaking his head. 'I know you think you're nervous, I've written it in your file. I'm not to use long words. I'm not to say "Aha" and I'm not to assume that you're brave.'

Life would be a lot more comforting for everyone, doctors and patients alike, if people admitted that they were very frightened when they are. You don't get a sudden strength from pretending to be brave, you just get treated like a brave person, while if you admit humbly to being appallingly feeble about things the chances are you'll get someone to be kind and gentle to you when they would have been brisk otherwise.

There's strength in unity, and if all of us cowards come out openly and honestly they'll have to take us seriously. They can't laugh us all out of the waiting rooms and the hospital beds, can they?

THE MAN IN SOUTH ANNE STREET

6 June 1979

The man in the phone box in South Anne Street was like a lighting devil. First he had lost his five pence, then he had lost his second five pence, and the box was full of litter and bad smells, and the walls were daubed with things, and, God, could things get any worse he asked rhetorically into the air and at myself. They could. At that precise moment a blast of electioneering nearly lifted us bodily out of the street, and the man's face turned such a frightening colour I thought he was choking. I tried to remember what you did when people choked and since it didn't come back to me immediately I was about to contact a competent-looking person but he recovered. It was Stress, he told me, Stress and Fury brought on by living in this country.

The pubs in Anne Street weren't open, mercifully, or I might be there still with him on the self-deluding pretext that I was actually interviewing him and getting an insight into how Stress-Filled Dubliners lived. As it was we just leaned up against the wall of the deserted post office and calmed each other down.

It was the electioneering that had finished him off. Send Your Best to Europe. Was he the only person who found that funny? If we were sending the Best to Europe, what were we keeping for ourselves? The second best? The worst? Answer him that. I said I didn't think that was the way they meant it. They meant more that if you were sending people to Europe you should imagine that you were sending great people. It was a measure of how important you thought Europe was. What he thought Europe was could not be printed. In fact it should hardly be said, I told him disapprovingly. Well, he couldn't help that. That's what he thought about it. Send our best. He'd like to send the lot, actually, and not only to Europe, further. What did I as a normal, ordinary woman think about Ireland these days? Wasn't I ashamed of my life to be living in such a madhouse? I said that I was sort of only half here, and half there and all round the place. He said he knew how I felt. I explained that I meant that I lived in England. His eyes went piggy with envy.

'You live in England?' he said like you might say to someone, 'You mean you eat as much as you like and you don't get fat?'

I explained that I did mainly.

'That would be lovely,' he said, calming down like the way a child forgets a tantrum when the thought of something pleasant is put into his mind.

'But it's lovely here,' I said with the fierce possessive love I feel for Dublin which I would never have admitted until a few years ago.

'In England,' he said, as one who spoke in a dream, 'you can post a letter. You can go out to a post office and buy a stamp, a postal order, send a telegram. You can ring up and get information, and directory enquiries. You can get petrol. They empty rubbish bins. And they're having no European elections to dement themselves further.'

Oh, but they are, I told him. They're definitely having European elections. In fact, I am meant to be there now writing about them.

Nothing could have displeased him more. People who wrote about the European elections were almost worse than anyone else in the whole sorry business. It was bad enough having to join up with a lot of foreigners in a meaningless sort of group to make the farmers richer than they already were and butter dearer than it already was. It was bad enough having to change our money system from what it used to be and to what everyone knew it was to desperate, complicated things which varied every day, and nobody could change for you in any bank in the world because nobody knew what it was any more. It was bad enough to live in a country which slowly collapses, and that was becoming a living joke, but people who wrote about these things only encouraged the decline.

I got fed up with him. I had been sorry for him about the phone box. I had lost two shillings in it myself and there was a rotten smell in it, but I felt he was taking things too far to deny any enthusiasm for Europe. 'What would cheer you up?' I said to him in a schoolmistress sort of way.

Before he could tell me, a girl with a nice, friendly face approached us with election literature for the Labour Party. The man studied it, his colour beginning to mount again. 'I hate people with double-barrel names,' he said about Jane Dillon-Byrne.

'At least they're good names,' I said. 'It's not Fossington-Fossington or Chomondly-Chomondly.'

'The trouble about people like you is that you see good in everything,' he said, and he tore the leaflet into a thousand pieces and increased the litter in the city.

A Magic Meeting

Published in My First Book *by Maeve Binchy* (Irish Times, *1976)*

'Hello, don't I know you from somewhere?'

It's always happening to Audrey Hepburn, but this guy was no Cary Grant either, so I decided that it happens to us ordinary people too.

'I don't know, do you?'

'Well I think I do, you look sort of familiar, like someone I would know, if you know what I mean.'

I looked windswept and wet, but then perhaps he was used to wet climates.

'I'm not desperately sure, I know a lot of people,' I said. Why did I say that? It sounds like boasting, it sounds idiotic. I rush on to say something that will take the harm out of it. 'I mean I'm from Dublin,' I gushed, 'and everyone in Dublin knows a lot of people.'

'I've never been to Dublin,' he said.

'You should, you should,' I said. Bord Fáilte would have been proud of me and taken me to their Baggot Street bosom instead of shying away from me every time I meet them individually or collectively.

'Dublin is lovely, especially in May. I always think May is the best month.'

'Do you?' he said, 'I thought it would have been appalling in May.'

'It's not,' I said, thinking that the magic meeting was palling a bit.

'But I do know you,' he said. 'I have a distinct memory of talking to you for hours and hours sometime. Can't you remember where it was?'

'I can't,' I said, biting back the next boastful thing I was going to say, which was that it could have been anywhere because I go so many places.

'We talked about tax evasion,' he said, happiness dawning on his face.

Now that's something I never talk about, because, honestly, I have nothing at all to say on the subject. Not, of course, that this would necessarily strike it from the topics I discuss, but it's something that would bore me rigid. People saying, 'You should claim for the light and heating of the room where you work,' or 'You write me a cheque and I'll write you a cheque.'

It's too wildly beyond anything I could grasp.

'Were you for it or against it?' I asked jovially.

'I was neither,' he said, 'but you were very well up in it all.'

This was taking a bad turn. He couldn't be some spy sent out from the tax office in Dublin to hound me down in a London street and get me to admit everything? There's nothing to admit, for God's sake, except that I pay too much PAYE because I can't understand the forms.

'I don't think I know anything about it at all,' I said, trembling with guilt, and reddening and prepared to hand myself over.

'I'm rarely wrong about these things,' he said. 'I have a memory of you smoking a cheroot and saying you had a scheme which would mean that you would never pay tax again.'

'I don't smoke cheroots,' I cried desperately.

'You were about to give them up at the time,' he said. 'I suppose you didn't, though, it seemed to be causing you some pain.'

Cary Grant was never like this. In one of

his pick-ups he would have remembered my eyes, or the song that they were playing at the time, we would have gone to a wine bar or a skiing chalet to discuss it. We would have fallen hopelessly in love. Cary would never have droned on about cheroots and tax evasion. I said what I should have said at the outset.

'I think that you must be mixing me up with someone else.'

A look of desperation came into his eyes. He was obviously for some reason determined to keep me there, which was flattering. He seemed to need to know me so badly, I almost relented. Perhaps he was just gauche and hadn't seen enough Cary Grant films, perhaps he was a rough diamond. Perhaps as the women's magazines are always saying, he was the strong, worthy type, few words, those few foolish, but worth a million of your other kind of man.

'Well, I met someone like you somewhere,' he said firmly. 'And I have an hour to kill and I was wondering would you like to come and have a hamburger so that we can think where it was. Oh, come on. You look as if you have nothing to do either.'

'You could read the evening paper,' I said, because I am so extremely kind I would never hurt anyone's feelings. I wouldn't tell him to get lost, that he was an offensive bore.

'I've read the evening paper,' he said.

I was silent.

'Well, make up your mind,' he said. 'It's starting to rain, do we have a hamburger or don't we? It's stupid standing here getting wet.'

All right, all right, in years to come you'll tell me I missed my big chance, that I could have developed an interest in smoking small black cigars and evading taxes even if it meant understanding them first in order to evade them. Perhaps we could have been sitting in his baronial hall with 28 guests and telling them the funny way we met all those years ago.

Perhaps you are right, and I was wrong, but I said, 'I hate people talking about "killing time". There's very little of it left, we shouldn't kill what there is. I'm afraid I must go on home. Thank you for the offer all the same.'

As I squelched off in the rain, he shouted, 'You were always too bloody intense, I remember that about you. Go back to your cheroots and your tax forms, I don't care.'

Oh Trevor Howard and Cary Grant, why did you have to louse up our lives making us think that chance meetings were great?

DO IT HONESTLY
OR NOT AT ALL

Published in My First Book *by Maeve Binchy* (Irish Times, *1976)*

I got a pen and paper and did the whole thing very systematically. It was on a train going to Ipswich and the man opposite me was doing it also, writing sneaky figures in the margin. Occasionally we would put our hands around the page like children at school who didn't want anyone to see how they were getting on. At first it looked pretty good.

Age group between 31 and 39, which is grand and vague, means that I should live until I was 77.

Place where you live. Greater London nowadays, so that's another year, 78.

I suppose journalism is laughingly called 'professional job'. It isn't 'skilled' in my case, and with all the modesty in the world I think it doesn't fit into their classification for 'unskilled' so I add another two years, 80.

How do friends and relations describe you? Fortunately you never hear most of their descriptions. Calm is not an adjective I have ever heard about myself in any of its variations like always, or usually, or even moderately. On the other hand, people are inclined to say things like 'hopelessly over-wrought again'. So to be honest define that as moderately tense, and subtract one year. Back to 79.

Single and under 40 I am, so it's down another two years. Why? Why? But actuaries must know their job is to know what weakens people. 77.

I knew it was coming — the cigarettes. I think I smoke 40, but I know I have to go into the third packet, so it's age 67 now.

Drink. What's an average day? Well if it was the previous Thursday . . . no forget that. If it were this particular Sunday there would be no drink at all. Come on, be honest, it works out at what they revoltingly call 'six tots' a day. I know, I know, but either do the thing honestly or not at all. Subtract five. 62.

Exercise. Run six miles a day? Are these actuaries *insane*?

Let's see. It's about three minutes to the bus, and about one minute from the bus to the tube. And about 30 seconds when you get off the tube. The same going home. Come off it. No exercise. Subtract five years, 57.

Weight. By the worst luck ever, hadn't I

weighed myself at Liverpool Street Station while waiting for the train. Otherwise I might have fooled myself a bit. No, the truth was just over two stone overweight. That was half an hour ago, there was no reason to believe that I had got thinner since then. Subtract six years. 51.

Now what's 'often ill', for God's sake? Does it mean all the time, some of the time? When you take the other alternatives, I suppose it *is* often. All that business about the gall bladder, and the limp I had where they were going to have me shot in the office unless I went to a doctor and had it cleared up. I get a lot of headaches . . . stop whining and feeling sorry for yourself. Subtract two years you silly hypochondriac and shut up. 49.

False teeth? Now this is embarrassing. I *have* one false tooth. Is it right to take the thing literally? They said teeth (plural), didn't they? But the principle is that one fang is gone. It didn't fall out by itself from age or being diseased, it was sort of assisted out in an incident. Still it's gone. Subtract three years. 46.

So, no plans for how I can spend the seventies, the sixties or even the fifties. It'll all be over at 46. I read that line about it not being scientific again and again. The man opposite me was doubled with laughter. He's going to live until he's 73, why shouldn't he laugh? He said I had been too harsh with myself about the false tooth as we did it again to check. I said he had been too indulgent with himself about his weight. He said that it was being dramatic to call myself 'moderately tense'. I said he was being insanely optimistic calling himself 'always calm'.

We both agreed that it was a very foolish and frightening exercise, that it didn't take anything into account like family history or ill health, like whether you had children or not, like whether your skilled job was steeplejack or draughtsman. It didn't bother to investigate whether you had money worries, came from a family of long-livers, or had your home in a war zone. The man said that it was rather unfair that he got extra years for not smoking and drinking. I said that perhaps when he got to 73 he could take up both feverishly on borrowed time. He then worked out his boss's life expectancy and was disappointed to find that was 85.

Anyway, according to the actuaries, you may not have to read me for much longer.

Though she may be best known and remembered for her features and regular weekly columns, Maeve Binchy was also a skilled news journalist. The following are excerpts from just two major stories she covered from the London office.

HOPE AND BITTER MEMORIES

24 July 1974
In the third week of July 1974 a Greek military junta backed a coup in Cyprus, prompting Turkey to retaliate with an invasion. Maeve Binchy had just returned from a holiday in Cyprus, and was asked to go back to report on the conflict. She has described this as the proudest moment of her career, because despite total isolation and terrible conditions, she got a story into The Irish Times *every day.*

Don't talk to any Cypriot about Geneva. Geneva is not on fire. What will Mr Callaghan and Dr Waldheim do about the sons and brothers who are dead? Will this high-power conference bring love and peace and co-existence with the men who are shooting at you to kill tonight, they ask. Are we all expected to live like dear friends after this week?

And not every country has known a military coup and a foreign invasion in one week. Tonight I talked to the Turkish Cypriot refugees, who sat spooning meat from tins and crying in the dark field where they wait to hear more news of their fellow Turks.

And the news they hear is not good. They know that whole villages have been wiped out. There are too few Turks here for comfort, they say. Where are the women, and the children from that little village and that little sector of the town?

An old man whose wife had been killed in a mountainous Turkish village near Platea told me that he had been saved by God, not Allah.

He was a Maronite. His poor wife was in heaven now. It was too terrible to tell, he said, but he told it with tears streaming down his old, brown face. They had a small shop, some Greeks in the next village, young and drunken, had come there late one night, ages ago, like three weeks previously, and demanded food. The old man said they were not open. The young thugs had put stones through the windows, and said they would be dead. Back they came on Saturday. Shouting and screaming that it was now war, they had worn uniforms; they came into his shop, to this one only, and shot his wife.

Another Turkish man confirmed his story. He said that they had been able to get lorries and get to the base quickly. They buried the old man's wife in the garden and said prayers and then drove past before any other villagers could be massacred.

They know nothing, nothing about what is happening outside, only that Ankara Radio tells them first it has come to help the Turkish Cypriots establish their rights, and now that these rights have been established. It must be strange, harsh news to hear when you sit spooning out tinned meat, and thinking of your wife buried in the garden.

But there is not general despondency among the Turks, not even those whose villages have been attacked. At last Turkey has really come, and the intense pride that this gives them will be some solace when it is all over and the problems of normal life begin again. Turkey promised to come before and didn't. Now it actually arrived and it will show the Greek Cypriots that the island is not all theirs, that a decent democratic way of life for all Turkish people will be maintained henceforward.

And in a strange way they have some reason for this wild belief, because their status, however personally disturbing, must be collectively improved when the bargains are being made, when the law-makers are yet again drawing up the rules.

I asked them did they not regret that the Turks had only landed in two areas of the Island, thus exposing the scattered villagers to risk. 'President Ecevit is sad tonight in Ankara,' said one young woman, who was a teacher in her town. 'He did not want so many Turkish Cypriots to be attacked but what could he do? He had to land somewhere. He could hardly drop a hundred men into each village. These are the sacrifices we must make.'

She went on to describe the sacrifices they had made. They had been a minority with titular representation.

Oh yes, it looked good at the beginning, they had been given Vice-Presidentship and positions for a small Turkish National Guard. They were second citizens in every way, except one, she said proudly. 'We are half of Cyprus. Even though our population is not half nor even a quarter, they must consider us one half of the population, and the Greeks the other when any decisions are made. That is what they never understood, but now that Turkey has shown real support and not forgotten us, things will be different.'

It all seemed so clear and so right that the Turks should be the victims in this mad war that I found myself agreeing with her from the heart. And the heart can change in a short walk through the section where the Greek Cypriot refugees are spooning meat out of tins.

There was an old Greek woman who thinks that her three sons are dead. Someone explained to me that she had not stopped wailing since Saturday morning when she was taken by friends to Dhekelia. They were in Kyrenia. They must be dead. Everyone is dead in Kyrenia. She was being looked after by a woman of about 40, her daughter-in-law, who refused to believe anyone was dead. The Turks had been pushed back into the sea. She had heard it all day on the radio.

An old Greek man thought that Cyprus would have to be partitioned sooner or later. Why not give the Turks Kyrenia since they had captured it anyway? Move the rest of the Turks in there, and let them feel happy with their harbour looking over at Turkey if that was what they wanted.

And what will happen to them all? The

mixed villages will have to go, for a start. When the whole truth of this week's fighting comes out it will be shown that many of the killings were to settle old scores, feuds and hatreds growing and festering in tight communities where the fear of fear grew and grew. Partition has never worked well anywhere else, as we all know, but it might be the only solution.

NUMBED DOVER WAITS FOR LISTS OF THE DEAD

9 March 1987
On 6 March 1987, the Herald of Free Enterprise *ferry on the Cross Channel route capsized near the Belgian port of Zeebrugge in a disaster which killed 253 crew and passengers. When reporters were cordoned off from the site, Maeve quietly bought a ferry ticket so she could access the passenger terminal to talk to passengers and relatives. This is her report from Dover.*

There was a fine coat of snow over the Cliffs of Dover making them whiter than ever at the weekend. The flag was at half-mast on Dover Castle . . . the town, which has always claimed to be the largest passenger port in the world, had a heavy feel about it as the reality seemed to sink in.

One of the FEs was not coming home. There are eight of the Townsend Thoresen ships called *Free Enterprise,* and, just as Sealink vessels are known by affectionate nicknames or initials, the Free Enterprises were always the FEs, and they were always considered unsinkable. All day long the local radio station broadcast the telephone numbers for enquiries, but stressed that there really wasn't very much more information.

From Friday to Sunday, distraught relatives moved in a maddened circle from Dover to Maidstone where the police headquarters had been set up, on to Gatwick where some survivors had been flown in, then back to Dover where 30 surviving crew members had returned unexpectedly on another ferry.

The horror of the first published lists was that nobody was utterly certain whether this was a list of known dead or known living. So to hear a name read from a list could have meant the best or the worst.

In Enterprise House, the company's Dover headquarters, the staff were red-eyed with lack of sleep and tears shed for friends and for the very fact of the catastrophes . . .

families sat in little clusters on the benches of the big departure hall, they followed the staff with their eyes and whenever a telephone rang on a desk, a small crowd would gather immediately, just in case.

Wearily, the ferry staff faced television teams and made statements. 'I have been asked to say that the Kent Police will answer any questions from now on.'

'Well what have we all been doing here for God's sake?' asked a man, distraught for news of his son.

'I don't know, I'm terribly sorry, but we realise that the lists are incomplete . . .'

The man, whose face was so drawn it looked like a skull, clutched at her hand. 'If you do know, I'd prefer to hear it now. I don't want his mother to go on hoping.'

The tired girl from the ferries swore that she did not know. She pressed several ten-pence pieces into his hand so that he could ring the police in Maidstone. 'I'm sorry,' she said again.

'I know you're sorry. He was only 19,' the man said.

A woman who was waiting for her sister-in-law to come back from this Continental shopping trip said that they might all be better off at home, looking at their televisions. A Salvation Army woman gave her more tea and sat down beside her on the bench.

'Tell me about your sister-in-law. What did she go to buy?' she asked.

'She might be drowned,' the woman was frightened to talk about her in case it might bring bad luck.

'But we don't know that. Tell me what did she go to buy?'

'Well she said there wasn't all that much in Zeebrugge and she would go on to this place called Knokke-Heist that was nearby. What will happen to her children if she's gone?'

'Don't think about that yet. The Lord will help, tell me about this place where she went shopping . . .'

Around the terminal building the crowds came and went as if by looking at that cold, grey sea they could somehow make it more likely that people had been taken from it the previous Friday night. And all around the Eastern Dock there were the distressingly inappropriate advertisements saying that the Continent is nearer than you think and perhaps the saddest of all, the big signs: 'They're here, the new big value luxury ferries.'

It was the endless waiting that was so hard to watch, even as an outsider. People passive in the never-never land of not being sure a full day and a half after the tragedy.

Gently, the police, the ferry officials and clergymen explained that there had been such a panic; nobody was too sure of what names were given and what names were taken. These English-sounding names would be unfamiliar to Flemish and French speakers. . . .

And in the town which has so strenuously opposed the building of a Channel tunnel, people said that it would be a crime if this disaster were to lead to the public believing that a tunnel was the only way to cross the sea.

Quietly, and without the usual excitement and fuss of people going on their holidays, the passengers filed on and off the rows of ferryboats in the harbour. And in a wet, cold, sad Dover, the ships sailed in and out under the white cliffs. The seagulls called as they always did but through the sleet and in the silence they seemed as sad as funeral bells.

■ ■ ■ ■

EIGHTIES

■ ■ ■ ■

THE RIGHT TO DIE
IN YOUR OWN HOME

17 February 1980

My neighbour in London has lived for 81 years in her house. She came there when she was five. Before that she lived in a cobbled mews where her father was a coachman but he lost his position because the family he worked for decided to go over to the horseless carriage. The mews where she once lived changed hands for three quarters of a million pounds not long ago.

They liked the new house when they came there in 1909 and had five nice peaceful years before the First World War. She remembers when that war ended in 1918 and all the excitement and the men coming back. And she worked in a big firm which gave a celebration party where George Robey sang. Every lady who worked in the firm was allowed to invite a gentleman and every gentleman a lady — the night is as clear to her as if it had been last week.

Much clearer, actually. Last week wasn't all clear.

Her sight is so bad these days that she dare not even boil a kettle in case she burns herself, so another neighbour, a woman from further up the road, comes in and makes her breakfast, her lunch and her tea. The State, through the welfare services, gives an allowance for this, called an Attendance Allowance, of £27 a week.

This is a fairly regular procedure now in London, where there is a real need for it. A lot of elderly people have no relations nearby, the very nature of big city living means they have few close friends.

Britain is a very ageing society, the contrast between there and here is extraordinary. Here the parks are filled with children, in London they are filled with the old. In Dublin you hold a supermarket door open for a mother with a pram, in London for an elderly couple with a basket on wheels.

The health cuts have meant that a serious attempt is being made to keep old people out of residential care. On a purely factual and financial level it has been worked out that it is much dearer to put a person in a home permanently than it is to provide what are called back-up services. Attendance allowances are a part of the back-up. The

State also provides a Home Help twice a week for two hours on each occasion, and a bath attendant once a week to assist in washing. The Home Helps often say that they are more needed to assist as company than as cleaners, and that sometimes they are followed around by the people whose houses they are trying to clean. The need for conversation is greater than for vacuuming.

The bath attendants say that very often they are told that the old person 'doesn't feel like a bath today'. It's too cold or they're too tired or whatever. It's not a police state, they say, they can't drag the person upstairs and insist on cleaning them.

So back-up services and a fair amount of people calling in and taking an interest have meant that this neighbour has been able to live in her home reasonably well for the past few years, since her sight and hearing and mobility have all so disimproved. She has resisted sheltered accommodation, rightly saying that where could be more sheltered than where she is? A house whose every floorboard and stair step has been familiar for eight decades. And people will find her, she says, if she has a fall. She has given the keys to people who will come and look for her if she doesn't answer the phone.

She didn't answer the phone last week. Her bed was empty when I went in. She was lying underneath it, unable to get up. There were no bones broken, so she couldn't be taken to hospital. The police, who now work the ambulances because of the strike, helped to carry her downstairs and settle her in a chair.

Snow white and shocked from who knows how many hours like that, she was determined to be cheerful. Part of the generation that doesn't like to worry the doctor, she agreed under duress to let him call. He is a determined man, he said she must go into hospital to be looked at, and because casualty departments will admit an ambulance with an old person if it comes with a doctor's referral, she was taken to Charing Cross Hospital in Fulham.

And that's where she is today, while they try to decide whether she will be able to manage at home any more. The last time she had a fall they built an extra rail on the stairs; the time before that they arranged a commode.

People have shaken their heads darkly and said, 'Thatcher's Britain!' They say the old lady is not able to look after herself and there shouldn't be all this cheeseparing and pussyfooting about, people like that should be given good residential care in their last years, they worked hard enough for it during their time.

But I'm not sure. I don't think it's as simple as that. I can see that, alarming as it might be to neighbours who are at the moment relatively mobile, an old woman might like to live and die in a house where she has been since the year Lloyd George tried and failed to bring in the People's Budget and Bleriot tried and achieved the first flight from Calais to Dover.

Yet, when I see her all clean and pink in a hospital bed with nurses around and company and no fear of falling and lying through the long hours of the night alone on a floor, then I think she must stay in care. She doesn't get frightened of burglars when she's in hospital.

She doesn't find her heart thumping in fright when someone knocks on a door after seven in the evening, thinking that it's muggers like she reads about in the local papers. And there is an argument that says since she can't really enjoy her own home maybe she should go into something more organised.

But there's another argument which says we only have one crack at life and if you protest so strongly that you want to be in your own place, regardless of falls and knocked-over tables and things not being as clean as they used to be, then that's where you should be.

And that is actually what Thatcher's Britain is trying to do for old people . . . keep them in their homes.

It doesn't, of course, give nearly enough in resources. You get the feeling that the Prime Minister wants a return to old-fashioned values of neighbourliness and concern, because the government doesn't have to pay for such things. And yet to my intense annoyance I can't disagree with her. I only wish I had her sense of certainty about everything. It would be great to know which bed my neighbour should sleep in tonight, and know it was the right place for her.

WHEN BECKETT MET BINCHY

14 May 1980

Beckett looks 54, not 74; he looks like a Frenchman, not an Irishman, and he certainly looks more like a man about to go off and do a day's hard manual work rather than direct one of his own plays for a cast which looks on him as a messiah come to rehearsal.

He has spikey hair which looks as if he had just washed it or had made an unsuccessful attempt to do a Brylcreem job on it and given up halfway through. He has long narrow fingers, and the lines around his eyes go out in a fan, from years of smiling rather than years of intense brooding.

He is in London to direct the San Quentin Workshop production of *Endgame* and *Krapp's Last Tape* for Dublin's Peacock Theatre. It will open in Dublin on May 26th. Beckett has become very involved with this San Quentin group since the early sixties when he heard what was happening in the big American Jail.

One of the convicts, Rick Cluchey, who was serving what might have been a life sentence for a kidnap and robbery but which turned out to be only 11 years, persuaded the authorities to let the prisoners do Beckett plays and they performed them in a studio theatre in what used to be the prison's gallows room.

The plays made such an impact on the prisoners, who immediately saw similarities between the imprisonment felt by Beckett's characters and themselves, that they were repeated over and over. The word got out and it even got as far as Beckett in Europe.

Nowadays, Cluchey and Beckett are

friends, something that the convict in San Quentin would have thought impossible. Cluchey and his wife, Teresita Garcia-Suro, have called their two young children after Beckett and his wife, Suzanne.

Rick Cluchey knows nearly every word that Beckett has written but when he is in a position of actor with Beckett as director, he says he tries to forget everything he ever thought himself, tries to strip his mind and memory of actors' tricks and his own interpretations, and just wait like a blank sheet of paper for Beckett to tell him what to do.

This is what was happening down at the Riverside Studios in London where they were getting the rather minimal set ready for a rehearsal of *Endgame.* They needed a chair for Hamm to sit in, a ladder for Clov to run up and down, and a dustbin for Nagg. Nell, the other dustbin inhabitant, hadn't arrived yet (she is Teresita and was coming over from America the next day), so this day Beckett played Nell.

He was endlessly finicky and pernickety about the height and shape of the props, he ran up and down Clov's ladder a dozen times to see was it the right kind of ladder, and if it gave Clov space to turn around and deliver his lines.

He sat in Hamm's chair another dozen

times raising it and lowering it so that it would be at the right angle when Clov came over to whisper in his ear. I thought I was going to die with irritation and impatience but the American actors, Bud Thorpe, Alan Mandell and Rick Cluchey, hung on every instruction and rushed to carry it out.

Douglas Kennedy from the Peacock Theatre in Dublin sat with his notebook, taking heed of all the requirements that would be needed in Dublin. Finally, Beckett got down to words.

The main thing you'd notice is that he thinks the play is a song, or a long rhythmic poem. He can hear the rhythm, he can hear it quite clearly in his head and his work as a director is to get the actors to hear it too. That's why he goes over and over each line, saying it not all that much differently to the actor (in fact you'd have to strain to hear the difference), but it has a beat the way he says it and, once that beat is caught by the actors, it sounds quite different.

He stands there in front of them, mouthing the lines they say word perfect in his own play, up to the pauses and the half pauses, quite confident that this conversation between wretched imprisoned people is almost the obvious definition of the human condition. He doesn't ever apologise for his own work, excuse it or say, 'What I'm try-ing to say here is this . . .'

In fact, it seems to stand there beside him, this play, as if it was an important state-ment, and he is just helping the actors to unveil it.

Beckett is courteous, he never raises his voice. 'Bud, may I suggest something here?' he says to a young American actor, Bud Thorpe, who thinks that, when he has grandchildren, they'll never believe this, not in a million years.

'Alan, Alan, take the rhythm. You have to knock on the bin, the rhythm comes in the knocks, it sets the speed for the conversa-tion. Come, no, I'll get into my bin.'

And Beckett sits down beside Alan Man-dell to play the loving scene between the two dustbin-imprisoned folk who can only remember, wish and regret. Mandell says he'll never forget it to his dying day.

He has ludicrous energy, Beckett. When the actors, all decades younger than him, were tiring, needing a break, a coffee, he was still as fresh as when he started, the tones, the rhythms were running through him; his spare body, in its almost traditional uniform of two thin polo-necked sweaters, moved from side to side of the stage, bend-ing, crouching, stretching. Even I, sitting silently on my chair, began to feel weary and wish he'd stop for a few minutes.

He did. He lit another of the small cheroots he smoked and came over to me. I looked behind me nervously, assuming he was going to talk to someone else.

It had been a very firm arrangement. I could watch but not talk. Write but not interview. I assumed he was going to ask me to leave.

He introduced himself to me as formally as if I might have had no idea who he was and assumed he was someone who came in off the street to direct the play. He asked how *The Irish Times* was getting on and I gave him the usual loyal craven tale about it being the best newspaper in the world. He only saw it from time to time, he said, but he seemed to go along with my opinion of its excellence.

'I remember it more in the days of Bertie Smyllie,' he said. 'Did you know him?'

'No, but I believe he was a bit of a personality,' I said, helpfully wishing that, when Beckett had decided to talk to me, I could find something entertaining to say to him.

'My memory of him was that he ran his newspaper from the pubs and that there were circles around him, listening to what he wanted to do and running away to do it. He used to drink in the Palace. Is the Pearl still there?'

'No, it's been bought by the bank,' I said.

'The bank,' said Beckett thoughtfully. 'The bank. How extraordinary.'

It seemed to upset him deeply. I wondered should I tell him about all the alternative drinking places we had found, but I decided that he was more brought down by the notion of the bank owning the Pearl than the actual deprivation of the drink in it.

'And I believe the Ballast Office clock has gone,' he said gloomily. I agreed and hoped that he might hit on something that was still there in Dublin. 'How do people know what time it is?' he asked.

'I think they sort of strain and look down the river at the Custom House,' I said.

'It's the wrong angle,' he said.

He was silent then, and I wondered was he really concerned about the people not knowing what time it was, or had he gone off on a different train of thought.

'Will you come to Dublin yourself to see this?' I asked.

'Not this time, no, I shan't be coming this time,' he said.

His accent is sibilant French with a lot of Dublin in it. Not as lispy as Seán MacBride but not unlike it, either. I was afraid I had given him a bum steer by letting him dwell on the Ballast Office and the Pearl.

'There's a lot of it left, you know,' I said.

He smiled. 'I'm sure there is, but I must get back to France and Germany . . . that's where my work is. . . .'

'What are you working on next?' I asked him.

'A television play, it will be done for German television in Stuttgart. I like Stuttgart, not the town itself, it's down in a hole, a deep hole, but I like when you go up on the hills outside Stuttgart. And I like the people there that I work with . . . I am looking forward to it.'

'Does it have a name?' I wondered.

'No name, and no dialogue, no words.'

'That's a pity,' I said.

After a morning of listening to his words, I could have done with more. Anyway, I'm rigid enough to think that a play should have words, for God's sake.

He saw this on my face, and he smiled a bit. 'It will be very satisfactory,' he assured me. 'It's all movement, activity, percussion, cohesion. . . .'

'Why do you like working with the people in Germany on this sort of thing?' I asked, the tinge of jealousy evident in my tone.

'Oh, they understand, we understand the rhythm of it . . .' he said.

He picked up the issue of *The Irish Times* that was on my lap, and looked at it for a while, not really reading, more remembering.

He had liked Alec Newman, he said, a very gentle man. He had admired Myles na Gopaleen and laughed so much at everything he had written but had been a bit disappointed when he met him because he had expected too much. There were a lot of things he thought of about Dublin from time to time. Niall Montgomery. Had I known him? He was a good man.

He decided that those young actors had had enough rest. He went back to them. They took up at a part of the play where Hamm has to say, 'This is not much fun.' Rick Cluchey as Hamm said his line, giving it all the weight it deserved. 'I think,' said Beckett, 'I think that it would be dangerous to have any pause at all after that line. We don't want to give people time to agree with you. You must move and reply to him before the audience start to agree with him.'

And Beckett laughed and lit another cheroot and settled in for hours' more work.

FIT FOR A QUEEN

23 May 1980

I met this woman at a party and she was quite drunk and had tears of vodka pouring down her face as she decided she was going to confide her biggest secret to me.

She had her bras and corsets made for her specially at a place in the West End, which also made bras for the Queen.

She told me that I'd love it, that it would become quite an addiction, that I'd never be able to buy an ordinary bra again without wincing and feeling third rate. She said I should go the next day and see them myself.

With difficulty she was restrained from taking off her dress there and then to show me their handiwork and I assured her I would check them out. She wrote the name on my cheque book, in my diary and, to my annoyance, all over some letters that I was going to post to other people. Then, happy that she had done her duty, she passed out.

I needed a new bra. It's never what I would call heady excitement going to buy clothes of any kind if you aren't a Stock Size, so I thought I might investigate the royal corsetières.

I hoped they wouldn't be snooty and put

me down. It's bad enough to be put down when you're dressed. Naked, it's intolerable. They live in South Molton Street, and you have to make an appointment. The place was faded genteel, lots of elegant-looking wraps and robes about the place and Christmas cards from the royal family; and discretion hung heavily over the whole place like ectoplasm.

The lady, whose name was Daphne, was crisp and welcoming.

She seemed quite confident that the outcome was going to be a spectacular success. She looked like the kind of person that would never discuss money in a million years.

There are a few advantages about being more or less grown up. When I was younger I would have sat there tortured wondering how much the damn thing cost; nowadays life is too short.

'How much will it cost?' I asked, brazen as hell.

'About £30. It depends on how much fitting we have to do,' she said.

It sounded a great deal of money, but then foul ones on which nobody has lavished any attention at all are about £18 in sickly pink and even more if they're any colour you might wear. I decided to live dangerously and have one built for me.

'That's fine,' I said.

'We'll call Madame,' she said.

Madame was tiny and from somewhere in Europe that gave her an accent which sounded as if she had come out the door of Central Casting. She was petite and charming, and she said ooh la la, twice. She had a tape measure around her neck, she had pins in her mouth. Together we marched in to the fitting room.

First she would make a model, she said, and when we got the model right she would make the bra. It would be like a kind of masterplan, she would work from it. It would be as good as having me there.

I got a feeling of rising panic. Surely she wasn't going to cover me in putty or plaster of Paris so that she'd remember my shape. I stood there unhappily, with my arms crossed modestly over my bosom.

'Oh, maybe you should just make it . . . sort of largish,' I said vaguely, looking around fearfully for whatever they were going to pour over me.

By this stage she had taken out a grand harmless-looking thing which was like two huge steel horseshoes covered in fur and kind of white cotton. She fixed it onto me and we scooped bits of me into it and I was delighted.

'Oh, it's great,' I said happily. 'I'll take it.'

With enormous patience she explained that this wasn't it. This was just what she was going to work from, the real thing wouldn't be dull old cotton, it would be satin and lace.

I felt very foolish but Madame didn't mind at all. She buzzed around me like a butterfly, nipping here and folding there and raising and lowering. I felt like the prow of a ship. I was delighted with myself.

Then she said she was satisfied and I got out of it with very bad grace and put on what I had come in with which was very humble by comparison, and we made another appointment.

I offered to pay a deposit and Daphne said that was super, but you got the feeling that if I hadn't they'd still have gone ahead and made it. On the stairs I met a woman who stood back to let me pass and I noticed she had a bosom like the nose cone of a plane. She had obviously been there already and was coming back for another fix.

A week later I went back full of confidence. This time Madame produced a confection of satin and little roses and lace. It would make your heart soar to look at it. I quite understood why the vodka-soaked woman felt the urge to take off her dress and display hers.

A frown on Madame's face, a few more little pulls and pushes, she buzzed and Daphne came in and purred and I moved in a stately way around the fitting room, and begged to be allowed to take it just as it was, but they said nonsense, the whole notion of having a bra made was so that it could be fitted. They said it would be ready on Thursday.

And it was. A final fitting . . . an enormous amount of mutual congratulation. No pressure whatsoever to buy anything else. I wrote a cheque for the remainder and they waved away the banker's card. In the privacy and peace of a corsetières, they assume a lady is a lady and not a bounder.

It is possibly the most cheering garment I ever bought. It is firm to the point of being like reinforced steel. It's so comfortable that it's like wearing a cushion around the bosom. It will look fantastic if I'm knocked down by a bus.

I don't know if it actually does anything for men in the sense of an infrastructure, which is what bras are meant to be about . . . but I know that if there's another revolution and I'm told to burn it, I'll abandon the sisters before I'd let it go.

CONTRACEPTIVE CONVERSATION

16 February 1981

Today I had an argument with a stranger, a real live argument with a woman I'd never met before as we waited at a bus stop for what seemed a considerable length of time.

'Very depressing kind of day,' she said.

'Grey,' I agreed. 'But it might cheer up later.'

'Nothing much to be cheerful about, though, is there? Look at the papers,' she said.

Obligingly I looked at the front page of *The Irish Times*. Compared to some days, I thought the news was fairly neutral. 'Do you mean Mike Gibson not playing rugby for Ireland any more?' I asked, not quite seeing anything that would cause gloom.

'Never heard of him,' she said.

It couldn't be the heady excitement of will we, won't we about the EMS; she was hardly brought down by the fact that the RUC may have been kidnapping Father Hugh Murphy, since he was safe and well; the talks were continuing in an RTÉ dispute, but that wasn't enough to lay anyone low. No, it had to be Haughey and the Contraceptive Bill.

'Do you mean about having to have a doctor's prescription?' I asked.

'Indeed I do,' she said.

'Well I suppose it does make us look very foolish trying to legislate for everyone else's morality and pass the buck to the doctors,' I said cheerfully. 'But then I'm a fairly optimistic person, and I'd prefer to regard it as a step in the right direction.'

There was a stony silence. I wondered had she heard me. After all, she was the one who started the conversation. 'So, even though it's a bit of a joke, it's not all that bad,' I said, keeping things going as I thought.

'Is that your view?' she said.

'Well it's not a very thought-out view,' I backtracked. 'But it's a kind of instant reaction, if you know what I mean.'

'You approve of all that sort of thing,' she said in a kind of hiss.

'Oh yes, I think people have the right to buy contraceptives,' I said, wishing somebody else would come along and stand at the bus stop and shout 'good girl yourself' at me.

'And you'd like to see them in public places,' she said, eyes glinting madly.

'Well not in parks or concert halls or places like that. But on shelves in chemists, certainly. Then, if people want to buy them they can and if they don't, nobody's forcing them to.' I thought I had summed up the case rather well.

'On shelves so that everyone can see them,' she said, horrified.

'Well they're in packets,' I said, 'with kind of discreet names on them. They don't leap up off counters and affront you.'

'And how might you know all this?' she asked.

'Well I've seen them in chemists in London,' I said defensively.

'If they're so discreet, how did you know what they were?' she asked, tellingly.

'Well, you'd sort of know. I mean people have to know where they are, for God's sake. I mean they shouldn't have to go playing hide and seek around the chemist's with the assistant saying warmer and colder.'

The woman wasn't at all amused. 'I'm sure you know where they are because you buy them,' she said.

I began to wonder why it is increasingly less likely that I ever have a normal conversation with anyone. 'I once bought a huge amount,' I said reminiscently. 'As a kind of favour to a lot of people. They knew I was going to be in London, and they kept asking me to bring some home.'

She was fixed on me with horror. All her

life she knew she would meet someone as wicked as this, and now it had happened.

'I didn't know what kind to get or what the names of them were, so I asked for four dozen of their best contraceptives and a receipt. They looked at me with great interest.'

'I'm not surprised,' said the woman.

'But imagine smuggling them all in for people, and not making any profit on them and not even . . . you know . . . well, getting any value out of them myself as it were.'

She stared ahead, two red spots on her cheeks, and mercifully the bus came. She waited to see if I went upstairs or downstairs so she could travel on a different deck.

THE HAPPY COUPLE

29 July 1981

It would be impossible for you to know the amount of goodwill there is directed towards the royal couple unless you were here in London. For a month, the shops and buildings all along the wedding route have been smartening themselves up. There isn't a space that doesn't have the faces of the young couple decorated with flags and coats of arms and loyal greetings.

Men and women who have sparse and

drab weddings themselves, people who had no honeymoons, even those who don't have a proper home to live in, let alone a palace, are out on the streets cheering and laughing and wishing Charles and Diana a happy wedding day. It's a combination of a lot of things. It's going to be a great spectacle; everyone feels like a festival; it's a day off but, most important, people think they know Charles and Diana now and what they know, they like. The couple are very, very popular.

Hundreds of thousands of ordinary people in Britain have been feeling a real concern for Prince Charles, and worrying about his lonely life. They read endless descriptions of the evenings he spent at home and how he is secretly a family man at heart. Now, they are overjoyed that he has fallen in love and is having a fairytale wedding to a beautiful girl.

Hundreds and thousands of girls all over the country are identifying like mad with Lady Diana, whom they see as one of themselves but a bit posher. They will never marry a prince and have carriages and horses and fanfares and the works but she is doing it for them, in a way. In fact, it is touching to see how little envy and how much genuine enthusiasm there is around the place.

Charles has always been very well liked in England. He was educated, if not exactly like an ordinary person, at least like an ordinary upper-class person, which gave him some kind of touch with reality. He was trained in the various armed forces and learned how to do all kinds of things like deep-sea diving and flying a helicopter and playing a cello. He also had to learn about meeting total strangers and expressing an interest in whatever it was that had to have an interest shown in it. At this, he has been very good. He decided somewhere back along the line that if he was going to have to do it, he might as well do it properly, so instead of saying 'how fascinating', he says, 'what is this, how does it work, what's it for?'

He is always courteous and able to send himself up. When he went through that stage of falling off every horse he sat on, he laughed at himself, and he even asked one of his aides to buy the disrespectful mug which has his ears sticking out as handles. He doesn't yawn and look at his watch like his father does, nor does he look as tense and strained as his mother sometimes does. Very few people envy him his wealth or his estates. Hardly anyone envies him his job.

He is a Good Guy.

Lady Diana is the living proof that men don't respect you if you give in to them, and that princes certainly won't marry you if there's even a question that you might have given in to anyone at any stage.

Lady Diana Spencer has had a hard few months and if she can stand up to this, she is thought to be able for whatever else is in store. After all, very few brides have to go through the embarrassment of having their uncle announce proudly that they are virgins. Lord Fermoy, the brother of Lady Diana's mother, made this statement, 'My niece has no past.' She has had to have a gynaecological examination to ensure that she is capable of bearing children, she has had to move in with her husband's grandmother in order to get a crash course on how to behave like a royal. She has been instructed to keep her mouth shut, to say nothing in public. She has been asked to lose weight and to lose some of her old friends because they are not suitable any more. To be the future Queen Diana is exciting but there are a lot of hard things to be done on the way.

But Diana Spencer is very popular too, not just because she is young and pretty. She has the kind of background that people like to read about. Old noble family, young princes as playmates when she was a toddler, nice exclusive girls' schools, Riddlesworth then West Heath and then a smart Finishing School in Switzerland where she learned to ski and speak a little French.

She had a lot of unhappiness, the kind that everyone can sympathise with; being the child of a broken marriage and because she wasn't very intellectual, she didn't try for A Levels. Instead, she asked her father if he could buy her a flat in London and she would get a job. Her father bought her a flat for £100,000 and she asked three friends to share it, they paid her the rent each month and very shortly after they moved in, she got a job helping at a kindergarten school which had been set up by two friends of hers.

She never did a season, or came out as a deb. She wasn't a girl who went to smart nightclubs like Wedgies or Tokyo Joe's. Perhaps because of her own lack of home life she tried to make her flat into a home. She and Virginia and Carolyn and Ann lived like other debbie girls who liked shopping at Harrods and having little supper parties but they were quieter than most and spent a lot of evenings looking at television.

The telephone directory is hardly big

enough for the list of names that Prince Charles was going to marry at one time or another, but very few of these are among his close friends nowadays. Only Lady Jane Wellesley remains from the old flames, and she doesn't count because she was always meant to be more interested in her work than marrying the Prince of Wales.

Another lady called Lady Tryon is a close friend. She is Australian and Charles calls her Kanga and takes her advice about everything, it is said . . . including the suitability of the new bride.

He has a hard core of male friends including Nicholas Soames, Lord Tryon, Lord Vestey and Lord Romsey . . . they are thought to be secure in their circle and don't fear that marriage will take the prince away from them completely.

For Diana, it may be different. Even though she was able to give her flatmates a phone number of the Palace at Clarence House and begged them to ring her up for chats, they keep finding that she's in the middle of this or that and it is frowned on to interrupt her. The flatmates have been so discreet and refused very tempting bribes to tell their stories about life with Lady Di that it is believed they may well be rewarded by being allowed to remain friends. The trouble is, of course, that they are not quite upper class enough . . . but if they behave nicely it may be overlooked.

It's easy to know all this kind of gossip and speculation about Charles and Diana. In fact in the London of the last month, it would be difficult not to know it. There is a determination to celebrate and indulge and even wallow in it all. People want to read the same old stories over and over — how he proposed, what she said, what he thought, what they said then. . . . They are like children wanting to hear the same fairytales over and over. And the best bit of the fairytale is today, which is why hundreds of thousands of men, women and children have been up all night to share in it, to be a part of a world where princes are strong and kind and princesses are young and beautiful and virtuous and if you position yourself rightly you might get a wave or a smile from them.

ENCOUNTERS AT THE AIRPORT

7 November 1981
At the shop in London Airport, there was a young man studying the display of post-cards. Then he went to a section which had simply big words on the front like THANK

YOU and I LOVE YOU. His eyes went up and down the shelves until he found what he wanted, and he bought 12 of the one that said 'SORRY'.

He was tall and fair-haired and blameless looking. I haven't had a wink of sleep wondering what he did. Two women on the plane were discussing a friend they had seen in London who had got amazingly slim.

'Unnaturally slim, I'd call it,' said the one with the velvet beret.

'You wouldn't even call it slim, it's downright thin,' said the fur hat.

'Fashionably thin is one thing, but this is verging on the bony,' said the Beret.

'Yes, the face is getting kind of gaunt,' said the Hat.

At that point the air hostess passed with the coffees.

'Two vodka and tonics, please,' said the Beret.

The air hostess broke the news that ordinary people aren't allowed to buy drink on planes any more; you have to call yourself Executive and pay a fortune and sit in the front, and they'll pour drink on you free. The Hat and the Beret received this news glumly, as indeed have we all in our time. But they thought back to their slim friend.

'Probably just as well,' said the Hat.

'Maybe it was meant as an omen,' said the Beret.

As we waited for the luggage to come out, my mind was a red blur of relief that we had landed and filled with resolutions never to go up there into those skies again. Dublin Airport is grand about luggage trolleys these days; there were dozens of them where you could see them, unlike a lot of places where they hide them behind huge cardboard walls. A woman and daughter who were having a hard time relating to each other were leaning on a trolley.

'There, now, the bank's open in the airport on a Sunday. Wouldn't that be a handy thing to know?'

'Why would it be handy?' asked the girl.

'If you wanted to cash a cheque, you could come out here.'

'God,' said the girl, 'twenty-four miles to cash a cheque, God.'

Mothers are slow to take offence at tones and dismissiveness. This woman chattered on about how the cases would soon be out and then they'd be on their way, and how grand it was to be home and how great it had been to be away. The girl grunted and eyed the crowd in a hopeless quest for an Airport Encounter with a young man who would whisk her away to less tedious chat.

'When all's said and done, I think it's best to fly by plane.' The mother looked pleased that she had come to this decision.

'Aw, God,' said the girl, 'what else would we fly by but a plane? Seagull?'

Out in the place where people wait to meet the Arriving Passengers, a family was peering nervously as there seemed to be no sign of their son.

'Is there anyone else left?' his mother asked me.

'There are a few people fighting with the Customs men,' I said with my terrific sense of humour, which was like a lead balloon.

The family went ashen at the thought of it.

'I meant talking to Customs men,' I said humbly.

That still didn't please them; what could he be talking to the Customs men for?

'Perhaps he bought presents,' said the father.

The mother's face registered a belief that he had been carrying a potato sack full of cocaine. 'Please God he's not in any trouble,' she said.

I went around and hid behind a pillar so that I could see what happened. In a minute he came out, and the family nearly fainted communally with relief.

'What did they want, what were they looking for?' demanded the father.

'Did they find anything?' begged the mother.

The unfortunate boy had been to the lavatory, had made a phone call, and his case had come off last anyway. He had walked innocently past the Customs men, he had nothing only one bottle of gin as a present anyway. What was all the fuss? What, indeed? I tiptoed away.

At the phones, which look like Space Age things with us all clustered around what seemed like a big squat tree with telephones growing on it, there was a man flushed and triumphant. 'I don't know what the country's coming to,' he said happily. 'I've got on to Wexford in no time, no crossed lines, nobody bit the nose off me. Maybe it's the end of the world.'

UP IN THE CLOUDS WITH CHARLIE HAUGHEY

4 February 1982

Charlie Haughey got up at seven-thirty a.m. yesterday morning and had a cup of tea. Later on he had another cup of tea and a third. That's his breakfast, not only during the campaign but always. 'I don't bother with breakfast,' he says fastidiously, as if those who do are somehow gross.

By eight o'clock he was washed and dressed and ready for the economic advisers who were going to prepare him for the morning's press conference. He emerged ready for anything. He likes to look presentable, he says, he knows that people often judge by appearances, and he doesn't find it a waste of time to have to keep himself looking Milan.

He thinks that if you are in the public eye you owe it to people to look well. He often remembers Seán Lemass telling them all in the old days that people are entitled to seeing you looking your best. 'Seán Lemass's great phrase was "who did your haircut?",' not just to Charlie but to all of them.

Charlie's own hair is very silvery and well groomed these days. If he hadn't taken his father-in-law's advice literally he has certainly taken the spirit of it. Did he give it a lot of attention?

'Well, Maureen Foley of Clontarf has always kept it in order for me. She's made me look respectable for the past while, and then for the debate my son Ciaran's girlfriend did it. She's qualified as a hairdresser so she had a go for that night.'

Was he pleased with the debate?

'Very. It's hard to know,' he says, 'how much the general public will be swayed by two men talking to each other,' but he thinks it was civilised and that they covered a fair amount of ground.

He had no complaints about Brian Farrell. He was a very professional chairman and he didn't favour either one of them. Was it nerve-racking? It was undoubtedly stress-creating. He had cleared the previous day to have a proper rest and time on his own or with just a few advisers to clear his mind and to marshal his thoughts. Did he sleep at all during the day waiting for the debate? Not really, a couple of snoozes but not going to bed and drawing the covers over him and going in to a deep sleep. Nothing as deliberate as that.

After the debate he had come home and there had been a crowd in and yes indeed they had talked about it. No they had not played it over on the video; they remembered the bits they wanted to talk about. Were people over-flattering to him, did he think, in fear of inferring his wrath? He smiled beatifically. Wrath? He seemed not to have heard of such a possibility. But seriously he said he did hear the bad as well as the good and his family in particular were all very frank with him.

There'll be no fear that he would live in an ivory tower out in Kinsealy. He had a busy day yesterday, not too much time to sit and brood over what the papers said about the confrontation. He is sunnier about the papers this time round. He thinks they have managed to dilute some of the more extravagant plunges at the jugular. He has always felt and still believes that there is a kind of media fog about things like elections, where everyone in papers and on the radio believes their own preferences.

Just look how wrong they all were about the divorce referendum, to take just one example. But he agreed that he's getting an easier passage this time. People are not hostile. 'Perhaps they've just got used to me,' he said. 'I've been around so long now they know I don't eat babies.'

Or indeed much else. Charlie Haughey wasn't planning on having any lunch. He doesn't bother with lunch on the campaign, he says, in the same way that he dismisses breakfast. But it's because he's never anxious to break the momentum.

It's a delay, a diversion, a bit of a waste of time to have to go and sit down for lunch somewhere. A cup of tea out of his hand would be enough for him. A sandwich if he was pushed. We drove from Kinsealy into the Berkeley Court Hotel in Ballsbridge, his mind now clear about what he would say at the press conference to launch the plan for an international financial services centre in Dublin.

At the hotel handlers and television teams and people in good suits who had all had their hair cut stood around. The lights, the thumping music played low but insistently, the television screens and the paraphernalia of a press conference were all underway. After eleven he would go to the helicopter pad in Vincent's Hospital and fly to Limerick, and then to Listowel. No, nobody was in trouble, just trying to get around and see everyone, that's all.

There didn't have to be a reason to go to places, a base party reason. Take today, for example. He'd be up in Killybegs this morning to launch their fisheries policy document and there was no question of looking for extra seats up there. No, it was quite possible to go to places for real reasons. Charlie Haughey had planned to be back in his home while it was still daylight and he would spend the rest of the evening in his own constituency.

He loves walking around the constituency with people saying hello to him, and telling him about the real issues of the election, about wanting a bit of hope and about how Charlie would give it to them. He thinks about that when he wakes up and that makes it easy to get up in the mornings.

ELECTION BRINGS LIFE TO AN AGEING SOCIETY

3 June 1983

For many old people, the huge rosettes and the bright young people coming to rap on their doors is a welcome chance to meet people. They haven't had people taking such an interest in them since the last election when the circus came around as well. The arguments about youth unemployment are almost meaningless on some streets where teenagers don't play and babies don't cry to each other from prams. In many parts of Britain, an ageing society, almost everyone on the electoral roll is on the pension as well.

They ask about the cost of living and the Tories tell them that four years ago inflation raged at 18 per cent, but now thanks to careful management it is down to 4.5 per cent. This simply is the best guarantee that they can afford to live. If they say, well it's still difficult to live, the answer is, imagine what it would have been like if inflation had been allowed to continue.

The Labour candidate will tell them that fuel costs have been forced up behind their backs and that Labour will cut these. Labour will freeze council and all rents for at least a year. Labour will insulate their houses.

The Alliance says one of the great wrongs pensioners suffer from is that they have to pay fixed charges for gas, electricity and telephone. All these fixed charges would go under an Alliance government.

Old people ask the candidates too about reducing the retirement age. In Britain, men retire at 65 and women at 60, and there has been increasing interest in a younger retirement age for men both from management and workers. So if a household asks the canvassers what the policies on retirement are, they will get these answers:

The Conservatives say that to reduce the retirement age would cost £2,500 million and is hard to promise. The Tories also say that they are against compulsory retirement at any age.

Labour says that its aim is a common retirement age of 60, and that if returned it will endeavour to get this organised, but it will first raise the pensions before it does anything else.

The Alliance has no very strong views, but says that it should all be more flexible.

A matter which worries many pensioners is the earnings rule. This means that if you earn any more than £57 a week and are in receipt of the pension, that pension will be reduced in line with your earnings. Many older people who feel capable of working on for several years after official retirement age resent this rule greatly.

The Conservatives say that it was their party which raised the earnings rule to £57 from a lower figure and they hope to take the top level away altogether eventually. Labour says that it doesn't intend to do anything about it at once since it's a matter that only affects a small number of the country's pensioners anyhow. The Alliance is in agreement with the Conservatives on this matter.

So far, no specific campaign has been spearheaded towards the elderly. The granny vote has not been isolated as an area of winning support. It is presumed that the elderly in society will follow very much the general view on matters to do with defence and the economy, and will share the opinions left or right on a normal statistical basis. But there are some matters, like the cost of living, law and order, and housing, where you would imagine that more specific attempts might have been made to woo this considerable section of the electorate. There's nothing to stop you being a floating voter at any age. Pensioners do not always vote according to the habits of a lifetime.

MAEVE'S OPERATION: THE WHOLE STORY

8 October 1983

First I'm afraid you have to have a little of the background. Since July, I haven't been able to straighten my right leg. This is of no consequence when you're sitting down or lying down which I seem to do a lot of, but in the odd bits where you have to walk from one place to another it is very harassing. Not to put it too finely, it means you can't walk.

I have arthritis in the other leg and so I thought gloomily that it must be spreading, like a rumour, or like one of those nice Russian vines that cover a wall in no time. But this knee took on terrible proportions, and by the time I found it easier for people to pour my gin and tonic into a saucer and let me at it on all fours like a big kitten I considered the wonderful Art of Medicine and went to a doctor who was very nice and said it seemed unmerciful to her and she sent me to a specialist.

I can't tell you all these people's names because it would be advertising, but suffice to say the country is filled with kind, sympathetic GPs and serious, efficient orthopaedic surgeons.

We had a merry month in August which involved great things like heat treatment which were really nice and didn't work and cortisone injections in the knee which were desperate and didn't work. 'Will these make my neck swell up?' I asked anxiously. I'm chubby enough already without gaining a lot of innocent fat from a knee treatment. It wouldn't, I was told. Then because we were all getting puzzled and I was like Quasimodo on two sticks now and I was wondering would I have to be fitted with a collar on my neck and led around . . . I went for an arthrogram.

Now I know I'm a long time coming to the hospital bit but honestly if you've never had an arthrogram you'd need to know about them. They call them X-rays. And you go like a simpleton to the X-ray department of a hospital to have one. I thought it was a great name for a start: arthrogram, like something out of *Minder* or a telegram from

Guinnesses.

By this time the scene had shifted back to London but I feel sure that the beauty and joy of an arthrogram is pretty much the same no matter what part of the world you're in. First it was in an operating theatre, second it took nearly two hours, third it involved a series of injections of dyes to point up little-known facets of the knee and lastly it had something straight from a James Bond film: they blow your knee up with gas like a balloon and X-ray it in its expanded state. I was nearly demented at this stage and trying to make conversation with people who seemed to be surrounding the operating table in increasing numbers. I saw a pile of papier-mâché hats and wondered did those who have to be exposed to radiation a lot wear hats as well.

'Do you often wear those hats?' I asked a tiny girl from Trinidad.

'They're sick bowls,' she said.

'Are you very uncomfortable?' the polite English radiologist asked kindly.

It was a ludicrous question. I tried to single out the most agonising thing about it all. 'There's some awful bit of machinery underneath my knee sticking into it,' I said, thinking it was probably a wrench or a hammer that someone had left there by mistake.

'That's my hand,' said the radiologist.

Ashen, I came out of it all and carried the pictures around my neck on a string until I got home. Remember I was now walking on two sticks and it's not easy to carry things and the arthrogram was not something I would repeat just because I lost the snaps. The snaps and myself flew back to Dublin and the serious but brilliant orthopaedic surgeon looked at them.

'Nothing,' he said after five minutes.

'Was there no film in the camera?' I said, tears in my eyes, ready to go back and bludgeon them all to death in that hospital with their own sick bowls.

'No, perfect pictures, just reveal nothing at all,' he said.

I waited for it . . . my poor big heart thumping, I waited and he said it.

'We'd better open you up.'

When the world settled down from the thunderous roar of terror that filled my ears, I heard myself saying in a high-pitched voice of total panic, 'Well, if that's it, then I suppose that's it. Let me look at my diary.'

I couldn't even see my diary. I just agreed like a big lamb to what he said, and a date was fixed. And I went to Admissions and an admission date was organised and then there was no getting out of it. I looked at the knee very dismally. What could it be, I asked myself in lay person's terms. Maybe my leg had just gone crooked to punish me for all my loudness and showing off. I was going to suggest this to the surgeon, but brilliant and serious he was, a person able to cope with an impish, ageing sense of humour he was not, so I said nothing.

I packed five books and a typewriter and 144 sheets of paper, and a manual on how to take up calligraphy and several tomes about evergreens so that I'd be an expert on them when I came out. I remembered to take some nightdresses and a wash bag too, but only at the last moment so I had to carry them in a plastic bag.

I put on my ingratiating face when I met the nurses on Floor Three of St Vincent's Private Hospital. 'I'll be a model patient,' I said. 'I'll be no trouble.'

Two of them remembered me from the gall bladder incident over a decade ago. 'She'll be a monster,' they said.

'I've got much calmer and older and more fearful since then,' I said.

They were possibly the kindest bunch of women I ever met in my life anywhere, and I'm not only saying that because one day I suppose I'll have to go back to them, to get a new hip, but they were kind. There wasn't one of them I could find fault with and let me tell you after a day or two I was ready to find fault with anything that moved. But not the nurses ever. Night and day cheerful and reassuring and they didn't even laugh at the typewriter and the books that just sat there untouched for two and a half weeks. They know we like to come to hospital with our illusions. I suppose there's a name for the operation. I didn't ask. I was so weakened by the memory of the arthrogram. I wanted no more definitions; anyway, a kind, efficient and nameless anaesthetist came the night before to tell me about it, and I closed my ears so that I wouldn't hear a single word while maintaining what I hoped was a look of alert interest on my face.

'Is there anything you'd like to ask?' he said politely.

'Might I die of a heart attack without your noticing what with being a bit on the plump side?' I asked.

'No,' he said.

They'd notice and stop me dying of a heart attack. They had a machine that told them that sort of thing. I lay in the dark and thought about people who have much worse things and wondered how they could bear them and I thought of all the bravery in the world. And big, sad tears came down my face. The night nurse who can hear silent tears at a hundred yards came in.

'I know you won't believe me. I was caring about other people,' I said.

'I know you were, aren't you a grand, kind thing,' she said.

And I told her that I now understood immediately why men married their nurses and if things had been different I would propose to her there and then, and we both said wasn't it great that I only had a silly old knee and not something awful and I went to sleep while she was talking to me.

They gave you three Valium next day to space you out and so of course I didn't know where I was but I was very, very happy. Unfortunately what often happens is that the schedule takes longer than they think. Some operation they think is simple turns out to be long and complicated then the lovely floaty Valium wears off and you know only too well where you are. And you can't keep asking to be topped up because that would be bad for you to tank you out of your mind.

So I remember the journey on the trolley passing ordinary people doing ordinary things. They had washed, or scrubbed I think it's called, my right knee so much I thought it wasn't going to survive it.

'I must admit I don't normally wash my knees that much,' I said humbly in case my own native filth was responsible for all the pain and we could now call the whole thing off, and put the pain in my leg down to common dirt.

They explained that they didn't either but this was to make it nice and sterile. Then they put gauze on it and a sort of red flag. I didn't like the red flag.

'Is that so he'll know which one to do?' I said in mounting panic, every story about people amputating the wrong limbs coming back to me in a line.

No, apparently, it was to keep it warm and sterile, they said. I wonder, but anyway it's not something you'd fault them on. And then to be honest I really don't remember much more. I have to rely on other people for what went on.

They say I asked the serious surgeon how old he was, which I might well have because it was something I had been speculating about. And he had said, 'guess' and I had guessed right, which had pleased the semi-conscious me enormously and horrified the acolytes who wouldn't have dreamed of asking a consultant surgeon anything at all. And apparently I had forgotten all about my knee and wouldn't listen when they tried to tell me what was wrong with it. Instead of listening I paid flowery compliments to everyone I met. 'How very courteous of you to come in and see me,' I said to one greatly loved sister who had been sitting there like a lamb waiting till I woke up. I used to say this to her graciously each time I woke up. She must have loved her vigil. When my other greatly loved sister came in I said it was extraordinarily courteous of her to have taken so much time off work even though this was the middle of the night and she'd had to fly home early from a conference in order to receive this level of conversation.

I had refused to allow my husband to come anywhere near me for the whole business, because he had a big broadcasting job in London that day and I couldn't have borne to think of him sitting in the corridor not understanding nuns and holy pictures and maybe thinking that I'd snuffed it. But I made an ill-timed attempt to ring him. He had been on the phone many times and quite unlike myself now knew what was wrong with me.

'Isn't it great?' he said.

'Isn't it great?' I said, miffed. My voice sounded as if I had drunk an entire bottle of some spirituous liquor ten minutes previously.

'But isn't it great what they found?' he said, happily determined not to be put off by this sporting drunk ready to fight with her shadow.

'I don't think they found anything,' I slurred. 'I forgot to ask.'

'You were full of Foreign Bodies. They got them all out,' he said happily.

'I think Gordon is very drunk,' I said, and hung up. Fortunately the angelic sisters got him back on the line and then I agreed to look at a jar full of ridiculous things, bits of bone, bits of cartilage, like the kind of jar a child might take home from a day on the beach.

'They were never in my knee,' I said. And then I looked at them with pride. Not everyone goes round carrying that kind of stuff in a knee; it reminded me of space debris. I was delighted with it, and then to be honest all was semi-oblivion for a couple of days.

I had no visitors only family and nurses so I felt safe in saying I love you to everyone who approached my bed. The paper lady was surprised but tolerant. And then came the dull bit, the bit where you think you're well but you keel over if you get out of bed, where you ache for visitors but after five minutes the room is spinning and you want to go to sleep. And in the end the only thing you yearn for is television.

And you won't believe this but just as I was sitting up and saying I'm going to have a whole night of telly and I won't look at one documentary or one serious analysis, I'll look at rubbish until they come and tuck me up, the entire television reception disappeared from the place. I joke you not — Thursday, Friday, Saturday, Sunday, Monday, we lay like mad bats in our beds, no Gaybo, no *Gone with the Wind,* no *Three Days of the Condor* that I once queued for an hour and a half in Fulham to see. I was purple with rage. Oh there were explanations, none of them made any sense to invalids. I wondered would I get a rebellion going and get us all to march on our crutches up to Phoenix Relays or to sister somebody and beat them all about the heads. You have no idea how awful it is lying there when you think you're going to have *Remington Steele* and instead you have your own thoughts. A fearsome fury descended on me and I staggered out of bed and tried to push the television out into the corridor. A nun tried to restrain me. She had been explaining yet again why the hospital had been five days without television. I wouldn't listen.

'Excuse me,' I said, filled with this new excessive politeness which seems to have been injected with the anaesthetic. 'I am moving this out to the corridor; if I do not have a room with a television, why do we keep up the pretence that I have?'

They told me people would fall over it in the corridor so instead I hung my dressing gown over it and went to sleep in a monstrous sulk.

I started to walk round the room. My leg was nearly straight. I had a frightening series of encounters with what calls itself the physiotherapy department but is actually a troupe of circus trapeze artists and acrobats who got stranded in Vincent's. They think you can lift your heel while you keep the back of your knee flat on the bed or the ground. Try it. No one can do it. They can do it of course because they are all the Flying Firenzes or something in real life and are just doing physio as a power trip. They also were one nicer than the other . . . and in the days when I was like a weasel with no television and no concentration, I couldn't even finish the *Evening Herald* . . . I couldn't find a fault with a physio. And then they said I could go.

I had heard awful stories that the bill was pinned by a dagger to your chest when you woke up from the operation but this was not so. It wasn't mentioned until the last day and delivered discreetly. And the nurses of the Third Floor all came and said goodbye and lyingly told Gordon that I had been as good as gold, which he didn't believe for two seconds, and in an odd way I knew I'd miss them, and I hoped whoever would be sleeping in my room that night would get well and strong like I did. And I cried to think of the people who hadn't been as lucky as I was with just Foreign Bodies.

Then I cheered up again and was the life and soul of the car until I saw Dalkey, when I started to bawl again, and most people there must think I have a wretchedly unhappy home life.

And then I came back to London which is where I am meant to be living though as people often say to me you'd never know it. And I asked Aer Lingus would they mind me having a wheelchair because that's a long haul on a weak leg uphill when you get off the lurching bus. They said there was no problem, and honestly, not that I'd wish a day's illness or incapacity on anyone, a wheelchair is your only man at an airport.

First a car into the gate, not a lurching bus, and then a great fellow called Joe who was from Limerick and off we went. Joe said that he'd have to take a bit of a run at the ramp if I didn't mind. Mind? I adored it. Imagine racing up past executives and eager, earnest walkers. I was crazed with power. I waved like the Queen Mother at everyone I knew and everyone I didn't, the latter being much the larger percentage. In fact I would have happily done a tour of all the terminals but the luggage arrived and Joe wheeled me to a taxi and Gordon packed in all the unread books and the typewriter and the tomes of evergreens and *The Art of Calligraphy* and soon we were home.

You know when you listen to hospital requests the way all the messages seem to be a bit samey, the thanks is so fulsome and it's always said in exactly the same words. Now I know why. There are no other words to express the relief and gratitude and amazement at the skill and kindness of people who were total strangers a couple of weeks ago, people who will hold your hand in the night and wash the back of your neck and root around for hours in a big silly knee full of Foreign Bodies. I hope they get satisfaction in their work. I really do. Because they give it. In spades.

Keeping Cruise off the Roads Is New Priority

16 November 1983

'They would have been more interested in the arrival of the New Beaujolais than the cruise missiles if it hadn't been for us,' said Laura, who has been at Greenham Common for 13 months. She spoke with tears of frustration in her eyes. The peace women have been outsmarted by the US Starlifters, which touched down while the protesters were either asleep or at the other side of the airfield.

The first missiles had arrived just before nine a.m. on Monday when the women were leaving their little tents to organise breakfast. Yesterday had been widely rumoured as Arrival Day and the women had been planning a serious rehearsal of what form their protest would take. So it was with disbelief and horror that they realised about noon that the long crates which had been slid out of the back of the Starlifter had been taken under heavy guard straight to the nuclear shelters. In fact, Cruise had arrived while they slept.

Trying desperately to rally, the women insisted that the missiles might be in the base but they would never come out. Greenham is intended to be only a storage depot for cruise missiles and they could not be fired from there, claim the women. The plans to settle the missiles in various other parts of the British countryside will now be the main focus of their attention.

'We could never have stopped planes and helicopters,' said Lynn Jones, a long-time resident. 'But we are not going to let them travel down our roads.'

Their candlelit vigil on Monday night was joined by many more supporters and when yesterday dawned cold and wet, the women were ready but on the wrong side of the airfield. This time the Galaxy aircraft and another Starlifter flew in accompanied by US military helicopters and guarded by British Army forces on the ground. Objects covered in tarpaulin and believed to be the actual warheads for the missiles were unloaded swiftly. Suddenly the singing and protesting women hundreds of yards away realised what was happening and ran for that corner of the fence, but too late to see the actual unloading of the weapons for which they have been waiting for over two years.

Two of the women who have been at Greenham since the beginning were sobbing openly. The two long winters, the lost springs and summers seemed to be in vain. They stood looking emptily from afar at the now unloaded planes. Their misery was like a long howl in the November afternoon.

But others reassured them and gradually got their spirits up again. So the missiles were in, but how could they get out? How could they get to their destinations if there was a massive campaign of civil disobedience? Suppose you had thousands of private cars blocking the cruise convoys? Suppose you had hundreds of pedestrians on the zebra crossings? Suppose even that you dug up the roads? It might be a crime of sorts digging up the roads with pneumatic drills, but it wasn't killing people or blowing them to Kingdom Come.

Arms linked, tears dried, they rallied. They told the press that they were still winning because they had brought the matter to the front of people's minds, and kept it there. The polls showed many more people objecting to the missiles now than there were in June during the election campaign. Even those who were for the missiles were jumpy about who had authority to fire them.

'Ronald Reagan played into our hands by being such a silly twit about Grenada,' said one tired, debby-looking girl, trying to wrest some good news from the crumbling day.

They barred the main gate again and lay down in front of it and cheered as young policemen first cautioned and then arrested over 120 of them. They don't mind appearing in court over and over just so long as they keep it all at the front of people's minds.

'At least they didn't come quietly,' said the peace women proudly as they settled down to guard the few possessions of their colleagues, who had gone off in the dark under arrest but also under the camera lights of television crews from all over the world.

DEVELOP YOUR OWN STYLE

30 November 1983
The only useful advice I ever got about writing was to write as you talk. I talk a bit too quickly and certainly too much, so that's the way I write as well. I don't know how it works for silent, thoughtful people who only speak when they have something to say. I imagine it should work rather well. Whatever they write would be worth reading. This is not artistic or literary advice, it is practical and down-to-earth . . . and if you are having difficulty beginning something . . . an

article, a short story, a novel or a play . . . ask yourself, 'What am I trying to say?' Then say it aloud and nine times out of 10 you'll have your first sentence. And once your first sentence is written down in front of you it's much, much easier to do the next one, and so on.

Unfortunately at school when we learn English we have to take on board a great number of words, expressions and forms of speech which are not used in everyday communication. This is necessary, I think, in order to fill up the gaps in vocabulary. It would be ridiculous to leave school with whole sections of the English language unknown to us just in order to clear the mind for easy communication. The language is rich so it's important to know the huge range of words and their shades of meaning. But, and it's a very large but, the trouble is that just because we do have to learn so many complicated and elaborate words we are inclined to overuse them. Not in speech, mind you, unless you happen to be a very pompous and mannered talker, but certainly in writing.

Time and again, I read short stories from young people — and oddly girls are the worst offenders — which are so choked up with words and phrases which they would never in a million years use in conversation that it makes the story itself unreadable.

An example: 'Untimely fingers of frost in what should have been the season of mists and mellow fruitfulness nipped Ann O'Leary as with furrowed mien she proceeded from the domestic portals and directed her steps to the main thoroughfare.'

She was trying to say, 'It was a cold autumn day when a worried-looking Ann O'Leary left her house. . . .' or something like that.

Now I don't know why we should think that the more disguises and padding we put on a thought the more respectable it becomes. It must be a throw-back to the days when we crammed as many words and allusions into a school essay in order to let the English teacher know that we were at least aware of them. Fine if that's what you're about, letting an examiner know that you absorbed a barrel full of vocabulary. But if you are trying to tell a story simply . . . or get an idea or a picture out of your mind and into someone else's, then it needs to be a lot more simple, a lot less cluttered. In fact a lot more like the way you speak.

Last year in Waterford I was making this point and a girl in one of the groups asked me a question which I couldn't answer. She said that if she was really to write as she spoke, it would be full of schoolgirl slang and local idiom and phrases that were currently fashionable but might be out of favour soon. Is that the way she should write, she wanted to know, because that was the way she talked? I've thought about it a lot since. She was right of course, her own school-speak was probably as unsuitable for getting her thoughts across to people outside her immediate circle as would be the awful essay-style crowded prose and jargon. Yet it would have more truth in it, and more honest attempt to say something simply. And as she grew to be aware what was in fact just the artificial group-talk that we all use at different times of our lives . . . she could discard it in favour of a direct and uncluttered style.

It's not easy to do at once, not if you have been used to writing as a vehicle for other people's thoughts and expressions. But once you start it becomes easier and easier and you will wonder how you could ever have begun a tale with some showy sentence full of words and hiding what you meant to say. It's a bit easier also to hide the real you, and what you feel if you use the disguise of other people's language. It's somehow safer to say 'within the hallowed walls of this esteemed place of learning' instead of saying 'here at school' because the first one has a kind of sardonic ring to it . . . the second is more naked.

You could begin with a diary. Just telling it like it is. No high-sounding phrases, no wishing to impress, because in a diary you are writing to yourself. You could say what it's like now in the winter of '83, what you feel, what you think about. Nobody will read it but you. But when you've done a page or two go back over it with a red pen and hunt ruthlessly for phrases and words that are not your own, for things that would be foolish and fussy if said aloud.

I think that's the best way to approach creative writing. To realise that it is creative, and you are the one creating it. Don't be content with other people's words, use your own. Don't worry about style, if you speak like yourself for long enough the style will be there. It will be *your* style. You will be writing like yourself. You will have found your own voice.

ONE EYE ON BARGAINS, ONE EYE ON ALSATIANS

9 January 1984
A cold, bright morning, and a small crowd

stands outside Harrods studying the free store map which the management wisely distributes at sales.

This saves endless hours of questioning, and helps the bargain hunters to work out a flight path from the main door to Fine China in the centre of the second floor, where a Wedgwood dinner service is reduced from £1,226 to £613.

Others were planning a quick gallop up the escalators to the Fur Rooms on the first floor, over on the corner where Brompton Road joins Hans Crescent — one floor above the spot where a bomb killed six people and wounded 90 last month.

There is nothing to show what happened here in December. No wreath, no flowers, no message scrawled in hurt or rage on any wall. Not even the broken windows. The whole menswear department has been fully repaired and was trading normally during the sale.

But there are no cars parked now in the side roads, and even a private car dropping somebody off at the door has barely time for the passenger to get out before it is waved on.

And all around stand policemen and policewomen, either speaking softly into the little radios which they wear fixed to their lapels, or just looking on with watchful eyes and a hand lightly laid on the collar of equally vigilant Alsatian dogs.

Lots of other men seem to be on the lookout too. These are plain-clothes Special Branch officers and members of the Anti-Terrorist Squad. They say that some of the people inside the store who might look like assistant manager or floor supervisor are in fact Special Branch as well.

The sale began officially on Friday morning, with the usual overnight campers pitching their tents early on Thursday evening. Some are paid to go and queue for bargains. One boy was paid £100, to get a television and video set which had been reduced from £1,000 to £500. He said that the fellow who paid him would still be able to sell the goods at a profit after that, so it was worth it to everyone. Including Harrods, presumably, who have the reputation of offering really gigantic bargains.

The store's managing director and chairman, Mr Aleck Craddock, said that the people who normally shopped in Harrods had no intention of staying away because of the bomb. In fact, he thought it had made them more determined than ever to come and buy. He announced that since the bombs, trading had not decreased at all, in fact it was 14 per cent up on the same period last year.

On the same factual note, Mr Craddock continued to express his belief that the store would be able to announce record takings of £25 million over the three-week sales period. More than 250,000 people attended the opening day. But not everyone is able to show such a calm and unruffled front.

Some of the 5,000-plus staff are very unhappy and distressed and don't mind admitting it. A woman in the china department said that on Friday there had been a great deal of noise and crashing about while people literally struggled over bargains, breaking crockery and china. She said her nerves got very bad and she had to sit down for a long time. She kept thinking that the bombers had come back to finish them off.

A young woman told me that if I went past the Staff Only door, I would see that the corridors were lined with messages of sympathy to the staff from the public — people had written from everywhere to say how terrible it was. A lot of people had wanted to send sympathy to the families of those people who had been killed or injured, but they didn't know where to write so they just wrote to Harrods. There were some letters from Ireland also, people writing to say that the Irish were upset too.

Some of the staff thought that these should be put up on a wall where the public could see them and realise the support that people gave the store, but the powers that be said no, that would be a bad idea. It would keep reminding people of the terrible thing that had happened, and really, it was best for people to forget and get on with living.

The crowds on Saturday morning seemed less than usual for the first Saturday of the sale, which is after all the first day that ordinary people who work Monday to Friday can get to it. There wasn't the stampede and throng that has been known and some of the staff were relieved to be able to breathe a little more easily than they expected. The tight security was adding to what was the normal tension of the country's biggest sale. But the big, silent police presence was obviously a great comfort to the shoppers, some of whom approached a little uneasily, one eye on the bargains and one eye on the big Alsatian dogs straining at their leads.

A Tipperary Robin Hood

7 December 1985

Twelve Christmases ago, when I had just come to live in Hammersmith, I was shocked at a notice which went in everyone's door telling them to look out for signs of old people who might be dead in bedsitters upstairs. They gave handy hints such as not having heard them move around, or milk bottles piling up outside the door. Then you were to say to yourself: aha, there must be a dead person in there. The notion that in bedsitter-land you wouldn't know who lived in the same house, or how frail they might be, was very hard to accept.

I think things have got much better. Social workers, who have got such a bad time over the deaths of children released from care back to families who were violent, also have the care of the elderly and it's not always easy.

There's a very cheerful social worker who has her hands full with the area round where I live. I'm not sure what her title or job strictly is, because they call her the Welfare, the Town Hall, the woman from the madhouse, Old Nosey Parker, the Labour, the Social Services, the Warder, the

Warden and the Minder.

They are half-afraid of her in case she will change their lives in some unacceptable way, like giving them a Home Help or putting them into sheltered accommodation. They are half-afraid that she isn't doing enough for them and that there might be free coal or another £2 a week if they play their cards right.

She is a marvellous woman, from Tipperary, and she is probably a saint. In her car she always has a dozen hand-knitted shawls. She gets the people in a local home to knit them; she pretends she has knitted them herself, so the old women with thin, shivering shoulders will take them because they think they're a genuine gift. She tells me she has hours of paperwork getting the money for the bloody wool and knitting needles, and she has to disguise it very deeply because they won't pass anything irregular or allow any hint of charity to come from public funds.

She has boxes of packet soup — she says she thinks she's turning into an oxtail by now, she has so much of it. She tells them it was a free sample and why don't they try it; she gets in, puts on the kettle and they all sip a mug of it and nod and say possibly, but she knows they will never stir themselves to buy it, so next week or next visit she will have another so-called free offer.

She picks up a lot of odd newspapers, anywhere — in restaurants, bus shelters. Sometimes she just swipes them from her own office. In some of the houses she visits, she thinks they would like a daily paper but it's a bit of an extravagance, so she casually says, 'I've finished with this' and sees it pounced on eagerly. They read out bits about the royals and Joan Collins to her, and she knows it was right to give them a few stories to think about.

She says that isolation is the real killer and that many old people just turn their faces to the wall and die in the winter from no disease, from no hypothermia; just from no will to go on.

Her priority is to keep them warm this winter, to explain that gas and electricity will NOT be cut off, that there are always funds from some public purse to meet a heating bill. It's hard to get that into the heads of people who have been brought up thrifty and in fear of authority which will punish them if they use two bars of the fire.

She thinks that the social services in England are basically very good and mean well; they have to cope with great cuts in funding, and every year there seems to be more to do and less resources to do it with. It's no use trying to explain this to Thatcher's government, it doesn't listen. Not to reasoned appeals, not to strikes, not to emotional demonstration.

She thinks it's better to get on with it; you keep more people warm by wrapping them up in shawls and giving them soup than you do by signing petitions and marching to Westminster. A lot of her colleagues disagree. They say she comes from a background where charity was acceptable, where people EXPECTED the Little Sisters, the Vincent de Paul and a dozen others to help. In the Welfare State, people don't have that system. They pay taxes all their working lives so that they can be looked after when the time comes.

So more and more she has to disguise her kindness in case it be defined by anyone as charity. She thinks that if she ruled the world she wouldn't give them a pension at all, she would give them free heating, get a certain amount of food delivered to their doors each day with a newspaper.

They should have vouchers for clothes, and there should be a law saying they all had to go out and eat lunch in a centre each day. That way they would meet other people. And all the pet-food manufacturers should be forced to give those tins they advertise totally free to pensioners, so that there would be no question of spending everything on the tortoiseshell cat called Margaret Rose and forgetting to buy any food for the cat's owner.

But then she sighs and says that's only ludicrous, you can't play God. And she's off again with a dozen small umbrellas. She bought them at £1 each from a man, without asking him which lorry they fell off. She will give them here and there, with some tale about having ordered too many in the office and the company refusing to take them back.

She thinks that a lot of the elderly get drenched when they go out and the damp goes into their bones. She'll probably never get the money through for 12 black-economy umbrellas, but it's not a fortune. She shrugs, the Tipperary Robin Hood who is the very acceptable face of the Welfare and the human side of bureaucracy, in a city which fears that its old people will die of cold this winter but hasn't the machinery to prevent it.

MAEVE ON
MARGARET THATCHER

19 June 1986

In February 1975, all kinds of women rubbed hands with glee that our girl or indeed any girl had become leader of the Conservative Party. Four years later when she made it to 10 Downing Street there was still an almost tribal pleasure amongst women to think that one of the sex had finally got there.

Now as she sails towards her 61st birthday in the autumn with the firm intention of trying for a third term of office, the gosh-imagine-a-woman-Prime-Minister excitement has worn off.

What has replaced it? Most women think that Margaret Thatcher is a mixed blessing. She has done one great thing, which is to take the giggle out of female political leaders. It is impossible to remember that newsreaders could hardly keep a straight face seven years ago when referring to 'The Prime Minister and her husband'. The very phrase 'Madam Prime Minister' was always said with such heavy inverted *commas* at that time that nobody believed it could ever be anything except a laboured joke. In the

House of Commons the irony with which friend and foe larded their voices when saying 'The Right Honourable Lady' was like very bad stand-up comedy.

Now there is no irony. Madam Prime Minister has gone into the vocabulary with much greater ease than say the word 'chairperson'. In fact, there are some who feel that there had never been anything except a Madam Prime Minister in charge of the country. She has done that, but she is not a woman's folk hero, she is not a role model for her sex. When people praise Thatcher, and many, many do every day, they praise her not at all for anything to do with being a woman. And perhaps that is her greatest achievement. She has almost single-handedly banished the notion that it is somehow unusual or special for a woman to be able to do anything. For that, if for nothing else, women in the future may thank her.

A woman barrister who knew her at Lincoln's Inn in the early fifties says, 'I cannot take her seriously as leader of the country because I remember her so well 30 years ago. She was fearfully impatient, quick yes, and bright but if everyone else doesn't understand every single thing immediately she goes spare. I can't think how she manages the Cabinet meetings. Just to discuss a case with her in the old days had us all in a frazzle. She was very hardworking, and you would never know that she had twin toddlers at home. She always said she had a good nanny and, unlike any other mother, literally never seemed to give the children a thought during the day. Perhaps I'm just being a bit bitchy saying that about her. But it seemed to us then a little unnatural. I'm not just saying it because she's Prime Minister.'

A woman social worker says that Thatcher has a genuine and utterly sincere crusading attitude towards equal rights for women at work and that she will pursue this very vigorously but in exactly the same way and at the same time as she will pursue policies against work shirking which she imagines she sees everywhere and regulations preventing local councils giving support to those they consider needy.

The trouble about Thatcher is that she gives with one hand to women and she takes away with the other. She's fine for the hardworking single-minded woman who wants to be an entrepreneur and who is somehow in some magic way able to get her children satisfactorily looked after all day. She is not so fine for the woman with three children who goes to the post office each week to collect her benefits. That woman is going to find the hospital giving her less under Thatcher and the schools giving less to her children.

If you are a woman like Thatcher yourself, you do well. But times don't move as speedily as she does, and most of the people who are like her are actually men. She is disciplined in a way that most busy people, men and women, would love to be disciplined even if they would abhor the manner and the message. A woman television executive who has seen her on several television programmes speaks of her with something like awe. 'She comes in here, her make-up is perfect, I mean it's not just good make-up, she has had a proper professional television make-up at home or in the office or in the car. I don't know where. Nor do I know how she gets the time. So it means that she doesn't have to spend any time at all being made up here and that gives her a certain importance. All the men are being powdered and toned down and she is sitting there calm as anything pretending to be interested in how we run a television station.

'She may be dying for a drink, but she won't have one, nor a sandwich or anything and we bring out nice ones when she's on.

She says, "No, thank you," she doesn't eat between meals, and you know that in her whole life she never has, any more than she ever went to bed with her make-up on.

'She will just smile at you coldly if you praise her and you realise that she has little time for anyone, like 99 per cent of the world, who are human enough to have a Scotch and a sandwich either before or after an important television programme.'

She just doesn't rate people who aren't as strong as she is. A woman publisher who has refused several books on the Thatcher enigma, on the grounds that no one knows yet what it is, says that she thinks the Prime Minister's much-vaunted courage within her own party is a distinct disservice to the cause of women rather than giving women something to crow about.

'Look here, we get a woman Prime Minister, who got in by turning on the guy who gave her all the honours and preferments. Sure I know that's politics, but it's also a characteristic that is often attributed to women, disloyalty, spitefulness.

'Then when she's in, what does she do? It's like the mad queen in *Alice in Wonderland,* Off With Their Heads. Stevas, Ian Gilmour, Jim Prior, Francis Pym, Cecil Parkinson, anyone who looks crooked at her or who has a bit on the side. Now if a man did that, we'd be up in arms and so we should about her too. She's making it harder and harder for any party to elect a woman again, they'll have their worst fears about bossy women confirmed in this administration. She may have the distinct achievement of being the first and the last woman Prime Minister of this country.'

A buyer in one of the big London stores says that Mrs Thatcher must have sat down carefully with a stylist and chosen her clothes with exactly the same care that she chose her War Cabinet. 'There's never anything really smart but there's rarely anything quite terrible either. She's dressing as Mrs Middle England. Do you remember that time during an election broadcast when David Dimbleby got so excited he called her Mrs Finchley and the name stuck, well that's the way she dresses, middle-aged businesswoman from Finchley. Spot on. And you do know that she's got four of every outfit, so that she always looks spanking clean but not too extravagant. She must have 10 of that blue houndstooth suit she wears with the blouse and floppy bow tie neck. I must have seen it on her a hundred times and it always looks as if it comes straight from the dry cleaners which it possibly has. And they did a great job on her hair and make-up as well as her voice. She looked quite mad at her wedding and in the early days. I wish all the 60-year-old women who come in here could get the same kind of right-on-the-button advice as she's got.'

She does not appear to have close women friends, but she has very little time for any friends. And she does seem to get on very well with her husband. She said in a revealing remark that it was great to have one person who would stand by you and understand what you were trying to do, even when nobody else seemed to. That was a touching reference to the much-mocked Denis Thatcher, who is now legendary for his hopes that the wife will give up the job and that they can retire to snifters and golf. But the wife hasn't given any indication of doing anything of the sort. In fact when she was going through a bad patch 15 years ago and had the nickname Milk Snatcher on account of proposals about taking away junior school free milk, her husband advised her to get shut of the lot of it and leave public life. She is said to have told him that she'd see them in hell first, before she would quit. It would be the same now.

A woman who worked with her in the Ministry of Education and always spoke highly of her said that she thought the remark about 'at least one person who will stand by you' was a very sad one indeed. She didn't find it human and showing the tender side of Margaret Thatcher. She thought it showed the hard and empty side. 'Most women have a friend or many friends who will be loyal to them, believe the best and put the most optimistic slant on what you do. It's a sad comment on Margaret, that after all her years and doing what she believes is right, that she only has her husband. She makes no mention of her children. And her children are not close to her and now they realise she was never close to them. It's a frightful object lesson of the loneliness of power-seeking. I hope she doesn't put all women off trying to succeed in any field.'

There's a shop not far from where I live where the daughter of the family is extremely bright and has ambitions to do law. She gets little help from the family, who want her to get behind the counter as quick as she can, marry a bloke who'll bring a few quid into the place and drop these notions about being a barrister. 'We aren't people like that, we're greengrocers,' they tell her, as if this was the last word on the subject.

'But look at Mrs Thatcher,' the girl was

unwise enough to say. 'Her father was a grocer in Lincolnshire, and look at her.'

'Yeah, look at her,' they all say, and heads shake and somehow she feels that no real battle has been won for her by the woman Prime Minister.

No Fags, No Food — It's No Fun Being Fergie

21 July 1986

When Sarah Ferguson wakes up this morning in the house of her fiancé's grandmother, she won't just stretch, reach for a cigarette, have a cup of coffee and toast and wonder what to do with her day, like many another horsey Sloane will do. Heavens no!

Sarah was put off the fags long ago when royal nuptials seemed likely and she wasn't allowed to have the normal pound of sweets a day that every reformed smoker needs for three months, because they said she was already a bit pudgy for a princess. Look at Diana, please, and learn. One newspaper set a cameraman on her at Ascot just to count the chocs she ate; then the paper delivered a diatribe against her greed. Another paper sent a spy to Madame Tussaud's to measure the hips of the wax model of Sarah and came up with a guess of 42 inches. No, there will be no breakfast today.

And she won't need to wonder what she will do when she gets up. Her timetable, hour by hour, has been handed out to press people the world over. She will read with everyone else that she has already packed for the honeymoon and that she has taken all the telephone calls that she is going to have time to take from friends wishing her well.

This morning there is yet another rehearsal at Westminster Abbey. So far these have been less than glorious. The adults have all been rooted to the ground with nerves and the children quite wild with excitement. There has been face-pulling and even punch-ups about carrying the train. This morning is the last try. The Archbishop and staff of Westminster Abbey are not the kind of showbiz folk who believe that a disastrous dress rehearsal makes a stunning first night.

Then it's back to Clarence House and a lunch party. Among the guests will be Sarah's mother, who will go into history for having asked innocently where else *could* one meet one's husband except at polo. Considering that she herself met two husbands at polo and that one of them is an Argentine, it might have been wiser to sing very low of the sport. Sarah's stepmother will also be there. The two ladies get on very well in public and all niceties are observed, but the crack is not judged to be mighty.

Then there's a rest of an hour — hardly to ingest lunch, since Sarah Ferguson hasn't been let near a plate of food in weeks, but to calm her down and dress her up for the next outings: a champagne reception at the Guards' Polo Club and dinner at Windsor Castle. Her future mother-in-law and father-in-law will be at both dos and so will Charles and Diana. Andrew will probably be allowed to have a drink and might even be given something to eat. The public hasn't developed any dangerous anxiety about the width of his waist yet.

The full guest list for both these glittering functions has not been made available yet to the press, but perhaps Sarah Ferguson knows whether the question mark over Nancy Reagan's name has been removed and whether she will have another delight ahead of her . . . earnest conversation with America's first lady.

The timetable suggests that it will be early to bed tonight for the future princess. Which indeed is to be devoutly hoped for. With a glass of nice, warm, fat-free milk, two super-strength Mogadons which would fell an ox,

and a very few minutes' last-minute won-
derings, could it all possibly be ever worthwhile?

It Was One of Those
Custard Heart Days

22 November 1986

'In five weeks' time it will be all over,' said
the woman with the neatly zipped tartan
shopping bag on wheels. She was full of
triumph at having worked it out. 'All over
and done with,' she said, in case any of us
thought that Christmas might linger on a
bit this year and trickle through until February. Her mouth was a thin line of satisfaction at having tamed the prospect of any
festivity. She cast a gloom over everyone
shopping in the late-night grocery.

It was one of my custard heart days.
Sometimes I'm like a weasel with these
killjoy people. But maybe she had a sad life.
It could be that her husband had died during the year, or that her daughter had got
married to someone they didn't like and
there had been a row.

Perhaps she had come from a home where
they didn't ever celebrate Christmas much,
or even something horrible could have happened at Christmas time and every year it

came back to her. In one of my rare fits of kindness I smiled and said that it was true that there was a lot of fuss made about Christmas all right.

The Lord punishes the insincere. I didn't mean it at all. I was only saying it to please her. It was the wrong thing to do. I had misread her signs totally.

'Well that's as may be,' she sniffed at me disapprovingly. 'And I'm the first to say live and let live. But I think it's a pity when folk can't have one short season of the year when they spread a little goodwill.' She looked me up and down sadly. 'I daresay that you have your own reasons for hating Christmas and I wouldn't presume to intrude and ask what they are. But perhaps I might say this, if you and the other people who hate Christmas were to think of the innocent little children who enjoy it, and the old people who have parties in the centre, and comedians and personalities giving their time free to dress up as Santa Claus in hospitals, then you might think a bit more warmly about it.'

Well, what would you have done? Tell her that you were lying in the first place, pretend to be converted to her bossy, cliché-ridden view of the world? Go deaf and wander off in the other direction? Abandon the wire shopping basket and run out of the late-night grocery? Wave at a mythical friend? Nod sagely with the all-purpose and meaningless cockney response, 'Well this is it. Isn't it?'

I was rescued. A man with the most bad-tempered face I have ever seen outside a cartoon came pounding in to the late-night grocery. He headed straight for the woman with the unctuous views and the tartan shopper on wheels.

'May I just ask you one question? Just one? Did you come in here for a conversation session with total strangers or was it possibly, as you claimed, for the shopping? I only ask because I have two traffic wardens up my arse outside, I've been round the block twice and we've missed ten minutes of *Sportsnight* already.'

I could see why she wanted a little goodwill in her life: both of them working late, London traffic being like a mediaeval view of hell, crowds, queues, short tempers. I looked at what she had bought as it was being checked out and she packed it neatly into the shopping basket on wheels which was totally unnecessary since she had a husband and car outside the door. She had a lot of cat food, three kinds of cleaning stuff and wire wool and big black plastic bags. She had one lamb chop, two apples and a tube of indigestion tablets. It seemed a poor haul for someone whose mate was missing *Sportsnight,* and I keep hoping that they do have a cat.

I have a friend who works in a bookshop and who is constantly amazed by the things people buy as Christmas presents. Men buy *Cooking for Idiots* and expect to get a tinkle of female laughter when the paper is ripped off it on the day. Women buy *The Duffer's Golf Guide . . .* and expect a similarly delighted response.

My friend, who hasn't the same wish to enter into other people's lives as I do — and has certainly not the time, sitting at a busy till in a large bookshop — says she arranges gift wrapping or personalised red Christmas bags for books without blinking an eye at the lack of wisdom involved in the choice. Until this week.

A nice young man, blond hair falling into his eyes, eager to a fault, hesitant and cursed with that over-apologetic manner which some people wrongly think is politeness, approached her. He wanted to know about this service called Post-A-Book, which means that you pay the shop for the postage, address the envelope, and they'll send it off for you.

The book was addressed to a woman, and he signed a card with what was presumably his own name since he paid with a credit card and it was the same name as on the card. 'Merry Christmas Darling, Love from Harry,' he wrote, and put it in with the book.

The book was called *A Guide to Better Sex* and the subheading said that it was a manual for those who found that the fizz had gone out of sex and who noticed that things were not as they used to be in the first heady days of their relationship.

Even the sight of a queue forming up behind the eager young man didn't stop my friend from making a last-ditch stand.

'It's a bit technical, this book, I believe,' she began.

'Oh yes, so it says,' the young man said happily.

'I wonder, is it a suitable Christmas present? It's more a thing someone might buy for herself or himself, or sort of after a bit of a chat, you know?' She was desperate now.

'No.' He was firm. 'No, I think she'd like it, and I'm sending it early because . . . well, she'll have plenty of time to read it in advance. Before the Christmas holidays, you

see. . . .' he said with the open, trusting face
of the fool that he was.

THE MAN WHO SET UP
OFFICE IN THE LADIES

13 December 1986

I went into the ladies' cloakroom of a hotel
and a man sat peaceably at a sort of dressing table. The place where you are meant to
be a woman and sit combing your hair and
adjusting your make-up. The man had his
briefcase beside him and he was fairly
absorbed in some kind of paperwork.

He certainly wasn't doing anyone any
harm, and I often think that the distinction
is fairly arbitrary anyway in cloakrooms.
After all, single-sex facilities are available on
the Continent and I've never been in a
private house where they made a distinction, except in one place in Australia where
they had 'Blokes' and 'Sheilas' written on
the doors.

It was a perfectly comfortable place to sit:
chair, desk and even a mirror to examine
himself in if he had any doubts about self-
image. He wasn't taking up too much space,
it was easy to sit beside him and adjust your
make-up. It was just a small bit unsettling
to know what exactly he was doing there.

This was an Irish provincial town, the man must surely have known the ladies who were coming in and out to what was after all their designated area. He had the air of a man who had been there some time. His ashtray had several butts in it. He was a man who had settled in.

There was a box of tissues on the table which he called on occasionally for a nose blow. He seemed quite oblivious of the lavatory flushing and hand washing going on a few yards away from him, admittedly round a corner. This part of the cloakroom was in sort of an alcove. I knew it would be on my mind forever if I didn't find out. He would join the other unsolved mysteries, like the man who wore a hair roller with an otherwise conservative city gent image; like the Christmas card I get every year signed SLUG; like the man who used to come into *The Irish Times* every day to buy yesterday's paper but not today's. He said it was because he didn't actually take it, he wasn't an *Irish Times* reader but people were always mentioning something in it that he wanted to follow up, which was why he bought the previous day's.

My head is too full of these confusing things. 'Damp old day out,' I said to him.

'Is it?' he looked up politely. 'It was all

right when I came in, but of course it's very changeable this time of year.'

'Have you been here for a while?' I asked, heading off a lengthy and generalised weather conversation.

'Oh yes, a fair bit, I have to meet someone, but there's no sign of him; still, I suppose it's the traffic, getting out of Dublin is a nightmare these days.'

He was going to meet another male in the ladies' cloakroom of the hotel. This could not be usual practice.

'Why do you decide to meet here?' I asked, with all the subtlety of my trade.

'It's sort of half way between us,' he said agreeably. 'Rather than have either of us drive 100 miles, we both drive 50, harder on him of course because he's got to get out of Dublin, as I said.'

'And do you always choose this place?'

He seemed so . . . helpful. I was sure he'd tell me.

'No, funnily, we usually go to the other hotel, but someone told us that there was more privacy here, you can have a chat without being disturbed. It's the divil to get service though, I'll tell you that. I've been here over an hour and nobody's come to take my order.'

I looked at him fixedly for a few moments.

'They mightn't think you were ordering in here, you know, people don't usually.'

He looked around him mildly. 'Why not, do you think?'

'I think that they'd never imagine anyone in the ladies' cloakroom might want coffee and sandwiches brought in,' I said.

'The what?'

I repeated it.

He stood up like a man who had been shot in the back in a film and was about to stagger all over the set before collapsing. 'I don't believe you,' he said.

I showed him round the corner, where two women were washing their hands, I showed him a line of cubicles and machines on the wall that seemed to prove conclusively where we were. His colour was very bad and I wished, as I always wish, that I had left well alone, and let him sit there all week if necessary rather than bringing on this distress.

'Mother of God,' he croaked. 'Is this where I've been all afternoon?'

'Didn't you notice?' I asked.

'I thought there was a lot of hair combing going on beside me and that women were getting a bit casual about doing up their faces in public. What am I going to do?' He looked utterly wretched.

I told him that since none of these fiercely combing and titivating women had complained about him to the management, it seemed to prove that there was no harm done, and that women were becoming generally more relaxed about things, which had to be good.

He wanted none of my philosophising. He had bundled all his papers into the briefcase and was looking at me as his saviour. 'Would you have a look out to see?' he begged.

'I wouldn't know your friend, why don't you go out yourself?' I said. 'I'll come with you if you like.'

I thought he needed somebody to lean on, he sounded so frail. 'No, I mean look out in case anybody sees me coming out of the . . . er . . . the Ladies,' he said.

I checked that the coast was clear. It seemed fairly academic, since anyone who had been in had already seen him. But perhaps he was more afraid of being seen by his own sex.

He straightened his tie and thanked me again. He assured me that he was not a mirthless man and he would see the humour of this. Not now, at this very moment, but eventually. I don't know when he saw the humour of it, but not I think when he found his friend, who was sitting impatiently on his third pot of coffee.

'What in the name of God happened to you?' the friend said. 'I've been on to your office, on to your home. I nearly had the guards out for you.'

The man recently released from the Ladies lowered his voice.

'We'll have a brandy,' he said.

'Was it the car? Did you hit anything?'

'No.'

'Is it your heart, any chest pains, any pins and needles in your arm?'

'No.'

'It's nothing to do with the firm, no redundancies or anything?'

The man who had been waiting all afternoon looked anxious.

'No, would you get us a drink, I've been all afternoon in the ladies' lavatory.'

'Were you being sick?'

'No, I was waiting for you.'

'I'll get the brandy fast,' said the man who had been waiting.

'I'll go up to the bar and get it myself.'

A Royal Romance Spelling Danger from the Start

9 November 1987

Things look bad when the popular papers

359

have started to ask solemn questions of Harold Brooks Baker, who is the publisher of *Burke's Peerage*. Suppose the royal couple wanted a divorce . . . he is asked in awed whisper . . . just suppose. Then would it cause constitutional crises beyond the wildest imaginings? Even more frightening, Harold Brooks Baker says not at all, no worries, or words to that effect. The heir has been provided, not only the heir but the spare. A divorce would be sad but that's all. Nothing would teeter, nothing would crumble. Diana would be called Diana, Princess of Wales, not The Princess of Wales. The problem would be if Charles wanted a new wife and wished to create her Queen. Brows furrow a little over that knotty problem, but they clear again when everyone realises what a good chap Charles is, and they know he wouldn't do anything silly to rock the boat, nothing unwise that would remind a nation of his mother's uncle and all the hoo-ha 50 years ago.

Charles is a luckless fellow in many ways. He will be 40 on Saturday, he has known since childhood what his role would be but never how hard it would turn out to be because he couldn't have seen how the world would change. When he was 16 his country was full of respect still for royalty, and there were decent attitudes like letting the young royals alone and giving them their privacy and not insulting them too much because they couldn't answer back. But the world changed all round him and nobody told him how and if he should change. His mother thought there was no way that things should change, his father was never very interested in him since he didn't like that terrible school where they all run up and down in their vests and knickers and it's called endurance or character building.

Charles means so well and tries so much that sometimes it would break your heart. He visits deprived inner cities and is taken on tours of areas where the very lucky have some desperate jobs in sweatshops and the rest have no jobs at all. His face forces itself into a look of concern. He says earnestly to the swarm of reporters and photographers that are like a permanent fog around him that one must do something, that one is so admiring of what has been done already but that one must never cease from doing more. His accent separates him, as does his attitude and his whole background, but there is something about him that saves him. Nobody is going to call him a stupid, unfeeling berk, because he genuinely seems to care. Like he cares about getting the *Mary*

Rose up from the bottom of the sea, and like he cares about giving his views on architecture and like he cares about shooting small birds at Balmoral or taking swipes with a sort of upmarket pickaxe at a ball from the back of a polo pony. When he straightens his tie nervously, when he admits that he talks to the plants and flowers in his estates, when he makes leaden attempts at humour, you'd be on his side rather than against him. Who else do you know coming up to a fortieth birthday who had so much and yet was able to do so little with it?

Diana, Princess of Wales is in many ways a luckless girl too. She was so shy when she faced the first barrage of press at her engagement ceremonies that her throat closed over and she literally couldn't speak. She was warned that it would be a goldfish bowl, but how could she have known just how many sides and how clear the glass? She did in many ways everything that the country wanted of her and did it so well that she is probably responsible for the whole royal industry all by herself. She was so beautiful for one thing, and none of the rest of the royals ever were, so she was the centre of attention.

She lost weight, she gained confidence, she learned style. The Sloane woolies and wellies went their way and the designer clothes came in, she was always ready to show a bit of bosom and a bit of thigh. The ranks of photographers following her trebled. But how could she have known that it was a dangerous game? When she was in a secret island, very pregnant and thinking she was alone, the papers sent cameramen to hang from trees and pass by in boats with long-distance lenses on their cameras.

She could be excused for thinking she was very important. If she read the newspapers and even believed a tenth of what they said about her then she would have had every reason for thinking that she was very important and powerful indeed.

The people, and not only the British people but the people everywhere, including Ireland, of course, loved a bit of romance and a lovely role model. Even though there were always aspects about the royal romance that spelled danger from the word go. The world believed that it was love at first sight, a strong prince and a beautiful shy girl becoming a fairytale princess, because that is what the world had always wanted to believe in one shape or another. It literally created that belief, and the popular papers and magazines were there to play back to the public exactly what was being demanded. In a secular and permissive society it should have seemed absurd that the strong prince had to marry a virgin but that was literally what had to be. Diana's uncle in embarrassed tones told a world that should have been equally embarrassed to hear the information that this was indeed the case. Everywhere it seemed like a reward for being a good girl. Look at what happens, you get to marry the prince if you don't give away that which is more precious than jewels. If anyone had paused to think about a girl 13 years younger than Charles, a girl with no real education let alone the strange sort of education that prepares you for being a royal . . . then it was obvious that there would be difficulties. If anyone had stopped to think about a decent, well-meaning guy who had no interest in pop music and who knew only women who found backgrounds into which to blend, then it should have been clear that there would be problems.

But nobody wanted to see the problems. And everyone was so relieved, the world had a fairytale wedding, the Queen of England really and truly believes that the succession is very important, as you and I might believe if we had gone through all that anointing and sceptre and Commonwealth routine.

Princess Anne, whose own marriage was far from successful, got the spotlight taken off her and turned into a reasonable person with a serious interest in raising money for children in need. Princess Margaret, also relieved that she was out of the firing line for having the odd cigarette in public, was delighted with it too. The Queen Mother, whose smile goes right round her face and who likes happy endings, thought that it had all turned out fine.

But the public appetite is never fully fed. Professor Anthony Clare has said that the people have created a romantic fairytale which, like all fairytales, should have ended at the point where the prince and princess have arrived at the altar. Perhaps even it might have been allowed to continue until the two blond little boys came on the scene and the family were seen in the sunset in one of their palace homes.

The appetite has been whetted by glimpses inside Charles and Diana's home, respectful and pseudo-relaxed interviews trying to show that they are just like everyone else, which of course they can't be because everyone else doesn't have small armies camped outside their homes wondering when and if they will speak to each other, smile at each other, or hold hands again.

They may hate each other by now, or it may in fact have been the mildest row that caused them to spend some weeks apart. Loves and marriages have survived separations of weeks and months even. But few other people have such huge pressure on them to have a public reconciliation. What other couple had to go through the hurt and upset with the eyes of literally the whole world on them?

The German visit was yet one more charade: Diana re-launches the mini skirt, wears a sultan's gift of diamonds, Charles straightens his tie and says what a pretty colonel in chief she is, news bulletins report that they are seen talking to each other, the world sighs with relief.

But meanwhile the Queen of England walks with her dogs and knows she cannot yet retire as she'd like to, and the princess's divorced aunt and separated sister wonder what all the fuss is about. And maybe 10 times an hour newspapers ring Harold Brooks Baker of Burke's Peerage and he assures them that a divorced Charles could indeed become king. Unthinkable a while ago but not unconstitutional, he insists. And the world becomes a less safe place for a lot of people.

Making a Spectacle
of Myself

8 October 1988

It happened at the Abbey Theatre a few weeks ago. The print on the programme had got all small and fuzzed around the bits where it told you what plays the actors and actresses had been in before. I was disappointed for them and felt they deserved better from the management. To my surprise the woman in front of me was reading bits out of it to her husband; I thought she must have got a clearer copy and asked could I have a loan of hers. To my surprise, by the time she had handed it to me, her copy had become small and fuzzed too. Sadly, I gave it back. 'I think it's the eyes,' I said to her in a doom-laden voice.

'Well, why don't you put on your glasses?' she asked, reasonably.

But she wasn't to know that it was my pride and joy, the ability to read the small print on bye-laws before others could see the noticeboard itself, the slight hint of envy and disbelief around one that one with so dissolute a lifestyle didn't need to fumble in a handbag or reach for a string around the neck in order to look at snaps or read the fine print of a menu in a dark restaurant. I, who used to read in the twilight when others wouldn't be able to find the book if they put it down for a minute, now I was going to have to get glasses.

Naturally, like every major event, I made a drama and a production out of it. I had no intention of going quietly into the dark night of spectacle-wearing. Nor was I going to delay. The very next day, when the plane landed me back in London, I made an appointment to see an ophthalmic surgeon. The receptionist and I consulted our Filofaxes. No, not early in the morning, she said, he would be operating.

'Operating?' I shouted down the phone in such a fright that strong men and women trying to reclaim their baggage from the carousels stopped short to know what was going on.

'Well, yes,' she said nervously.

'I don't think I want that kind of an eye doctor,' I said firmly. 'I want one that will either say tut tut, it's just that you're a bit tired and it will be fine when you've had a nice long rest, or else give me something that will bring out the cheekbones in my face and make me see everything again.'

There was a silence. You could see her wondering whether this appointment should be written into his book, whether this encounter was to be encouraged.

'Who exactly recommended you to us?' she asked, in one of those tones that frighten me to death and bring on a huge sense of middle-aged respectability.

'Fearfully sorry,' I said. 'Where were we? Yes, indeed, eleven-thirty would be fine.'

They had property magazines only in the waiting room. A woman with a hat and gloves asked me was it my first time.

'You'll like him,' she said positively. 'Great soap and water man, of course, says a lot of the problem is caused by all these creams and scrubs and grains and peeling.'

I felt a wave of nausea. Nobody had ever told me anything about any of these things in the care of the eye. And I had always thought you should keep soap and water out of your eyes. It turned out, of course, that the waiting room served several specialists. Hers was a dermatologist. There were other doctors in the building that might have been more alarming — she could have told me that he always suggested a bypass or a hysterectomy. I was calm by the time I was called.

It was like a dentist's chair without the

instruments. You kept looking at things and answering lovely bright-child questions like whether you see more green than red. Then there was the sort of cartoon-style 'can you read the bottom line?' bit and a few drops in the eye and a reassuring pat and the news that I was luckier than most people, the average age for it was 44 to 46. I had lasted a few years longer. This made me feel like a champion. I thought of going down to the Savoy Theatre and having a word with Mickey Rooney, who is there in a song-and-dance musical and talking about us old survivors. It was the only doctor's surgery that I left without the customary instructions to have lost three stone the next time I came in. I told him that, praisingly. I said he shone amongst fellow medics in his attitude. He said diplomatically that he was sure his fellow medics were very right in whatever they advised, but it had no adverse effect on the sight.

'Probably helps it,' I said cheerfully and went off in search of a place to get the specs. I told the girl I wanted something showy. She found the description too vague.

'If you could tell me what kind of showy, like do the glasses of any personality appeal to you?'

I thought for a little and decided I wanted

them like Edna Everage's, not exactly like hers, but in that area. The optician was regretful. They didn't do that kind of range.

'Huge, then, like dinner plates,' I said. I wasn't going for half moons or something restrained. We tried on every pair in the shop, and to my annoyance the ones that met with the most approval from everyone, including myself peering at them in a mirror, were extremely discreet ones with mainly colourless frames around the eyes and a bit of blue on the bits that go over the ear. They look very dull on the table, and I can't really see them properly on my face because they're not meant for looking at faces in mirrors — they're meant for books and papers and theatre programmes and telephone directories.

I can see all kinds of things with them, including a sort of numbering on my typewriter showing you how many spaces you've gone. I never knew it was there, and apparently that is the explanation for all those irregular sort of paragraphs over the years.

There is only one puzzlement. The glasses have a name on them. It's written in small letters inside one of those bits that goes over your ear. I suppose in posher spectacles it would be a Designer Label. But what it seems to say is 'Happy Pouff. Paris France'.

I've asked other people who can read it with their own glasses on to check this out, and indeed this would appear to be the name. Maybe everyone has awful silly names written on the inside of their glasses on the grounds that the poor weak-eyed people wearing them won't be able to read them. It would be worth finding out.

MADAM IS PAYING?

Published in Maeve's Diary *(Irish Times, 1980s)*

Today I took a man to lunch. It's something I have done many times before in my life, and hope to do again. It's not something that makes me feel aggressive, butch or dominant. It doesn't seem to emasculate and weaken the men who have been taken to lunch either. Never did I feel I should be groping under the table, fumbling to get past his knees, to hand him the fiver or the tenner. Never did I think the table should be booked in his name.

Today was a beauty, however. I had booked a table for two for one o'clock. I arrived on the dot and gave my name.

'Mr Binchy's table is this way, madam. I don't think he's arrived yet.'

I said nothing. Sometimes, it's not worth

the whole business of explanations, especially when it wasn't going to change anything. I mean, I was getting to the right table. I ordered a gin and tonic while waiting.

The waiter looked mildly disapproving. He felt there was an outside chance that the man who had booked the table might hit the waiter across the face for having let a female guest order a drink on her own. He brought it along, grudgingly.

The man I was taking to lunch rushed in, apologetically. He is an engaging-looking American, who has written a book about Californian way-out lifestyles and meaningful relationships. He is, I think, about 60 or 65. His main emotion was shame at being five minutes late. The waiter hovered about in a worried way.

'I have brought your guest an aperitif, Mr Binchy,' he said to the American author, fearfully. The American looked back at him fearfully. Was this some terrible plot? Would he have to pay for the meal? Was I passing him off as my husband or my father? He was filled with unease.

'What will you have, I'm paying,' I said firmly, and he ordered a highball, with a marginal air of relaxing.

All through the meal it went on. He got

the menu with the prices, I didn't; he was shown the wine list, I was ignored; the tray of cigars was brought to him at the coffee stage, even though we had both made it perfectly clear to this dumb, chauvinist waiter that I was the one who was in charge of the lunch.

Then came the bill. You must remember that this man and I had been discussing the whole role of female assertiveness in a West Coast marriage. We had agreed that patterns had changed beyond recognition because of the women's movement nowadays, women no longer saw marriage in its traditional role of giving security or stability.

Over the cheese we had marvelled at how much had happened in how short a time. And there stood the waiter, discreetly trying to catch the American's attention so that he could present him with the piece of paper which couldn't possibly be shown to a woman.

'I'm in the lucky position of being invited to lunch,' the American said engagingly, waving over to me as if to indicate that funds unlimited were available at my side of the table.

The waiter stood still.

'Madam is paying?' he asked in a voice full of doom.

'That's right,' I said cheerfully, getting out my chequebook.

'By cheque,' he said defeatedly.

'Oh, they let women have them these days,' I said with an attempt to cheer him up.

As an attempt it failed. He took my cheque and cheque card like a butler in a film might pick up a tousled gypsy child to remove it from his lordship's eyes.

There was no service charge included so I left a 10 per cent tip, which is, I think, what people do. He looked at the money as if it were the worst humiliation he had ever undergone. I was desperately tempted to snatch it back, since I had got no service, I had only got a patronising sneer throughout. But then, that would have given him further fuel about women if I had taken the money back. So, even though I didn't feel like it, I grinned at him and thanked him for the nice meal. And though he certainly didn't feel like it, he grinned back, and said it had been nice to see me and hoped he would see me again.

As we came out into the cold sunshine, the American author looked back thoughtfully at the restaurant and shook his head.

'It'll be some while before he'll let it all hang out with an assertively laid-back female,' he said, disappointed that the time was changing so slowly after all.

∎ ∎ ∎ ∎

NINETIES

∎ ∎ ∎ ∎

Even the Presidents Are Getting Younger

1 December 1990

It's one thing to notice the guards getting younger, to look over people's shoulders at their passports and realise they were born the year you left teaching but truly it's a bit hard to become older than the President of Ireland *and* the Prime Minister of Britain all in one month. Only the comforting lined face of George Bush gives me any hope that there are some elderly folk out there trying to run things. I keep expecting some fresh-faced boy that I taught up to First Communion class to emerge as the Pope.

It's not something that will darken my brow for the rest of my natural or anything, it's just that these things seem to come all at once. A letter in flawless English from a Dutch student who is doing a thesis on Irish women asked me would I talk to her about what I and all my friends felt the day we got the vote. A girl's school having a sale of work wondered could I donate any mementoes of the old days like a fan or a dance card so that people could get the flavour. A kindly and we hope short-sighted woman told a whole bookshop that she remembered me climbing through the window of the nurses' home in Vincent's in 1935.

A child doing a school essay asked me for advice. They had been asked to imagine that they had been alive the day decimal currency was introduced in Ireland. He wondered what the place had been like then. It was tempting to draw a picture of gas lamps, and cobbled streets and coaches rattling by but since a lot of the teachers probably wouldn't remember it either, there was no point in being ironical — the child might have got a low mark and been deemed stupid.

I told him the truth about that day, and that it happened to be a day that a deeply unsatisfactory romance of mine was over, and like everyone in such a situation I was On the Verge.

One cross word from anyone and the floodgates would open. Determined to begin a new life full of sharp, clear decisions and snappy dialogue, I got on the bus. Everyone else was saying 'a shilling', which was the fare. In a voice that could cut through steel, I asked for 'five pence please'.

The conductor may have been having a crisis of his own. He looked at me without much pleasure. 'If there's one thing I hate it's a smart alec,' he said. I looked at him in disbelief and then I began to cry; the bus was racked with sobs, and heaving and whooping. Every single passenger took my side, they had no idea what it was about, but he had grossly offended me, a paying passenger, trying to coordinate with all these instructions about trying to Think Decimal. Scant thanks you got for thinking decimal, only dog's abuse from public officials. They were going to take his number and report him for upsetting the poor woman who was only struggling like the rest of the population to cope with what we all knew would be our ruination and our downfall. I was now terribly sorry for the conductor and trying to get people not to report him, which only made me look nicer and him look even more foul.

New passengers getting on were told of the horror of it. By now he was meant to have called me a smart arse, he had shouted at me, he had frightened me, he wouldn't hear the end of this. Oh no.

No fare was taken from me in either the old or new money, and I staggered off the bus eventually red eyed and thanking my loyal supporters. They all waved at me out the window as the bus pulled away, some of them made fists of solidarity, and the unfortunate conductor ashen with fright was trying to cover his badge number.

The child said it was interesting but probably not what the teacher had in mind. Sadly I agreed, these kind of tales are never what the teacher had in mind.

I would like to thank the seven readers who wrote in saying that they agreed with me about working at home and the nightmarish difficulty of actually starting the damn thing when everything else on earth seems more interesting.

One woman listening to the radio when she should have been working heard an item about bees, and went out and bought two hives. She has a lot of stings, very little honey, a fascination with bees and no income from her real work, she tells me. I would also like to thank the 23 readers who wrote to correct me about the previous Governor General of Canada being a woman, not a man. I was going to say it was just a little test, or I'm glad you're all awake, but it might have looked as if I were flailing on the ropes so I didn't say it.

And if you are reading this in Canada

tomorrow night as you might well be, it's because a couple called Kevin and Meta Hannafin of the Irish Newspaper and Book Distributors bring in national, provincial and Sunday papers. At eight o'clock on a Sunday night you can get them, and they have to wait until Wednesday in Chicago, the Hannafins say with some pride.

I would particularly like to thank the reader who said that there was a message on her telephone answering machine asking how to get rid of fleas from a cat or dog's cushion. The person hadn't said who they were but it sounded like my voice and the kind of thing I would ask. Since I hadn't left a number, she wrote to me at the paper and the answer was to stuff the cushion with dried ferns. Ferns are said to frighten off fleas. She gave no address to save me the bother of getting in touch again.

Again? If she thinks I rang her and left this request on her machine then surely I should know her address. I have a friend who always says, 'Let it pass, let it pass.' How can you let something as mystifying as that pass? But then there could be something about some people which actually goes out and attracts the confusing, the incomprehensible and the downright barking. It has nothing to do with being loud and extrovert and claiming to enjoy unexpected experiences.

One of the quietest and most demure authors I know got a postcard the other day from a boy, man maybe . . . saying, 'My grandmother says you know everything; how is CWRW, the Welsh word for beer, pronounced? Trusting you can oblige.'

The flattery was very pleasing; someone's grandmother thought she knew everything . . . Of course she did no work that morning looking through dictionaries and Books of Unusual Facts. She eventually had to ring a newspaper in Wales and found that the answer was Koo Roo. The whole thing took forever but she felt it was somehow more satisfying than finishing the chapter that was already a week late.

And I agree, it's so much better being thought a person who leaves messages about fleas on the answering machines of strangers or someone who knows how to pronounce beer in Welsh than to be thought capable of nothing.

I heard two students talking glumly about their mothers. One apparently obsessed, day and night, about the house. The other was in a worse state. 'She just sits and looks in front of her as if all her brain cells were dead,' the daughter said sadly. 'Of course she will be 50 at Christmas; what's left for her when you come to think of it?'

My Theodora Story

6 April 1991

Last week, when I was writing about sauces in a restaurant, I felt the familiar sense of fear that Theodora might read it and tell me that even now at this late stage I had still learned nothing about cookery terms.

But last Saturday the pages were full of appreciation and memories of Theodora FitzGibbon, and I remembered my own Theodora story and how she had said I must always tell it after she was dead, since it reflected huge credit on her and George and none at all on me.

I *think* I was the one who hired Theodora on a regular basis for *The Irish Times*. The more famous she became, the more often I say that it was I who found her. Anyway, when I became women's editor in 1968, knowing nothing about fashion and cookery, it was great to have that side of things handled by experts. In the beginning she used to discuss recipes with me, but the feeling of talking to a brick wall must have overcome her, because she eventually gave up. One inkling of my limitations may have

385

come when she typed out a recipe that included one to one and a half pounds of split peas. The way it was written, a 1 and then another 1 and a 1/2, made me think it must have been eleven and a half pounds that she meant, and I amended her copy accordingly.

It was around that time that she decided to take control of her own column, and sometimes her husband, George Morrison, would send us a picture to go with the piece that Theodora wrote. I loved it when he did, but it was always just a little bonus.

So there was this day when it came to getting the cookery page ready and it was one of the days that George hadn't sent an illustration. The recipes were for various ways of cooking veal. Of course, because I wasn't well organised there was no time to ask the *Irish Times* photography department to set up a nice, relevant picture, so I looked through what I always called my Emergency Cookery Pictures File. These were things that had come from various sources, you know, pots of marmalade beside oranges, and picnic hampers. Nothing seemed very suitable until I saw a nice, vague-looking picture of a casserole with a lot of spoons and servers and forks sticking out of it. It wasn't the *best* but it would do, I told myself. A swift caption was typed by me: 'Tasty veal casserole, excellent for a winter evening.' And with the totally undeserved feeling of a job well done, I took the train out to Dalkey at the end of the day.

My father and I were looking at the nine o'clock news on television when I saw something that made me deeply uneasy. I saw Dr Christiaan Barnard, the heart transplant surgeon, getting off a plane somewhere after yet another successful operation, and I knew suddenly where I had seen that picture before. It was in fact a picture of open-heart surgery. What I had taken to be forks and servers were in fact clamps and forceps.

I telephoned the paper and asked them to hold the cookery page. As a request at ten past nine at night, it was poorly received. I was asked why, and the explanation was met with disbelief.

'I think you had better get in here as quickly as possible,' said the editor in a voice that I knew was holding on by only a thread.

We had no car, so I started to run the nine miles from Dalkey to Dublin purple-faced, panic-stricken. An unknown man with a car gave me a lift, and when he heard my errand he abandoned his car in the traffic in D'Olier Street and came in with me, a total stranger, saying he had to see; he loved to know how other people coped in a crisis.

Grimly, I discovered, very grimly. They stood around my desk searching hopelessly for any alternative picture; not having unearthed the Emergency Cookery Pictures File, they found only a cache of Kit Kat wrappers and a bundle of magazines of much lower brow than I would have liked it known I read.

The replacement picture had to be of the same size. There was now no time to enlarge or reduce anything that emerged from the file. Eventually I found one, an egg in an egg cup . . . I think it was a picture from an advertising agency trying to show the charms of some china.

Underneath the picture, and under the grim glance of Top People, I typed out, 'Why be content with a boiled egg on a winter's evening when you could have all these tasty veal recipes?'

Theodora was on the phone bright and early.

'You didn't exactly kill yourself getting an illustration,' she said to me frostily.

But she was delighted with the explanation of the terrible happenings the night before. She said she had lived a colourful life and it would have been entertaining to have added a prosecution for cannibalism to her other achievements. She seemed to regret my last-minute discovery and heroic dash to save us all from turning out a cookery page that would have been a collector's item.

She said almost wistfully that it would have been something that would make people remember her . . . as if there were a chance that any of us will ever forget Theodora.

HEADING FOR THE HUSTINGS

4 April 1992
Even though a heavy cloud of greyness is hanging over the British election, there's still a whiff of intrigue about it all. I'm excited already at the thought of going to the press conferences and looking them all straight in their weary eyes and seeing how they're bearing up.

And it also reminds me of the great happiness of going back to school knowing that a hated teacher has gone, you can hardly dare to believe it. She won't be there in the hound's-tooth suit baying at the back of the hall, turning with reptilian cunning to the cowering ministers on either side saying those dreaded words, 'I think that's one for you, Home Secretary, or Chancellor,' addressing any number of men whose nervous systems and political futures she unsettled over the years.

I have no nostalgia for those Thatcher days when the sun always shone and we were sure of a good row story every outing.

I think the place is far better without her, and for once she may have done the wisest thing by leaving town. Because she sure as hell did everything else wrong a year and a half ago when she was leaving. She waited to be booted out, she patted the head of the little grey boy who was to be her successor and she even chose the wrong little grey boy to be her puppet because he cleared his throat and found his own voice and lived perfectly well without her.

She should have gone six months earlier and sat watching them running around like headless rabbits tearing each other to bits.

That's what I would have done. I would have sat there with a false smile playing around my chops saying that I was absolutely certain that they'd all manage *much* better without me.

And then I would have laughed all the way to the Thatcher Institute listening to a chorus of world opinion trilling that everything would have been perfectly fine if only I'd stayed.

But then she's not the only politician who stayed too long in these islands. It seems to go with the territory.

What is beyond comprehension is how a woman who loved free enterprise and what she called the cut and thrust of the market-place could have made such a monumental cock-up of writing and selling her memoirs. She was months dillying and dallying and allowing everything that could possibly be said in her book be said elsewhere. She was said to be taking the advice of her son, someone whom she had rarely consulted on anything during his whole existence.

A forthright, if inelegant, American publisher said she should have done the deal when she was red hot or not at all. She should have held an auction, promised to name names, say that she was going to right wrongs, avenge grievances, and possibly describe some of the frostiness of Her Majesty the Queen during their weekly conferences.

If she had done this, her asking price in dollars and sterling could have gone through the roof, the publisher lamented sadly.

She would not be human if she did not feel some small satisfaction at the way the boys in the nursery are messing it all up now that Nanny has been sacked. She would not be normal if she did not take a small *frisson* of pleasure from the polls. But had she only gone in time, she could have been regarded forever as the Monarchy in Exile, and she could have had her ego massaged until she lived to be a hundred.

But she's gone, and though her shadow hangs over the country she ruled for so long with such certainty and so little self-doubt, she will not be a consideration this time round.

It can hardly be a presidential-style election since the candidates trail so little glory. Just from my brief four hours a day spent watching the campaign on television, they all seem to me to be in pretty poor shape. John Major has almost blended into the background, they're afraid to photograph him against anything except primary colours. Neil Kinnock is as white as a sheet and as hoarse as a crow, Paddy Ashdown's famous lopsided smile seems to be held on with putty, and they are all moving into the most important week of their lives.

It will be very exciting to get back to it all. To see them again, lining up each morning striving for the newsbites, the one phrase of burning sincerity that will catch every news bulletin, the one lashing out against the other side in a phrase that 20 script-writers worked on all night. I will sit with the press corps, the lay analysts who try to spot victory or defeat in the red-eyed faces on the platform. And I'll walk through the streets of Hammersmith, one of the safer Labour seats in London but with pockets of bright blue resistance in the most unlikely places.

There are a few times in life when Irish journalists are greatly in demand among the British media, usually to explain the Third Secret of Fatima, or the artists' tax-free exemption scheme. But at general elections, people always want us to explain proportional representation in case it might ever become a real issue.

And this time, for the first time, it just might.

PLEASE DON'T FORGET TO WRITE

2 January 1993

There's a great advantage in being grown up. You don't have to swim if it's pouring rain. You can sit and look at the others being dragged in — to get value, or because they've come all this distance, or just because it's Christmas morning.

I'm a great believer in not doing things just for some ritualistic principle; or that's what I said as hot tropical rain lashed down on Bondi Beach.

The people in the next car were not so lucky. They didn't have the Inner Zen that would enable them to sit there and drink the ice-cold champagne anyway. They also had three screaming sons with bodyboards who wanted to be in that surf at once. 'They'll be trampled on — the place is full of Poms,' said the mother anxiously.

'Piss off, Poms,' screamed the children in excitement, quoting a graffito seen on every Qantas advertisement: a polite way of registering disapproval of British Airways buying a stake in the national airline.

People were setting up little camps on the beach in the rain which everyone knew would pass soon. They were planting Canadian, Greek and Italian flags in the sand.

'Where's ours?' asked one little boy.

'It's *all* ours,' said his father, shivering in his bathing trunks.

That pleased the elder two. The youngest one was interested in a well-developed lady shaking the drops off her bosom as she came out of the tide.

'That lady lost her bra,' he said, looking at her with deep interest and some sympathy.

'Not all she lost, I'd say,' his father said.

'She's still got the bottom bit.' The boy

was a stickler for accuracy.

'For the moment.' The man looked knowl-edgeable about such things.

'Perhaps, Brian, you might take your son out to the sea, which is the reason we came here, rather than embark on any further instruction, sensitive as it may be, on the Facts of Life.'

It would have been interesting to know how their Christmas Day went on, but then wouldn't you want to follow almost every-one home? Like the two men in their braces and hats on the back of their heads, sitting on the Promenade in Bondi, saying to each other sagely, 'Better to stay out of the house. Women don't like *people* in a house when they're cooking.'

Or the girl all dressed up to meet the boy's family who asked, 'Is there anything I shouldn't talk about?'

'Communism,' said the boy.

'Right.' She took it on board with a puzzled expression. I felt she should have enquired further but the young probably know what they're at.

Our own Christmas was fine thank you and, apart from chickening out on the swim, went as forecast. There was a moment though when the soft, warm night air came in the open windows and the lights of Sydney Harbour twinkled beyond the gently moving curtains when one of our number asked, 'Do you think that with four people out of five fast asleep during the video we could say that a democratic decision might be to turn it off?' And we all woke up angrily, denied having dozed at all and fought to keep awake to the end.

And then came the Sales. The biggest one is in Grace Brothers, where they had the usual attractions of televisions at $50 and washing machines at $70 to get the crowds in. These special bargains were called 'Doorbusters', a name they'll probably drop now, since the crowds actually did break the doors down in eagerness to get at them, and glass was everywhere, wounding a lot of the shoppers. But still the buses and cars and even the ferry boats are weighed down with huge parcels, brightly coloured sheets and duvet covers, huge terracotta pots for the garden, deck chairs, garden lights — all the luxuries for summer living.

At a party I met a woman who asked me could I tell her absolutely honestly whether I thought she had a mad face. With total honesty I told her that I did not, and wondered why. She said that for the second year in succession she had been photographed for the newspapers as a sort of face in the crowd to illustrate Sales Frenzy. Once had been bad enough but twice was something that would make you think.

At the same party I asked someone who the man was that had just walked in.

'Someone whose face I had hoped never to have looked upon in what remains of my life,' said my informant, who told me the newcomer's enormities and how he had wrecked the particular part of the media he worked in. I heard of his sleazy way with women, his betrayals of trust, his sailing close to the wind financially and that he owned a Rottweiler. By the time I was introduced to him there was nothing he could say to redeem himself.

'I'm not surprised you like Sydney,' he said. 'On a gossip level it's just like Dublin.'

And of course he is absolutely right. I just hadn't realised it before.

I feel as if I have always lived here. The neighbourhood is so familiar now. There's not a day that you'd leave the house without meeting someone you know. On the road where I live I meet Siobhan McHugh and her marvellous baby Declan; in the Dry Dock pub they know our table; in Manjits Indian restaurant they bring the poppadums and chutney before we sit down. In the hairdresser opposite the police station — which calls itself 'The Crop Shop Opposite the Cop Shop' — they'd remember you after one visit and make you feel like a friend. In Ralph's delicatessen, they keep hoping I'm going to emigrate there; they like the reckless abandon with which I buy food. There are three gorgeous cats where we live and sometimes I go into Heavy Petting to consider gifts for them, and they are full of advice.

Fireworks over the harbour for New Year, everyone out in the warm night air, windows open and the old or the children waving at the festivities.

And before going to bed we all light those green coils that smell slightly like incense and burn through the night, killing, we hope, any mozzies that come in the open doors. And the cats sleep peacefully out of doors on the warm wood shavings that are ground cover, and there's a wonderful yellow plant called Kangaroo Paw that is all lit up in the dawn at about six o'clock when it's bright enough to read in bed but there's no anxiety-related pressure to get up just because you're awake.

And tonight it's off to the Sydney Opera House for the gala opening of *Lughnasa*.

It's over four months since we left Ireland

but thanks to the friends, colleagues and family who have been so great about keeping in touch it doesn't seem anything like that.

It *truly* has been so good to get letters from home that I have resolved for 1993 to write to the Irish abroad. We may seem over-confident, as if we almost preferred where we are to where we were. But the truth is that we are all desperate to hear from home.

CASUALLY ELEGANT MEETS THE MOB

9 January 1993

You never know exactly what they mean about dressing up in Australia. We spent a couple of nights in a resort called Terrigal, in a smart kind of hotel where they left a note in each room saying that guests would probably appreciate some advice about Dress Codes. Fearfully we read that the Executive Lounge was Casually Elegant in the evenings, and Smartly Casual in the mornings. They defined Smartly Casual as meaning no bathrobes or swimwear, which left the field fairly open.

But it was confusing because Casually Elegant in the Key Largo Lounge meant

No Runners. What could they want in La Mer, the gourmet dining room? The instructions were Elegant Resort Wear. I put on all my jewellery and a lot of eyeshadow and hoped that would compensate for the ordinary summer dress. Gordon bought a tie.

Everyone assumed we were the cabaret. Elegant Resort is taken to mean open-necked shirts, shorts — and one woman was definitely barefoot, but she had cunningly draped tinsel around her legs so that it looked like exotic twinkling Roman sandals.

So back in Sydney at the opening night of *Dancing at Lughnasa* you wouldn't know *what* they were going to wear for a glitzy night out, and there was the usual rainbow of clothes: little black dresses and pearls; great Hawaiian-type shirts over psychedelic shorts; marvellous beaded and brocade-type Asian jackets. They came in from the warm night air around the harbour to the cool air-conditioned Opera House.

In the row just in front of us a line of people came in, all the men dressed in smart dark suits. I speculated about them happily — they might be coming from a funeral, or possibly serious negotiations within the Mob. Then one of them, who was Martin Burke, the Irish Ambassador, introduced me to another of them, who was Paul Keating, the Prime Minister of Australia, and that sorted out who they were.

There's huge rivalry between Melbourne and Sydney, so Martin Burke had to go to the play's opening in both cities, which he said was no hardship at all. I explained the Cork–Dublin thing to Paul Keating in case it was something he would ever need to know and he listened gravely, adding that if you lived in Australia and didn't live in Sydney you were merely camping out.

The night was a huge success and there was one unexpected laugh in the script: when Gerry the Welsh Romeo describes his kind of dancing as 'Strictly Ballroom' there was a cheer. Australians are as proud of the success of this film as they have been of anything for years, and love to know that it's showing in cities all over the world.

There was a reception afterwards where I realised from the photographers that the gorgeous woman sitting beside us who was about one inch wide was in fact Judy Davis the film star, and I was having a great, happy conversation with a man called Michael Bailey who worked in television. We were getting along fine until someone whispered to me that he read the weather forecast and my brow darkened.

'I don't make it up, I'm not a Met Man. I

only read it,' he pleaded.

But the magic was gone. The Australian weather forecast is as helpful as our own; it says things like sunshine mixed with showers or showers mixed with sunshine and everyone thinks that this is useful.

They are so conscious of equality in this land I was horrified to see an advertisement on television for one of the January sales. It was for a women's dress shop called Katie's. And the ad was a male voice over scenes of empty office desks saying that no female employees could be expected to show up for work until Katie's sale was over.

It was so uncharacteristically sexist in a land which is making great strides against the old macho Ocker image of beer-swilling Australian men liking women to be in the kitchen, the bed or at the filing cabinet, I wondered whether to ring up and complain; but then I decided that was being tiresome. It's not my country. It was late at night. I didn't know the number of the television station.

But enough people *did* ring up. The very next day there was an announcement saying that the advertisement had been withdrawn because it had unconsciously given offence.

The managing director of the company bleated a bit and said that there had been women involved in the advertising agency which dreamed up the account — which was a bit of a last-ditch flail I thought — and he kept referring to the *ladies* who had phoned in telling the store that they wouldn't shop there unless the ad was removed. He said that of course he hadn't intended to imply that *ladies* would put shopping before work. He realised that it might have been unwise to have had a male voice, implying that employers were male and employees were all *ladies.* I know nothing about the shop, but everyone says that it's not a question of any publicity being good publicity; the whole thing did it nothing but harm.

And now for the clear-up. How can seven weeks have gone in this little house when it only feels as if we had just arrived? Where did all the stuff come from? It was lean and spare when we came into it.

There are going to be endless trips to various recycling areas before we leave. I hated throwing out the cards that came the whole way from the other side of the earth, but to carry them back again? That way madness lies.

And now everything has a sense of being the last time. The last lunch out in Bondi on the balcony of Ravesi's watching the world go by. The last sneaking into a five o'clock movie on a wet afternoon, with a choice of maybe 20 in the huge George Street cinemas. The last breakfast in the garden watched by three solemn cats wondering why we like mangoes so much. The last drive out to Long Nose Point to see the ferries cross the harbour. The last night out with friends.

And this morning we will be moving backwards out of the little house, cleaning as we go — just as I remember doing so many years ago in Ballybunion when it was a matter of honour to leave the lodge in just as good shape as you found it.

And then it will be time to go to the airport, with yet another bag added to the luggage, faces rounder and redder than when we arrived here, and check-in at Departures.

I'm not expecting the destination to give you any great sense of pleasure as the winds blow and the rains fall, but the ticket actually says Bali.

Someone's got to do it.

THEY'LL NEVER LET HER GO

4 December 1993
Of course it won't be goodbye. The public

will never let her go, the girl who lived her whole adult life in front of their eyes; the awkward, blushing, stammering Sloane whose main and possibly only qualification for marrying the prince was that she was a virgin.

Daughter of a broken marriage, step-daughter of Raine who could have been sent down by Central Casting to play the wicked stepmother, step-granddaughter of the marvellous, batty old Barbara Cartland, who could out-hat and out-pink the Queen Mother any day and who had written nine million novels about gels keeping their virginity and landing nice princes as a result. And daughter of the burbling, con-fused old Earl of Spencer, who barely made it up the aisle with her, who was seen taking photographs of the crowds who were taking photographs of his daughter.

In addition to her purity, she had all the right credentials, including her Julie An-drewsesque job as sort of nanny-like teacher to lovely little posh children. . . . She was awkward, shruggy and young when she was introduced to the cameras and the horrific lifestyle that was to follow.

Then the world watched her change. She lost her puppy fat, she stopped wearing woolly cardigans, she showed her bosom and her legs. She smiled at people because she realised that they *liked* it rather than thinking they might sometimes *deserve* it, as her mother-in-law and sister-in-law had always done.

And when she saw how much they liked it, she did it more and more. She smiled upwards at photographers, laughed and threw back her head, and it wasn't long before she was on the cover of every magazine that wanted to increase its sales by a minimum of 40 per cent.

Diana sold papers, magazines and books. So many that the market couldn't keep up with the demand. There is no way they are going to let her go now, no matter how many messages, coded or otherwise, come from Buckingham Palace.

For years people have followed the Diana story. They went through her eating disorders with her. Mothers whose daughters had anorexia or bulimia watched her anxiously, willing her to get better, to become happier, so that their daughter would too, thinking that it was all more understandable somehow if a lovely princess could endure such an illness.

Diana made motherhood fashionable too. They waited out on the streets for news of her babies. They stood cheering as she left hospital with the little boys. Nobody could say you were just a breeding machine if you looked at the youthful Diana running with her sons held by the hand.

Then they saw her marriage grow cold and sad. And everyone who had a bad marriage, or even a row within a good marriage, felt better somehow when they saw that such problems and sorrows could even befall the charming princess.

They suffered with her over the humiliation of the Camilla tapes. Whether she loved Charles or not, it was degrading to have the intimate conversation of a husband and mistress broadcast and published all over the world. . . . And the evidence of previous cover-ups, of friends who had been false friends, made ordinary British people feel weak with sympathy for Diana — for Diana who had done nobody any harm, but who had brought warmth and charm to the endless round of royal duties, for Diana who had picked up children and cuddled them instead of waving at them royally, for Diana who had sat on the beds of dying AIDS patients and held their hands. She was pilloried in the gutter press and called an associate of sodomites when she did this, but she had taken no notice and altered her schedule not at all.

Then the accusations came that she was running a rival court.

Almost all the press and most of the public thought 'good luck to her' . . . but there was a fear that the monarchy might not survive such antics. So, bit by bit, heavy pressure was put on Charles to get involved and to get on with things and to make his voice heard.

Charles couldn't compete with Diana in looks, which was not his fault and it was very unfair of the Diana supporters to mock his appearance. He couldn't compete in terms of charm either, because he was literally brought up to believe that he was special, important and different, and descended from lines of that stuff, and couldn't just behave ordinarily. It's a nightmare for him to try to be ordinary.

But what he did was to have an affair — and then did nothing about it when it became public knowledge. He should have apologised to everyone involved and tried to make a go of his marriage instead of being aloof and glum. Or else he should have apologised to everyone, abdicated in advance, married Camilla and got a divorce as everyone else of his nationality, religion and class would have done.

Instead he has played a wounded nobleman whose camp is trying desperately to build him up into some kind of king material.

Diana hasn't put an elegant foot wrong in most people's opinion. If she has to cut down on her public duties, there are many who will see this as part of a bad-tempered, weaselish palace conspiracy.

They will all regret that there's a possibility we may be seeing less of her and more of the other. The other hasn't nearly as much to recommend him.

They are sorry they won't see her crowned queen. But they are not going to say goodbye to a girl who seemed to do everything according to the dream. Ordinary people are still going to want Diana on the cover for a long time to come.

THERE IS NO EXCUSE

26 March 1994

I regard people who say they'll meet you at eight p.m. and then turn up at eight-thirty as liars. I had a colleague years ago in my teaching days who used to smile and say that she was *always* late, as if it were something outside her control, like having freckles or a Gemini star sign. At first I went through agonies thinking she had been mown down by a bus. After that I would arrange to meet her, not on the corner of a street or at the cinema, but in a café where at least I could sit down while waiting. After that I stopped meeting her. There were too many main features beginning at five-twenty missed, too many buses gone, too many houses where I had to be part of an apology for an unpunctuality that was none of my making.

She lives in another country now and I met someone who had been to see her. Just as nice as ever, apparently, just as good company. Much loved by her children but treated as a dotty old lady who can't be relied on. She would never turn up to pick them up from school, so they just adapted to doing their homework in the school yard. So she is still at it, thinking she can say one thing and do another, and everyone will forgive her because she is unpunctual the way other people are left-handed or colour-blind.

Of course she got away with it because people are so astounded by the unpunctual that they forgive them and allow them to roam the world as ordinary people instead of as the liars they are. It's our fault for putting up with it in every walk of life and I advise people to declare war on the unpunctual. It's no longer acceptable to consider it an attractive, laid-back, national characteristic. It is in fact a lazy, self-indulgent, discourteous way of going on. Already there are a lot of signs that people do not accept it as charming.

I remember a time when the curtain never went up on time in a Dublin theatre because, as the theory went, the Irish were all so busy being witty and wonderful and entertaining in bars they couldn't do anything as pen-pushing, meticulous and prosaic as coming in and being seated before eight o'clock. But enough protests from those who objected to people shuffling in late to performances has led to their not being admitted until the first interval, and it's very interesting to see how that has concentrated the ability to get to the place before the lights go out.

Staff of Aer Lingus don't think it's charming and witty to leave late because their wonderful free-spirited clients can't be hurried, and likewise with trains, the DART and the buses. Religious services don't take account of some quirk in the national psyche by having Mass at around eleven or Matins at approximately ten. Races, football matches, television programmes start on time. Why should business appointments and social engagements be let off this hook? And yet this week I was talking to an American publisher on the phone who said that she was expecting an Irish author in her office but he was 40 minutes late. She laughed good-naturedly and even though she was 3,000 miles away I could see her shrug forgivingly. 'Oh well, that's the Irish for you!' she said, as if somehow it explained something. To me it explained nothing.

As a race we are not naturally discourteous. In fact, if anything, we wish to please a bit too much. That's part of our national image. So where does this unpunctuality come into the stereotype? Has it something to do with being feckless and free and not seeing ourselves ever as a slave to any time-servers or time-keepers? It's a bit fancy and I don't think that it's at all part of what we are.

Not turning up at the time you promised seems quite out of character and if we do it, it must be because it has been considered acceptable for too long. If nobody were to wait for the latecomer, then things would surely change. If the unpunctual were to be left looking forlorn and foolish when they had ratted on their promise, then people would keep better time. We shouldn't go on saying that it's perfectly all right and, nonsense, they mustn't worry, and really it was quite pleasant waiting here alone wondering was it the right day, the right place, or the right time. We should never again say to latecomers that they're in perfect time when the meal is stuck to the roof of the oven and the other guests are legless with pre-dinner drinks.

Sit in any restaurant, bar or hotel foyer and listen while people greet each other. 'I'm very sorry. The traffic was terrible.' 'I'm sorry for being late. I couldn't get parking. . . .' 'I'm sorry. Are you here long? I wasn't sure whether you said one or half past. . . .' 'I'm sorry, but better late than never.' I wouldn't forgive any of these things. In a city, people with eyes in their heads *know* that the traffic is terrible; they can see it. Unless they have been living for a while on the planet Mars, they're aware that it's impossible to park. If they couldn't remember whether you said one or half past, that shows *great* interest in the meeting in the first place. And as for better late than never, I'm not convinced.

FEAR OF FALLING
OFF THE WAGON

23 April 1994

A very agreeable, social sort of man, he says he won't come to Ireland for this particular gathering because he couldn't bear all the flak he will get about not taking a drink. He remembers Ireland in the old days, he says, when you brailled your way from the early Bloody Mary to the lunchtime pints and everyone was defined by the amount they could put away, while abstainers were mocked as Holy Joes, Cute Hoors or possibly Not Real Men.

Not the place for a man four years into a different way of life, he says. Why draw it on himself? He's not afraid that he'll weaken or anything; it's just that he couldn't take all the explanations, the defensive attitude he will have to adopt, the rationalising, the assuring people that he doesn't object to their lifestyle, it's just that his own is not the same. He's been here before, he says; he knows of what he speaks. No, life is too short to take on that hassle. He's going to miss the reunion.

I advise him to think again and ask a few people, as well as myself, before he pleads an excuse not to meet classmates who were great pals in the years gone by. He may be very pleasantly surprised. The Ireland of his student days, 20 odd years ago, which he revisited 10 years ago, is not today's Ireland, regarding attitudes to drink.

He will not find people calling him Matt Talbot or Father Mathew if he asks for mineral water. They will not ask for an explanation, nor will they want one. And best of all, they will not turn red, watery eyes on him and sob into their own drinks about how they wished they had his strength. There are lots of nice pink livers in Ireland.

Ah, but Maeve was always one to see what she wanted to see, he says. I would like him to come and meet his fellow students so I could be expected to create a rose-tinted world for him, where people are mature and wise and tolerant. This is not what he hears.

Right, I tell him, this is what I hear and see and notice. I notice that pubs, which love selling soft drinks anyway and always thrived on the mixers because they constitute almost pure profit, not attracting any tax, now have a whole rake of alcohol-free beers and low-alcohol lagers, and they are being wooed senseless by the various mineral-water manufacturers, dying to get their particular shade of bottle and label in.

Publicans, who used to collapse like a Bateman cartoon if anyone asked for coffee, now want to know if you want decaf or cappuccino. In recent years, I cannot have heard a barman make a joke about serving a Real Man a non-alcoholic drink. I haven't seen a sigh, or heard a groan. I have never heard an explanation about someone being a Pioneer, it being Lent, or the breathalyser, or the price of gargle being offered. Maybe I don't go to enough macho bars but I do go to a reasonable cross-section and in recent times I have never heard anyone being challenged after ordering the drink of his or her choice.

I agree that years ago the order would go, 'Four pints, two gin-and-tonics, three large Paddies and a Cidona for your man!' Your man was thereby marked as being outside the tribe. Nowadays it's just as often the reverse; it could be a round of white wine and soda and many varieties of non- or low-alcohol drinks and someone saying apologetically, 'Do you mind if I have a short, it has been a bad day?'

Like smoking. People don't say they've given up apologetically. The apology is from the one who asks for the ashtray. I told the man who thinks that attitudes are frozen that when I gave up smoking I was afraid to answer the telephone in case I had to have a cigarette before I spoke; I was so unused to the experience of one without the other. Not a good example, he says. The phone wouldn't take me by the throat and say I was no fun without a cigarette — go on, have just one.

But I told him that he was guilty of over-dramatising himself. Everyone he will meet at his reunion will have read the bad news about how many units are safe per week. Some of them, admittedly, may have decided to take no notice, but they will know about them, they will not think he is wearing a hair shirt and chains around his middle if he doesn't lower a bottle of sherry at the reception. Some of his colleagues and friends will have read the tests under the heading 'Are you an alcoholic?' and by question three realised that they should be in treatment. Some will have done something; some will have said these questionnaires are run by some backlash pressure group. But they will have read them. There will be colleagues who have had friends die of drink-related illnesses, or passed over for promotion because of being a bit unreliable in that department.

He will discover that the liquid lunch is

no longer a permanent feature of Irish middle-class life in the mainstream, as it might have been when he left. Not an eyebrow is raised if a captain of industry or a politician or even a successful journalist asks for a glass of water; heads will not wag. They will not say that's what has him where he is, either for good or evil. It's just one more choice people make. Like having no car and walking to work can be as high in the pecking order as having a car the size of a house. I advise him to give it a lash.

The profession that he is in has changed. Its ideas of machismo have altered greatly and not just because his colleagues have become middle-aged. New attitudes are all the more apparent among the younger generation. He may not find Ireland an entirely pluralist society but at least he will find his countrymen and women broad-minded enough to know that we owe no explanations for what forms of pleasure or madness we deny ourselves. And he will also have a great time.

GETTING IT RIGHT
AT THE END

14 May 1994
Years ago, there was a different code. You

went to see a friend who was terminally ill and you looked into the eyes which would not see for much longer and you swore that the person had never looked better. You could see a terrific improvement since the last visit, and it would be no time before everybody was as right as rain again. The more hearty and jovial the protestation, the better you thought the whole thing had gone. At least you felt you had handled the performance as it should have been done, and you were hugely relieved that nobody's guard had broken down and there had been no danger of anyone saying anything important about life and the leaving of it.

We don't know what they felt about it, the people who were at the receiving end of all this histrionic pretence that everything was normal. It might have been some consolation to them, but surely they saw through it. In the dark hours of the night, they must have wondered why there was no communication left between friends who had once talked about everything. Just when they needed real conversation most, they got reassurance, platitudes and, in fact, lies and this from friends who used to sit up until dawn to discuss the meaning of the universe, the future of art, and the likelihood of getting someone you fancied to fancy you. Why should it turn to 'Ho ho ho, and aren't you looking well today?' It was because the well could not bear to admit the thought that the rest of the world was not well. So what do you do if a friend is terminally ill? You do not want to go in with a face like the tombstone they know is not far away. You might not wish to bring up unaccustomed spiritual reading, likely aphorisms or new thinking on reincarnation.

Last year I had a friend who was given three months to live, and I asked him to tell me what were the best things people could do and what were the worst. He said that the very worst thing to do was to send a Get Well card, one with bunny rabbits crying into spotted handkerchiefs and saying, 'Sorry to hear you are not so well.' He used to look at these cards blankly and knew that they were the conditioned response and automatic reflex of people who meant desperately well, but who had to hide behind totally inappropriate greeting cards. He wanted to reply on another card, saying, 'I'm trying, God damn it.' But he didn't. And he didn't because he knew that the idiotic bits of card with hospital beds and sexy nurses and thermometers and bad puns hid the real message of sympathy and huge distress. He said that he really didn't like people urging him to get another opinion and saying that it couldn't do any harm. It would do harm, he thought, because it would waste time, the one thing there wasn't much of left. He preferred people to call it cancer if they spoke of it at all, rather than use some euphemism, and he also wished that he didn't have to spend so much time thanking people politely for their suggestions of healing crystals, prayers Never Known to Fail, or the laying on of hands by someone who lived half a continent away.

Those of us who knew him well and asked him how he wanted to do it were told. He wanted to remember the good, laugh at the funny, hear all the gossip, and try to be as normal as possible. Even though he could no longer eat, he wanted to come to restaurants with us and didn't want to see anyone wince when he told the waiter he was on a diet. He said that three months was a terrific bit of notice to get. You could make all kinds of arrangements, ask people to take a book from your collection, burn incriminating letters, heal old enmities, and send postcards to people you admired. Once upon a time he had thought it would be good to die in his sleep or in a car crash.

Something instantaneous. But there was a sense of time borrowed about this three-month sentence. Without being in the slightest maudlin, he said it was something we should all be lucky to get.

He said that he didn't really like bunches of flowers, there was too much of the sick room and even the funeral parlour about them arriving in great quantities. But what he really liked was a rake of stamped post-cards or a couple of colourful tracksuits which he could wear around the house, and a few videos to watch at night. He didn't like letters telling him that lots of people had conquered this and surely he would too. But neither did he like the letters saying that he had a good innings and that, at 60, he had done everything. He wanted to be the judge of that. But he did love to hear from the many people he had known during his life, saying briefly that they had heard about his diagnosis and that they were sorry. Letters that then went on to say things he could hold on to, things about time well spent, marvellous places seen, and memories that would live forever. All this brought a smile to his face and made the tapestry richer and less laced with regret. He said that if at all possible, he would like there to be no tears, but he knew this was hard, and he didn't mind unnaturally bright eyes, because he knew this was a sign of grief felt but bravely fought back. He could understand why some people hadn't the guts to come and see him, but he wished they had.

It has taken me a year to get the courage to write down his advice to those who want to do their best for friends who are about to die. A year in which I have never ceased to admire his bravery and honesty and to believe that there may be a lot of it around if we could recognise it. We planted a rose tree, a Super Star, in his memory, and at last I feel the strength to pass on his advice to those who might learn from it.

FOR TIRED READ TERRIBLE

25 June 1994

It was a lovely sunny day on Bloomsday and I was sitting in the hallway of the Joyce Centre in Dublin, delighted with myself. Why wouldn't I be? I was watching all the comings and goings, the people dressed up, the American tourists, the faces I hadn't seen for years. I was waiting to do an interview and was given a glass of lager to pass the time. Not many people would be having as good a time on a Thursday afternoon at one-thirty, I said to myself.

And then a woman came in whom I used to know years ago, when we were young teachers. She was a very positive person then, I remember. She used to take her pupils on great trips to France, which they never forgot. She had amazing projects in her classroom, and she used to go around with a box on the back of her bicycle asking people who had gardens if she could have cuttings, and then she used to get the kids to plant them around the schoolyard.

She was a leader in everything, the first to give up smoking, the first to organise lunches where people were asked to contribute the price of a meal for the hungry, the first I knew to go to America for the summer and work as a camp counsellor. I had nothing but good memories of her.

She seemed glad to see me too, but then her face fell. 'You look desperately tired,' she said sympathetically. 'Are you all right?'

Well, the sun went out of the day and the fun went out of the Joyce Centre and the taste went out of the glass of lager and the sense of being as free as a bird went out the window.

Tired is not a good thing to be told you look. Tired is terrible. And the really infuriating thing is that I was not tired, I had been in bed nice and early the night before. And

I was tidy. Tired can often mean that you look like a tramp, but no, I had gotten all dressed up, complete with white collar, to be interviewed. And I wasn't sweating or collapsing up flights of stairs. I was sitting calm as anything in the hall.

And if I was 25 years older than when we last met, so was she.

So, stupid as this may seem, I looked upset. I must have bitten my lip or may have looked as if I was going to burst into tears, because she said at once that she was sorry, and wanted to know what she had said.

'I'm not tired,' I said, like a big baby.

She tried to explain that tired was okay. We were entitled to be tired. By God, we had earned the right to it. We worked hard, we had done so much. It would be an insult if we *weren't* tired.

She was backtracking, trying to dig herself out of it, I said.

No way, she insisted, and wasn't I the touchy one trying to read other words into a perfectly acceptable observation, and more meanings than were implied in an expression of concern?

But what was she going to do about my tiredness? Suppose I had admitted it? Just suppose I had agreed that I was flattened by fatigue and had been waiting for someone to come in that door to identify it. What was her cure? Had she ginseng or Mother's Little Helpers in her handbag? Did she have a personal fitness trainer, a protein diet, a Seventh Son or shares in a health farm?

We argued it away good-naturedly, as we had always argued in years gone by. She had always been a woman of strong views, a characteristic I admire. I have even remembered many of her maxims, such as 'Avoid restaurants that have strolling musicians', 'Never play cards with a man named Doc' and 'Don't resign before lunch'.

But what's the point of telling someone that they look tired, even if you don't mean it as a euphemism for old, ugly, unkempt or rapidly going downhill? Was it a kind of sympathetic come-on . . . expecting an answer along the lines of Nobody Knows the Trouble I've Seen?

She was spirited about it. And she nearly won the argument.

Would I prefer, she wondered, if we were all to turn into those dinkleberries who greet each other with an effusion of insincere compliments: 'Oooh, you look marvellous' and 'Oooh, you've lost loads of weight and honestly, I never saw you looking better, what have you been doing?' The greetings and the compliments becoming like a ritual dance where the vain and the self-centred rake through a form of words, wondering if there is a 'marvellous' too few or an expression of astonishment not heightened enough. Surely we haven't reached this stage?

But then, when she said tired, did she mean that as some sort of shorthand, to be a jovial punch on the shoulders between old mates, a kind of bonding between the worn out?

She thought about it.

She thinks she meant that she liked me from the old days, and it was good to see me again, and when she came upon me I had a serious expression on my face as I had been talking to a woman about her late husband and maybe she remembered me roaring about, not sitting down. And in a sense, she didn't want to be one of those people who always said twitter twitter things and assumed other people had lives that were free of care. And on reflection, she said, now that we had argued the thing down to the bone, she would never as long as she lived tell another human being that they looked tired again.

Traveller's Tales — The Call of the Check-In Desk

Two years ago I went around the world, heading west into the sun all the time, and I loved every bit of it, except the two and a half days in Las Vegas and the memory of an unmerciful row in Los Angeles Airport. Looking back, I don't know how we did it. If it's Monday it must be Arizona, if it's oysters at five pence each, it must be Auckland, if it's police horses with red tinsel necklaces, it must be Christmas Eve in Sydney. If it's people playing tinkling music and wearing flowers in their hair, it must be Bali. And this for two people who normally sit with two small cats looking at the television at night, or else in other people's houses, staring mystified at bridge hands and wondering how many points you need to respond to a call of 'one diamond'.

So now the urge has come again: the call of the check-in desk, the unpacking in strange hotel rooms, the day tour of a new city, the heat in October, the factor 15 sun lotion in November, the postcards home, meeting friends in far-off lands, the sense of something new going to happen every day,

428

the writing of a weekly travel diary, of working out what possible time it could be at home if I wanted to ring the family or friends. I want to read newspapers again in different countries, obsessed with different issues, utterly unaware of our concerns. I'm looking forward to celebrating other people's festivals and thanksgivings, lamenting their political systems and weeping over their ludicrous weather forecasts, where Met men and women look into the entrails and forecast, in different accents, sunny periods with some showers or showery periods with some sun and get paid salaries for doing this.

I don't have four and a half months to examine the world this time, only about half as long, in fact. But I met a marvellous couple last week in County Clare, who told me they were doing the entire cosmos in three weeks and they found it a satisfactory kind of undertaking. The secret is having early nights everywhere, they confided, and drinking a lot of fluids — mainly bottled water — and not going to any country where the people were in any way hostile to your people.

Boastfully I mentioned that I was in the habit of touring the cosmos myself, and they wanted to know my secrets. These were different secrets; they had nothing to do with early nights, bottled water and wondering whether anyone would be hostile to my people. They had a lot to do with only meeting people you wanted to meet, seeing things you thought you would like rather than you should like, late nights and much bottled wine. I told them happily about packing half-a-dozen Ella Fitzgerald and Liam O'Flynn tapes — great for evenings far away — about bringing a small torch, having nothing that needed ironing and always going to airports an hour early to keep the blood pressure down. They looked at me steadily and thanked me for sharing this with them.

Younger friends wondered why would I visit a lot of the same places again when there were so many new places left to see. It's hard to explain that if a dozen Australian sunrises are good, then two dozen are better, if laughing all night with great friends thousands of miles away was good in 1992, it should be just as good in 1994, and would not be long enough this time either. Last time I missed a general election, which was heart-breaking, but good friends sent faxes with essential information like the results of each count in Dún Laoghaire/Rathdown — good deeds like that will never be forgotten.

I have four weeks before I go, and now that I'm not in the business of dishing out advice any more, I'd love to receive some — if you have any ideas about travelling light or making things easier in some way, it would be great to hear from you. Nothing about travelling irons please, or sheets of tissue paper to make sure the creases fall out. No hints about putting jewellery in hotel safes; this would fall on deaf ears. I had four great dresses made by a friend of mine, who is actually a rather important person in costume design in a theatre. I gave her one dress as a sample, and asked her if she could find an assistant or a student who would make four like it, the only requirements being no discussion about it, no fittings and no ironing. She said she had to make them herself because she spent her working life telling others that you must discuss everything down to the bone, have a fitting twice a day and never use these horrible synthetic fabrics, but have everything natural and crushable. Her entire credibility would have been shot to pieces if it were known that she had a friend with such base requirements.

But out there, somewhere, there are people with marvellous ideas, like the journalist who told me that when you bought books abroad you should send them home by surface mail, which costs hardly anything and then they arrive as a lovely surprise weeks later when you'd forgotten about them. A photographer who told me that if I wanted great holiday snaps, I should look first at the main postcards of wherever I was and go to where they were taken, since these were the guys who had figured out the best angle to take the shot. And since there should be a pool of brilliant travellers' ideas, I'll publish some of the ones that appeal to me most.

Last time I went looking at the cosmos I swore I would be better informed when I went to examine it again; I would know intelligent things about the places I was going to visit. But, somehow, two years passed by and I never got informed. I greatly look forward to hearing any advice which might be put into practice during my second crack at the cosmos.

Love's Last Day Out

11 February 1995
The last Thursday of every month, their mother came to Dublin for an outing. There was a day excursion fare and if you got to the station nice and early you got a great

seat on the train. Then, at what she still called Kingsbridge, one of her daughters met her. This was Jenny, the daughter who didn't go out to work. They would meet Nuala, the daughter who did go out to work, at lunchtime.

It was a wonderful routine, never broken over the years, except when one of Jenny's babies was inconveniently born in the last week of a month and once when their mother had a chest infection. The outing took the same form always. Jenny would drive down the quays, and her mother would cluck at the changes she saw on every visit. It had all been altered, the implication being for the worse, but they knew it wasn't since last month or last year; their mother was thinking of 30 or 40 years ago, when the world was young.

Jenny would then park and her mother would sigh at the way so many people brought their cars into town for no reason at all. And then they would head for Brown Thomases. It was always said in the plural; if you said it in the singular it meant you didn't know it. It was like people who said St Stephen's Green. The tour took two hours, never less. In fact, Jenny thought that had the time been available it might have taken all day. Her mother stood at the front door and sighed with pleasure. Everything that lay ahead was like a wonderland. In a changing world this place remained as it always was, a temple of comfort and luxury.

They would start at the cosmetics counters. Mother knew a lot of the elegant women who demonstrated and sold the various fragrances and creams. Well, she didn't really know them but she remembered them from visit to visit. 'When I was here last month you were telling me about this new firming cream for the throat,' she might say to one. They were invariably helpful and interested and often gave her a spray of something new and very sophisticated that had just come in. Years ago there had been a very nice woman called Caroline Mahon who mother had got to know. She had wept and sent a letter to the store when she read of Caroline's death in the paper. But all these girls were very helpful and took all the time in the world. Which, as Jenny said grimly, was more than duty required since her mother's face, with its dusting of face powder and merest touch of lipstick, was not going to be an arena on which the great cosmetic wars of the world could be fought and won.

Then they went to look at scarves and ribbons and particularly at the kind of ribbon comb attachments that someone going to a glittering evening do might wear in her hair. Mother had short grey hair, hidden on the day of the outing by a hat. She never wore these hair ornaments but she fingered them, lovingly clucking over the prices, but saying that of course if you had the right dress then these ribbons could set it off and make the whole thing into a coordinated outfit that would be very striking. And then they might go to the cookery shop where they would examine whole ranges of coloured cookware and mother would discuss 12-place settings and easy-care napkins.

They would try on jackets, a nice jacket. A nice jacket paid for itself a hundred times over, she would tell the salespeople. And as they would nod and agree, she would see the price and cluck that it was steep but then you were paying for the cut. 'And the material,' the assistant might say. 'Pure wool.' 'And the name,' mother would say and put the jacket back on its hanger.

The tour almost always ended in the bed linen department downstairs. Real down was debated, the kind of goose that had delivered up the feathers for the duvet was identified, queen size and king size beds were clucked over; in the old days there had been just a double bed. Mother nearly always bought a pillowcase, it was wrapped carefully in the distinctive bag of the store and she would leave reluctantly for lunch with Nuala.

Since mother did not walk far, lunch was in Dawson Street or Wicklow Street. It was a nightmare for Nuala, who worked on the southside. She gave up trying to find lunchtime parking and took a taxi instead, arranging for another taxi to pick her up an hour and a half later. This meant nearly two and a half hours away from the office, unheard of in the place where she worked, but Nuala said that not to have it for her mother's outing was unthinkable. She worked longer hours to compensate and always felt slightly guilty about it.

At lunch mother would talk about the tragedy of growing old on your own without knowing love and a family. Nuala would clench her teeth and smile ever more brightly as she said in a tinny voice that one never knew what was around the corner. And, at the age of 43, with the same relationship, of which her mother knew nothing, she found it harder and harder to play this role. Then it would be Jenny's turn, what a pity the children had done such odd things, gone to Australia with no job and no plans, didn't write letters to their gran, were never there when she came to the house. Jenny smiled and shrugged and said that was the way it was, and what could you do?

The sisters' eyes met across the table. Twelve times a year they felt united by this huge resentment of the mother they both loved. Then Nuala's taxi would come and she would go, and it was always too soon and nothing had been said and she worked too hard and perhaps that's why she hadn't settled down like a normal person. And then Jenny would get the car and take mother home for afternoon tea, never sure whether she wanted one of her children to be there and possibly bring up an argument about the Church, or whether it was better to face into an empty house. And she would put Mother on the train. All the way to the station and as they boarded the train, Jenny's mother talked about the great visit to Brown Thomases. It was a tragedy that it was going to change into that Marks and Spencers.

Last month at lunch she told Jenny and Nuala that she might cease these outings to Dublin. After all, with no lovely visit to Brown Thomases what was the point? Her two daughters looked at her blankly. Nuala began a useless attack, saying that the place had always been a bastion for the rich and privileged and that it was absurd to say it was for ordinary people. Jenny, trying to be a peacemaker, said that BT's would be across the street and that everything would be just the same. But their mother would not be consoled, without any idea that she was writing off over 20 years of being welcomed warmly to Dublin by her two girls. As far as she was concerned it had been maybe 250 visits to an escapist paradise.

She was 71, too old to have the shining, glittery toy snatched away from her. Too innocent to hide from her children that the disappointment was so great it had clouded her judgment and her love for her family.

A WALK ON THE WILD SIDE

25 February 1995
It was usually with a group of friends in those days and they would all make sure to buy a different Sunday newspaper so they could go and have a drink afterwards and read four papers instead of one. It was very companionable then but of course nobody had time to do anything like that now; they were all in marriages or relationships varying from uxorious to deeply unsatisfactory and they would corpse themselves laughing if she were to suggest anything as ludicrous

as walking down the pier on a cold Sunday and going to have a few jars.

Nowadays they asked each other to dinner parties, at infrequent intervals, to drinks mornings or to charity dos; the days of sharing newspapers and glasses of lager were long gone. So, if she were to go down the pier, she would go alone. But it might look odd if she met someone she knew, which was part of the purpose of the trip, so she borrowed a dog from a neighbour. She could always say it was a keep-fit exercise. The dog was less fit than herself and seemed to have had enough after a few steps. But she dragged him along behind her. She noticed that everyone else seemed to be following behind bounding hounds who were straining at leashes — she had obviously taken the wrong breed. This was a sleep-by-the-fire-and-wait-for-bits-of-roast-beef-after-lunch kind of dog.

She had dressed quite carefully: a smart jacket with a white shirt coming out over it; dark pants and boots; no handbag or anything prissy like that; hair wind-blown but not messy. If she met anyone from the past she would look fine. She would also have her explanation — her husband was at the golf club for a special competition so she was released from making Sunday lunch and she thought she would blow away the cobwebs. It was mainly true. It was a bit true. And anyway, one of the great things about growing older is that you know people don't care about your circumstances all that much.

After 10 minutes she met a man she hadn't seen since they were students. He looked in very poor shape, she thought, and she could hardly believe that he must be the same age as she was.

'Are you at the same game as myself?' he asked her hopefully.

'What game is that?' She felt she might be. A game that involved beating back loneliness, trying to banish the growing feeling that life had not turned out as she had hoped it would.

'Waiting for the pubs to open?' he said, as if it were obvious.

She didn't want to have a drink with him, his story was bound to have been worse than her own. 'No, no, purely exercise,' she said, and bounded on.

He had been such a firebrand at college; they all thought he would have been a politician. She would not allow herself to be brought down by him, he was not someone she had been fond of, there was no room in her heart to feel sorry about acquaintances, people she half knew. She had enough things she really did care about. She met a couple with their teenage children. The children were polite and shook hands; the parents were holding each other's gloved hands as they shivered in the sea breeze. They told her she was looking terrific and they laughed at the lazy dog who had been so delighted with the pause for chat that he had fallen fast asleep at their feet. Their praise sort of made up for the fact that they were happy and together on a Sunday and holding hands still and that their children would bother to go out walking with them and be courteous enough to greet someone who was introduced.

And she met another couple she knew, walking together in animated conversation. They stopped to exclaim briefly how healthy and young she looked. They went back to their argument, which was about *Riverdance* and whether people were building all kinds of fantasies and wish fulfilment on it, or whether people who said that were just a shower of begrudgers. They seemed pleased to see her and each hoped to recruit her to their own side of the argument. They assumed she had been to the Point and shared the experience.

She felt nonplussed as she walked on.

Imagine, people thought that she had the kind of marriage which involved joint outings to something like that, which she would have loved. It must have been two decades since she had been in a lively discussion with him about anything except the latest crisis concerning the children, or the fact that he hadn't come in for a lunch or dinner that she had prepared. And everywhere she looked, it seemed that they walked the pier as if it was the gangway into the Ark, they went two-by-two, unless they were accompanied by eager, happy children who seemed perfectly content in the company of their parents. The single people that she did see were young, determined and obviously going somewhere.

Perhaps this had not been such a good idea. Then she met the man in the anorak. About 50-ish, hands in pockets, nice friendly face. He was carrying a small exhausted Pekinese in his arms.

'At least yours is on his feet,' he said, nodding at her exhausted charge who was gasping for air and for mercy beside her.

'He'd be a bit heavier to carry than yours,' she said. And they were friends.

They decided to turn back. They walked companionably back to the mainland, laughing over things like dogs having no stamina.

And it was the most normal thing in the world to go and have a drink. When the boy came to the table, the man in the anorak said he hadn't a penny on him. It would have been nicer if he had been just a little bit apologetic and said that by some amazing chance he had come out without his wallet. But he didn't; he just said he had no money. So she bought him a pint and a gin and tonic for herself and then another pint and another gin and tonic.

They talked about the football match and Northern Ireland and the new plans for Dún Laoghaire, and Joe Duffy on RTÉ and the divorce referendum and Bishop Casey and the DART and then it was time for the pub to close. And he said that maybe he might see her on the pier next Sunday if she was a regular. And they woke the sleeping dogs and went their ways without exchanging names or family circumstances.

All week she had been wondering if she would walk the pier again. There were so many things to put on one side of the scales. Including the knowledge that it's always women who feel low and unappreciated, who walk blindly into the most ludicrous situations. And would she be buying him pints all her life? But there was a bit of ballast on the other side too. It's a long time since she had a proper chat on a Sunday and a bit of fresh air and, in a sense, it all depends on the weather tomorrow.

PETER PANIC ATTACK

6 January 1996

The Messer will be 59 in February, into his sixtieth year he said on the phone, mystified as if it had suddenly crept up on him unfairly from behind.

It had been a long time now, 10 years maybe since I had talked to him; he sounded just the same, like he had sounded in UCD a long, long time ago.

He was calling from London on New Year's Eve. He was on standby for a flight to Dublin, and had suddenly thought it would be great to see the New Year in with the old gang.

The Messer sounded so enthusiastic about the people of the past that you would get carried along with it and think they were all there waiting to gather in Neary's. He spoke about them as if we were all still in duffle coats in Earlsfort Terrace. He spoke of people who would be spending New Year's Eve with their grandchildren, people who had lived abroad for 30 years, people who had become recluses and disappeared from anyone's lives. He asked warmly after two men who had died, and seemed shocked by the news. He must have known, he must have.

I remember telling him about one myself 10 years ago, and the other was so well known even the Messer would have read about it. And yet you couldn't feel enraged with him; he was so grieved, and said such warm and appreciative things about them both, remembering the good and the positive.

And after all he had been abroad.

He only came home rarely, on spur of the moment goodwill visits expecting to find everything frozen in a time warp of 35 years ago, a perpetual student life where people would assume he had only been away for a matter of weeks.

And where was he staying: in Dublin?

The question was always asked to the Messer with some trepidation, but even as it was asked you remembered the hollow nature of the request. The Messer always said that he was fine, and he would get fixed up, he never asked straight out for a bed for the night. He knew that the offer of a bed was increasingly refused as the years went by, because it was never for the night; it was for many nights and usually involved other

445

people coming and going and irritation turning into conflict and guilt, huge, huge guilt, because the Messer was a decent person and none of this ever seemed to be his fault. Directly.

But somehow, even though he said he was fine and would get fixed up he never was fine and never did get fixed up, and someone always had to look after him because nobody could be so awful to him as to walk out and leave him there, or so patronising as to give him the price of a hotel room.

So what happened over the years was that you'd try to second guess the Messer, arranging to meet him somewhere in the city centre for a specific time in the middle of the day before things got to the stage that he would come home with you, being firm about your own commitments while assuring him that you were enormously enthusiastic about seeing him again, which was actually true.

His life is lived entirely in the past; he has painted the edges of everything we lived through then with heavy silver, and sees it all through the rosiest of spectacles.

He never remembers any incident that reflects anyone in a poor light, yet he makes us all uneasy because we have felt that time has marched on. Maybe we are all dull and middle-aged and middle class and the Messer who is older than any of us is the gilded youth, the Peter Pan who somehow kept the faith when the rest of us lost our wish to be free spirits.

We even pretend in his presence, people who meet rarely and casually. For his sake we let it be thought that we are all together the whole time and resist asking each other questions that would prove us to be near strangers.

The Messer gives little information about his own life: there was a wife and son a long time ago, and then another wife, and a long-time companion and someone in Prague who might or might not have been a wife. But they are never brought along to meet the friends of his golden youth — they are spoken of vaguely and benignly but with a slight raising of the shoulders, a near shrug, as if their responses and unpredictability are beyond the Messer's comprehension.

Work seems too dangerous a topic to bring up. Certainly it's not something that the Messer would introduce into the conversation.

He is interested in an astounded sort of way to hear what the people of his generation did with their degrees or often without them. His own was never conferred, because it was never given, 'too many' confusions and mix-ups and situations at the time.

And there are pen pictures of cities far away, all of them great places in their own way but none of them a patch on Dublin, which of course is greatly pleasing and flattering — but doesn't hold water.

If Dublin is so great . . . why isn't the Messer here all the time?

Anyway, as a standby he got on a plane. Of course he did. Quite possibly a passenger with a ticket may have ceded a seat to him. That's the kind of person he is, charming and helpless and bewildered and good-natured.

And because it was a No Room at the Inn situation on New Year's Eve he just wandered around the Old Haunts as he calls them looking for ghosts, waiting for the crowd to turn up. You just could not ask the Messer to anyone else's house, too many years of people in floods of tears, fights in kitchens, the wrong thing being said over dinner tables, unlikely candidates being found in bed with the Messer or even more unlikely candidates being tight-lipped and furious because they were not in bed with him.

All those promises made and broken, all those cars over the years having to drive 30 miles in the rain to collect some late arriving friends that the Messer had assured of a welcome.

And as the clock struck 12 and those of us who had sort of grown up in our different ways celebrated in various parts of the forest I would say a lot of us thought briefly of the Messer and wondered for a little instant had we been selfish to exclude a man who thought so well of us all, and who had written a memory book in which we all had starring roles.

But I looked around my gathering and felt deeply grateful that he wasn't there, unwittingly upsetting all the good-natured people I was with, starting a political argument with one, an affair with another and with the sure knowledge that somewhere out there a crowd of Other People were hovering, waiting to join us.

The Messer rang from Shannon Airport last night. He was on standby for a flight out.

He had a great time in Dublin, but when had he not? God, wasn't it a fantastic city; no, he hadn't run into anyone from The Old Gang, they had all been tied up or out of town but he had gone to some of the Old Haunts.

And he had met a gorgeous girl celebrating her twenty-first birthday, and she had said to join them and they all went on and on, to pasta in one place and really lovely people, and then a nightclub. Imagine Dublin full of nightclubs! And then they had plenty of room in their place so he stayed, which was just as well because the poor girl had this awful row with her boyfriend on New Year's Eve as it happened, and it was good that she had an older, wiser man to pick up the pieces, and a lot of their friends were going to the west so he went along too and it had all been great and he was so glad he had just acted on impulse and come to Ireland for the New Year.

'Do you ever do anything on impulse these days?' he asked me.

'Can I write about you?' I said suddenly.

He said he'd love it and then his coins ran out.

He won't be back for many years, he may never read it. None of what he calls the Old Gang has an address for him, we never had. We must never feel guilty about him, never ever again.

Fortunes have been invested by pharmaceutical companies seeking the secret of eternal youth, and we happened to meet a man called the Messer who found it all by himself.

450

He didn't grow up, simply because he didn't want to . . . maybe it's as simple as that.

LITTLE PERSON! TINY PERSON!

13 January 1996

At the hairdresser sat a woman who was, to my mind, the client from hell. But what do I know? They seemed to love her and fawn over her.

'I'm going to have an entirely new style,' she said.

'Right, now do you want it close to your face?'

'No, no, not close to my face.'

'Away from your face then?'

'No, not away from my face.'

I wanted to fly from my chair in my protective gown and take her by the throat. But they were interested; it was, after all, a challenge and they decided to call another stylist for a consultation.

The other stylist appeared and the woman who neither wanted her hair close to her face nor away from it gave a screech that froze everyone in the salon.

'But you've lost so much weight. You've lost stones and stones. Little person! Tiny person! How did you do it?'

'Well, it's not all that much and I . . .' She didn't get an inning.

'But you're a tiny person; you used to be a huge, huge person. Remember those great jowls you had? Real jowls, they were darling, and look at you now. A little person. How super, no jowls. Don't ever let it creep on again, will you?'

I thought about it for a long time. Would the little person, the tiny jowl-less person, like all this praise? Was it the reward for the diet, the self-control, the exercise? Or might she resent the spotlight and the attention of 30 people beaming on her and the memory of an earlier, more hideous self being brayed all over the salon? It was a mystery.

And I was so glad that I am not in hairdressing. It would be so easy to let that scissors slip.

FIGHTING FEBRUARY

10 February 1996

A hairdresser told me people do desperate things to their heads in February. They are so fed up of life being cold or wet or dark or whatever, they make reckless decisions and get the lot lopped off, or the colour changed radically to counteract a pallid face.

They sit discontentedly in their chairs

before and after the transformation and even though it's not good for business, she would often suggest to them that they do something else, rather than a revolution with their hair which they might spend a year regretting and growing back to the proper shape or returning to the proper colour.

'Like what?' a gloomy woman said to her last year.

It was a puzzlement but the hairdresser was a woman of courage. 'You could go to line dancing,' she suggested. And the gloomy woman did.

And on the very first night, she met a man in the line as they were dancing whom she liked much better than her husband. And he tilted his hat forward and talked in a nice jokey country and western style. The gloomy woman seemed to be cheering up by the hour.

Her husband just looked up from the paper when she came home in the evenings and he said they were all cracked to be doing that sort of thing, and there was someone, somewhere making big money out of eejits buying fringed skirts and laced boots.

The children were grown up, but still mystified when they heard their mother was leaving home and moving in with the man from line dancing; their father was philosophical.

'She was always that way in February,' he said. 'It was a kind of a thing with her. It was as if she thought the good weather would never come again.'

Apparently, he shook his head about it, accepting it as inevitable, just one more of the many bad hands that life dealt. His wife walking out on him.

Whether there might also have been something wrong with their lifestyle was something he never paused to speculate about in the following months, when the good weather had come back but his wife was still with the man who tilted his hat.

The hairdresser said to me that from now on she's keeping quiet: if someone wants a head shaved to the bone in February, she'll do it. But I said no, the gloomy woman was somehow waiting for that man in the line dance. The hairdresser must not feel responsible, she must go on interfering in people's lives. Doing that is just proof that we are alive.

This friend of a friend, also an anti-February person, gives a St Valentine's Day party every year. The simple rule that nobody who is officially or emotionally attached can attend. The theory was you wouldn't have lovebirds canoodling and making you sick, or old staid married couples nodding and patronising everyone to death. No, this was to be a gathering where the mind-set of everyone was unencumbered — her phrase, and a fairly horrible one, it has to be said.

Anyway, it turned out to be a fine gathering over the years as the group changed from being twentysomething to thirtysomething, and a new decade is approaching.

Some people have dropped out because of getting involved and attached, which presumably was what a lot of it was about.

Some have moved from one state to another and back.

Everyone brings a bottle of good wine and they can ask to include new blood as well. If these people are unattached and come along bearing the requisite bottle, that's considered great too.

But last year two deceivers were at the party. Men who were certainly committed officially, and as far as their wives believed, committed emotionally as well. Dublin is a small city; they were unmasked at an early stage. Now a shadow hangs over this party.

Everyone had thought it was for real. Now,

you might just as well go to a nightclub, they all say.

One of the parents at a school I know has a cookery class in her home. She has children round each Tuesday in February and they all bring their own ingredients. They are boys and girls and they all sit and watch her do it first; then she gives them boards, dishes and part of the kitchen table each and they do it themselves.

They have made gingerbread, pizzas, cheesecake and pancakes. That was last year's repertoire.

The children and their parents would have been happy for it to go on all year, but the woman said no, it was only February, in order to beat the blues.

I said I didn't know children felt low in February.

'Who said anything about them feeling low?' she asked. She was doing it to raise her own spirits.

There are two men I know in Dublin who have hardly noticed February for the past 20 years.

February is quite simply the time they put their heads down and make money. They'll dig your garden, cut things back mercilessly, they'll teach your children to drive in your car, take your rubbish to the dump, they'll collect dry cleaning, stack trolleys in super-markets, clean windows and cars, clear out garages and attics. I know they offer their services to drive drunks home, and I suspect they also drive other people's hackney cabs.

This is all on top of their day jobs, which could be described as office work.

They have regular clients; they strike a rate and work almost around the clock. But only for this one month of the year.

Why only February?

It's the month before March, stupid. And March is when you go to Cheltenham. Do you know nothing?

Since I left teaching and got more or less in control of my own life, I always tried to have a holiday in February. The sun on your shoulders seems to do you twice as much good in the month when you know it's go-ing to be dark when you wake and dark while you're still at the keyboard. So today, I should be in South Africa.

I have the highest of hopes about the sun, despite the telephone interview I did for a radio station there. I was burbling on about how much I was looking forward to the heat, and the talk show host said I should bring my umbrella, which I thought was a weak but good-natured weather joke, so I laughed immoderately.

Apparently it wasn't a joke at all; the rain was bucketing down outside the studio. She was giving me practical advice.

I tell you this so that you will not hate me for having gone to the sun yet again.

SHE DIDN'T DO SO BADLY

8 June 1996

Forty years ago this week I did my Leaving Certificate. The biggest, laziest, youngest girl in the class, my head was full of lollipop music that summer. I think my whole life must have related to it since I have no other memories at all of the time all my revision was done to the tune of 'The Man from Laramie', and 'Hernando's Hideaway'. If I kept the record player really low in the bedroom I was allowed to play it but they could apparently hear it everywhere so I used to sit on the floor beside it reading my North and Hillard and rapping out the words.

'With ask, command, advise and strive. *By ut* translate infinitive.' It went almost magically to the Johnston Brothers' version of Hernando. Try it. And you could sing the prime ministers of Britain to 'Cherry Pink and Apple Blossom White' too, if you had a mind to.

It was too late to put anything to the tune of 'Rock Around the Clock', because we knew the real words too well and it wouldn't work trying to put in the French verbs that were conjugated with *être* or whatever had to be sealed into the brain in those last weeks and days.

There was a thing in trigonometry, the proof of a sine or a cosine I think, it went beautifully to 'It's Almost Tomorrow', and in fact I liked it better at the time than the Dreamweavers' version. But some songs were sacred. There were a lot of things I could have sung to 'Memories Are Made of This' but I didn't want to destroy the sound of Dean Martin's lovely velvet voice by listing the terms of the various Land Acts or Home Rule bills. And of all the songs that summer, it was the one I loved best.

I was terrified that somehow I mightn't have any memories. That life would pass by and I wouldn't have enough fresh and tender kisses to look back on, not to mention stolen nights of bliss. I was dying for a stolen night of bliss. It was the only thing that kept my head down to do any study at all. Whatever chances there might be of getting together a stolen night of bliss if you had the Leaving, if you hadn't, then there wouldn't be any chance whatsoever.

I remember that I got a small piece of steak with my tea when the others would just have sausages. My father and I, the workers, would get steak. It was meant to give me great energy for all the studying I was doing but in fact, of course, it only made me feel guilty.

The great surge of energy only went into dancing 'Mambo Italiano' round the bedroom to myself wondering did I look like Rosemary Clooney and singing 'Rock and Roll Waltz' in what I thought was a terrific take off of Kay Starr. The steak fed my delusions that I would in fact be a performer and that the Leaving Cert was not only not essential, it might even hold me back.

But I was the eldest of the family so there was more than usual depending on this result. They would get some kind of inkling from my score whether the show was on the road, or if they had been fooling themselves and we were all as thick as planks.

So I decided regretfully that I would have to get it to keep the peace, and to reassure them. And once it was got I could go off on stolen nights of bliss and be 'discovered'.

I would be an Educated Rock Star and when Dickie Valentine would lead me on stage with him to do a reprise of 'The Finger of Suspicion', pointing at me all the while, no one need ever know that I had got my Leaving Cert, I could just keep quiet about it.

I suppose it all proves I wasn't nearly old enough to leave school or indeed to be allowed out anywhere if these were my views. I am trying to be honest, but 'discovery' is definitely what must have been uppermost in my mind that May and June. Suez hadn't happened, Hungary hadn't happened; Ronnie Delaney's Olympics were later. I sure as hell wasn't thinking about knowledge for the sake of it or an academic career, just scrape in, do law, be a judge or something until I was discovered. I thought a lot about Grace Kelly and Prince Rainier and a bit about Khrushchev and atheistic communism, but much, much more about someone, hopefully Tony Bennett, who was going to 'Take My Hand' because I was a 'Stranger in Paradise'.

I remember the first day of the Leaving Cert and there being some idiotic row at school about whether we should wear our uniforms or not. There was a View that said we should, it would sort of straighten us up, make us realise that this was all work and part of the studying process. There was

461

another more liberal View which won in the end that it didn't matter if we went in our vests and knickers as long as we tried to write down what we had been learning for over a decade.

We would meet girls and even fellows from other schools on the way home and compare the questions. You didn't really want to talk to anyone who hadn't done it. We all hated showing the papers to the teachers and our parents.

The poor teachers would say, 'Well at least you knew that, didn't you?' stabbing at something and you wouldn't remember whether you had known it or not.

And at home the exam papers were always spread out on the kitchen table and studied by everyone. Even Smokey the disdainful cat used to come and look at them as if he could have got through them with no worries. And they assumed I would have done brilliantly in English.

'Aren't you always telling long, rambling stories about things, the essay would have been no trouble to you,' my mother said proudly.

'And those are grand straightforward questions about Shakespeare,' my father said approvingly. They were indeed, but only for people like himself who had read and understood it all. Not so straightforward for those who had tried desperately to set the Tomorrow and Tomorrow and Tomorrow speech to the tune of she wears red feathers and a hula hula skirt. And none of them were any good at Maths or Irish so that had to be an unknown quantity, and I did a lot of dealing with the Almighty about good behaviour and putting Stolen Nights of Bliss on hold for the foreseeable future if I got the exam.

And then there was an endless, endless summer waiting. I think the sun shone every day but Met Éireann, of course, will tell me that it never came out at all.

And then there was the day the results came. We were in Ballybunion, and we had a Fuller's cake for tea and I was allowed to eat two of the four solid chocolate drops on top myself. And compared to all the Einsteins in Kerry, of course, my Two Honours were a poor thing. And only a Pass in English. Imagine!

Still it was worthy of being celebrated. And it was. In style.

I wish they knew that of all their children, I was to be the least educated of all. But Two Honours in those days served fine to start me off for the rest of my life.

And of course if I had it all over again I

would have worked harder, read more, opened my mind, made them prouder of me. But that's only what I think now as I look back on a summer that seems like the other day.

CURMUDGEONS OF SUMMER

9 July 1996

'I don't like summer myself. Personally,' said the girl in the pale pink shorts and the dark pink halter top. She was eating a huge ice cream cone and waiting in the crowds to see the USS *JFK* come into view in Dún Laoghaire.

She looked like an advertisement for summer, with her shiny hair, her 97 small, healthy teeth, her light suntan and her air of well-being.

'I know,' said her friend, who was no use as a friend. She had said 'I know' to people for all of her 18 years and you could tell she would do so forever. 'I know what you mean.'

The girl who didn't like summer, personally, was at least a person of views; she was prepared to elaborate on her stance.

'You see the thing about summer is that you expect so much from it,' she said earnestly. 'Every time you open the papers

464

or turn on the television there's someone saying, "Here comes summer," and you get all excited and then nothing much happens at all.'

'Oh, I know,' said the other one.

Socrates had a friend like that, didn't he, when he was writing the Dialogues, some dumbo who said 'Assuredly' every two pages or so.

Deeply depressing, I would have thought, and wouldn't have crossed the road to meet the guy again. But look at it this way: they remained mates, at least until the end of the book, so people might just appreciate that kind of attitude in other people. Anyway, the girl who didn't like summer, personally, seemed perfectly pleased with the response.

'Like they're always saying that the deep dark days of winter are behind us — I love winter.'

'Oh, winter's great,' said the other.

'And you could stay in bed on a winter morning without being demented by the birds, they've all gone down to the Mediterranean or died or something in winter, you'd get a bit of peace.'

'The birds are brutal,' said her friend.

'You know where you are in winter, you're cold and wet and you know that's what it's going to be, you haven't a clue where you are in summer.'

'Not a clue.'

'It could be pouring rain or roasting the skin off of you, and what's there to do anyway?'

'Tell me about it,' said the other.

They were both gorgeous-looking, and getting many admiring looks from what I would have thought were fine young fellows as they stood scantily clothed, staring with dulled eyes out at the *JFK*.

The girl in the two shades of pink finished her ice cream and licked her fingers.

'You know another thing about summer, you end up eating 300 calories of this stuff without realising you're even doing it.'

The other one nodded until her head nearly fell off.

'You're right,' she said. 'You're too right.'

I didn't wish the pink girl a more sunny attitude, or a sense of priorities. I was sorry that she didn't have anyone to disagree with her and to sing some song in praise of summertime. I wished her a better friend.

The woman polishing her brasses was dying for a chat. 'It's a nightmare trying to keep the house right in summer,' she said. I told her she was doing a great job of it. But no, apparently the bright light of summer was the enemy. You could shine and shine and some smear always showed up. But the very worst thing was the way the bit of brass polish comes off on the door, well, that kind of thing goes unnoticed in winter, but at this time of the year it's a nightmare.

I thought to myself that a nightmare was putting it a bit strongly, and though a lot of people have very exacting standards about housekeeping, there's a question of going too far.

'You see there should be some method which means that you only clean the brass and not the door,' she said. What I should have said of course was, 'I know, this is what you're up against.' Why do I never realise that this is the right thing to say almost all the time?

But I said that there was a woman who lived near us in London who had little cardboard shields cut out and she used to lay them over the knocker and the letter box and just clean within them so that the brass polish didn't get on the door.

Well, if I had found the Holy Grail or the Missing Link she couldn't have been more interested. And was it heavy cardboard and did you stick it onto the door, or just hold it, and imagine my doing that. She'd never have thought it about me, just goes to show

how wrong you can be about people. She was going to go in and make one immediately, and would a cornflake packet be strong enough, or should it be something sturdy and what did I use myself?

I was purple in the face trying to tell her that I had never done it, but she didn't believe me. If you had a wonderful hint like that, then of course you'd use it. I had transformed her summer for her, she said. But don't you like summer anyway, I pleaded.

I wished she did, but in fact she didn't. The sofa covers faded, the net curtains looked grimy after three days, you realised how much of the place needed painting. One good thing about winter, she said mysteriously, was that everyone was in the same boat.

There's this couple who have been given the loan of a mobile home for a week. They were delighted because they thought they could have one last real family holiday before the kids grew up and wanted to go off on their own. There's only one problem. The children think they are grown up and have planned to go off on their own already. They're 15 and 16, for heaven's sake. What would they be doing going on a holiday with their parents?

A holiday is what it says it is, it's time off to enjoy yourself, to be free to do what you want. The mobile home would be like home, but even more uncomfortable. You'd have to be in for meals and clear up after them and you wouldn't be allowed go anywhere.

Now they don't quite say it like this, but that's the drift.

And they don't buy the idea of it being one last holiday either. You can be absolutely certain that come next year there'll be one more 'last holiday', and so on until they are old and grey.

The kind thing to do is to cut it now and let the parents realise that it's not on packing Scrabble and a family-size Nivea Creme any more.

I know I'm a softy, but I wish there could have been a compromise. That the children could have come to the mobile home for just a weekend. That way things wouldn't have looked so bleak for good, warm people whose only crime was to want to enjoy the summer.

THE FALL

19 October 1996

Years ago, before I knew that people called things by different names, we knew an American person named Martha and she used to talk a lot about the fall. I didn't know it was autumn for ages because she had so many other marvellous expressions and dramas in her life that the thought of a huge upcoming fall off a roof or a wall or something was only too likely. After all, her father had lost all his money in the Crash, and we thought it was a car crash and asked why he didn't go back to the scene where the crash had happened and look for it. And when she talked about little cookies we thought she meant small people in chefs' outfits.

I call her a person, not a girl or a woman, because we thought she was oldish, almost bordering on being an adult. She was the cousin of a neighbour and she came to spend four weeks' vacation every year. She used to clean the house from top to bottom as payment for her keep. She talked about Jell-o and turnpikes and trashcans and how her uncle used to take the paddle to his sons if they behaved badly.

Mostly we didn't know what she was talking about, but she seemed to treat us as equals, which was great. It was a time when it was much more important that people were of goodwill and occasionally had candy to offer than that we understood what they were talking about. We were always pleased when Martha arrived, and we listened, bewildered, to some of the things she said.

Like, back home she worked for a tightwad who ran an old folks' home, and her brother hoped to hang out his shingle and her sister had saved for a muskrat coat. And always she said she wished she could stay in Ireland for the fall. She would love to see just one fall in this part of the world. It would be wonderful what with there being so much greenery already.

I didn't ask anyone about it because, to be honest, I got the impression that the grown-ups thought Martha was a bit soft in the head and I didn't want to let her down and I thought it was odd to look forward to and be wistful about seeing a fall of any sort. And I had no idea what greenery had to do with anything.

And the years went on and her uncle's wife died and he didn't see any need to drag the unfortunate Martha back to be a skivvy in the house. Those were his words. His late wife had always referred to it as giving the girl a holiday. But anyway, Martha didn't come. And sometimes she sent us the funnies from American newspapers — Blondie and Dagwood and things — and we got a lot of the jokes in them.

And one day some years later her uncle said that some people were just born for trouble, and that Martha had all the hallmarks of that kind of person. It wasn't bad enough that her father had lost all his money on some cracked stocks and shares, her brother had been forbidden to practise law because of some misunderstanding, her sister had left home without a forwarding address. Martha's mother was in a decline, so they had arranged that the mother go in to the home where Martha worked — no wages for Martha, but then no fees for the mother.

I was about 14 then.

'It's not fair,' I said.

Martha's uncle said that in his opinion life was rarely fair.

Martha didn't remember what age we were or else she thought we'd still like the funnies, and when I was about 16, I actually got her address and wrote to thank her. She wrote back to tell me she was in love.

And this was fantastic. Firstly nobody

talked much about love, no one old like in their twenties, which Martha was, and she told me that his name was James and his aunt was a patient in the home and that when his aunt died James would be very rich and they would get married. And I was very excited by this and asked what kind of things James said, and Martha rather innocently wrote and told me and I told them to the girls at school.

And Martha said that when she and James got married they would come to Ireland for a honeymoon — they would come for the fall. I knew what the fall was now but I didn't rate it much in those days. I wrote and told her that she shouldn't bother, the summer was nicer, and of course she wouldn't have to clean her dead aunt's house now. I even said that she had been very good to do all that years ago. And she wrote an odd letter saying that she looked back on those days like heaven, the work was so much easier than here in the old people's home. She would love to leave but of course there was her mother to support there, and then James coming in twice a week to see his aunt.

I always thought she was a nurse there but she was a lowly cleaner, she explained. She said that she had never claimed to be anything else. She asked for a picture of Ireland in the fall.

We didn't have colour films in our cameras in 1956 and our garden looked desperate anyway, and my mother said why wouldn't I take a snap of it when there was something to see instead of everything straggling and dying. I found a wet-looking picture post-card which looked as if it were taken in Famine times and sent it to Martha. She didn't reply and then we lost touch.

And when I was 20 and saw the colours of my first fall in New England I remembered Martha and wrote to the old people's home that the tightwad had run. I didn't know his actual name, but a woman wrote back and said that Martha didn't work there any more, adding that the management had entirely changed.

And I felt somehow that Martha had been annoyed with me for sending her that hor-rible postcard so I wrote again and won-dered did they know where she was, because I wanted to send her a proper picture of Ireland.

And the woman wrote to say Martha was in a penitentiary, she and a young man had been convicted of the unlawful killing of the young man's aunt. . . . It had always been thought that Martha was very much under the young man's influence.

Martha's mother had died shortly after it, her brother had been in some kind of trouble and there was no trace of her sister.

Her uncle in Dublin is long dead.

Martha would be 65 now.

It's not her real name, but if she were out there and on the internet? Maybe.

On this lovely autumn day when the fall in Ireland never looked better, I would love to find her, and to take her back to see it just once. I don't want to hear about James. I don't imagine she sees much of him.

There are greater coincidences in the world than that I should find her and show her the Irish autumn she wanted so much to see.

LET'S TALK GRIDLOCK

30 November 1996

When I went to live in London in the early 1970s I used to be knocked backwards by the amount of traffic-conversation that preceded every gathering. If you went to someone's house for dinner you were expected to give an account of how you hacked your way through the jungle to get there, as if the place was some kind of forest clearing in Borneo instead of a suburban house in Ealing, and in turn you had to listen to everyone else's story.

I decided it was a ritual, like the way a dog often turns round a lot before settling down; London people had to tell you where they left the M4 and how they had skirted round the back of Paddington. Then, when it had all been said, you could talk about real things.

It was very boring and I used to thank the Lord that in Dublin there would never be endless traffic stories like this because there weren't a dozen alternative ways of getting from one place to another; you sort of went on the main road. So we could start the real conversation immediately, I thought. We were ahead of the game.

Wrong.

They're here.

And if you want to unleash them on yourself, just mention the three words Traffic Management Plan and you'll get worse than you would believe possible.

And the really bad part about it is that there's no real solution except to leave three hours earlier than you need for everything, like in the middle of the night. And buy tapes with sounds of water rippling over the little rocks, things that will calm you down, and keep saying 'ohm, ohm' and try to loosen your grip on the wheel if you see bones coming through white flesh on your knuckles.

That, and the knowledge that you are not alone, may help.

Listen to the conversations all round you, know that everyone else is in the same position. Get solidarity and comfort from realising that the city has come to a standstill for everyone, not just for you. Listen, listen and calm down.

In a restaurant, a couple waits for their host. He arrives in the door with a face like thunder, nearly taking the door of the restaurant, the waiter, and the people at two tables with him in his path to his own table. He starts dragging off his wet overcoat, his gloves; his face is purpling up by the moment.

'Jesus Christ' are the first words he gets out, and the place is treated to a description of how he waited for 20 minutes at one set of traffic lights, and 10 at the next and there was no parking and there were wardens and guards like spare parts at a wedding, walking round leering at people, and *Jesus Christ!*, again bawled at the top of his voice.

The startled couple, who had been waiting for him more than half an hour, lied and said they had only been there for five minutes: the crumbs of 10 bread rolls proved them to be dishonest.

'Can I take your coat?' the waiter asked, politely.

'Look, I don't need any hassle today, let me tell you.'

The waiter moves nervously away. The man who owns the restaurant arrives to take the coat, which is thrown half on a chair, half on the floor, with the gloves and a scarf and the man looks as if he's about to strip down to the buff unless somebody stops him and calms him down.

'A nice drink, perhaps?' The owner cannot find the right word. There are no right words.

'Nor do I want to be patronised,' cries the purple man in a choking voice that terrifies the wits out of his two lunch guests, who had wrongly thought they were going to have a nice meal out.

On the bus, the woman got up three times to ask the bus driver was there no way he could go any faster. The first two times he explained politely that there wasn't. The third time there was a slight edge to his voice when he asked had she any suggestions. Like maybe ploughing through the solid line of traffic ahead of him? Or revving up seriously and taking the bus into a flight path 10 feet above the line of trucks, cars and buses below?

There were tears in her eyes.

'I'm sorry,' she said, and went back to her seat.

People were kind and came up with suggestions. Could she get off the bus and walk? No, she walked with a stick, she wouldn't be any quicker.

What about a taxi?

Wouldn't it be the same snail's pace?

Yes, but at least the taxi driver could take a different route. People will understand if you're late, they told her, everyone's late these days. It just can't be helped. Everyone understands.

The woman could not be consoled. It was an appointment with the bank. Everything depended on their getting this overdraft. The bank had a feeling that they had been unreliable in the past.

We all had the feeling that she might have been — the tears of mascara didn't make her look like a good risk.

The bus was silent thinking about banks. Someone gave her a tissue and someone else loaned her a mobile phone. She made a poor job of explaining the traffic situation. None of us had any hope for the loan.

A boy stood at the bus stop — like everyone else he had been waiting forever as things went slowly by, grim-faced people from an adult world staring unhappily ahead.

'Did you have a nice day at school?' asked an old lady anxious for a conversation — any conversation — to pass the time. The bus was 200 yards away, it might take 15 minutes to get to us.

'No,' he said.

'Why was that, dear?'

'The bus was late getting there and the teacher said how was it that the rest of the class got in, and I said they had fathers with cars and they all got up at six o'clock in the morning and I was told not to give cheek.'

'Yes, well,' she said.

'And then we all got late to the football pitch because the bus didn't come and there was no football, and now the bus hasn't come and I'm going to be late home and they're going to say how is it that I'm the only one late home, and none of them go out but if I said that I'd be giving cheek again.'

'It's a hard life,' the old lady said.

'It's a shit life,' said the boy, ending the

friendship between them.

Outside a solicitor's office. An awkward meeting, two one-time friends have fallen out, a business is being wound-up, there are still areas of disagreement about some outstanding debts.

'Let's try to get this done in as civilised a way as possible,' says one of them.

'Yeah, well it would be easier to be civilised if your bloody lawyer had turned up.'

'He's stuck in traffic, his secretary said.'

'Secretary? Gargoyle, more like. Where's she coming from not letting us smoke in the building, for God's sake?'

They stood glumly in the rain smoking while traffic inched by.

Once they had cursed the traffic to the pit of hell, and counted the number of cars that had only one person each in them, there wasn't much to talk about. So they inhaled. And they talked about the old days, when they were starting out.

When the solicitor arrived yelping about gridlock and the car scrappage scheme and nobody caring and cities coming to a standstill, the two men were looking at each other as normal human beings. One of the few success stories of the Christmas traffic.

'They've Gone and Dumped
Portillo . . .'

3 May 1997

As soon as the sun started to shine in London it was as if someone had shouted 'Strip'. They stood half naked outside the pubs, pints in hands and faces upturned to the hot sky. In the parks they lay out on rugs in shorts and bikinis, their skin glistening with oil. They had dragged tables and chairs out into front gardens and people without gardens draped themselves over steps and footpaths. It was only the first day of May but there was terrific heat in the sun — and those who live in a city of nearly 12 million people will take any opportunity at all that might suggest closing their eyes and pretending it's Midsummer's Day.

And even at the polling station in a west London school there was a holiday air. A woman with sunglasses on her head, two small children by the hand, came to the gate of the little school.

'Don't talk to anyone at all, just look at all the lovely pictures the other children have drawn while Mummy votes,' she said.

'I want to vote,' said the five-year-old.

'Not now, darling, later . . . look at the

nice pictures on the wall.'

'You never let me vote.'

The seven-year-old was examining the artwork. 'These are no good. Our school is better,' he pronounced.

'Shush, darling, they're doing their best, it's a very little school.'

'It's a *normous* school,' said the child.

'I meant they don't have all the marvellous classrooms and lots of good teachers like your school does.'

'It's an awful school, Mummy, why are you voting here?'

'It's where we vote, darling, now *do* look after Charles.'

'I *want* to vote,' said Charles in the querulous tones that he may still have in 13 years' time when he is allowed to vote.

'Charles, darling, just a little patience for Mummy then we buy mangoes and ice-cream, all go to Grandmother's garden for a lovely, lovely visit.'

'I hate Grandmother,' said Charles.

Most people smiled tolerantly at each other as if to acknowledge that children always speak their minds.

'I bet she hates you, too,' said an old unshaven man bent over a stick, a bottle of ginger wine peeping from his pocket.

It did the trick and silenced Charles and

his discontented elder brother. They stood fearfully in the small, run-down school, worrying about what the future might hold for them.

In the restaurant the waitress said that she was doing her own poll. She asked every single person who came in which way they had voted and amazingly as soon as they had got over the shock of breaching the secret ballot, they all told her.

'It's going to be a landslide,' she said cheerfully to the owner as she bustled through the In door and the Out door of the kitchen.

'You wish,' said the dour owner, who had worked out with two accountants and a man from a money house that he would be marginally better off if the Tories won, but that the country was going down the tubes no matter who won.

'Aren't you excited?' the waitress asked him.

'Takes a lot more than a bit of unscientific research bothering the customers to make me excited,' he said.

'It's not unscientific, we get them from every walk of life here.'

'I'll bet my whole week's wages Labour gets in with a majority of over 160,' she said.

'Your week's wages? Don't be so foolish, woman.' It was easy winnings but he didn't want to bankrupt the staff at the same time. She was determined, however. She asked three customers to be witnesses to the deal. Even those of us who were not regulars could telephone and make sure that he would honour the bet if she won — or lost.

'Don't be specific about the majority,' people warned her. But she was a confident, New Dawn Woman. She wouldn't reduce it — 160 or more, she said — and went on serving tables, her face full of smiles.

I rang the place yesterday to check the situation. Apparently they had all stayed up most of the night watching the television. When the majority topped 160 the waitress had bought champagne.

'Fine bloody socialist she turned out to be,' said the owner glumly. A hangover, a lost bet, the wrong government in power — it was not a good Friday.

'Did you tell her that?' I wondered.

He had, of course, several times during the night but as she poured the champagne she had said that this was what it was all about, champagne for everyone, not just the fat cats.

'Fine bloody grip on reality she has,' the owner added, as he bid me farewell.

A woman who works in a factory reports that they all began the day yesterday by dancing round in a conga line singing 'They've gone and dumped Portillo . . . They've gone and dumped Portillo . . . da da da da da.' And it proved so catchy that even the supervisors and management side of things thought it was funny and sang it too.

The phrase got into people's heads and at lunchtime when they went to the pub they started it again and this time the whole pub joined in.

'What's Portillo done to them?' the barman asked.

'He looks like a prat,' said a man at the bar.

'Not fair to judge the poor fellow by his face,' said the barman.

'He talks like a prat.'

'Oh well, then,' said the barman, as the pub danced on.

Mrs Perfect

13 December 1997

Mrs Perfect got married in May 1970 and to this day she has never forgiven Charlie Haughey for upstaging her at the wedding. The guests talked of nothing but the arms-smuggling charges that had just been announced. She felt nobody gave her even a passing glance as she walked up and down the aisle. Their wedding seemed only like a supporting act to the dramas that were going on elsewhere. She was 25 years old, she looked wonderful — she can show you the wedding pictures to prove it — but they were more interested in Blaney and Haughey that day.

She knew that you have to work at marriage — her mother told her that long, long ago. Let nobody tell you that running a home was easy, her mother had always said; it involved ceaseless vigilance and planning.

So Mrs Perfect had done exactly that, and never more so than at Christmas.

Hers was going to be the Christmas that would be remembered by everyone. Planning began in early summer, when she would start the present list. Her gifts were never extravagant but very thoughtful.

If you ever said to Mrs Perfect that you liked chutney, she would write it down, and she would cross-reference this on her chutney list.

She made two summer shopping trips to the North, where many things were much cheaper, and she never travelled without her list, plus the list of what she had given for the past five years.

She knew how dangerously easy it would be to give the same person an aromatic herb pillow year after year if you didn't keep proper records.

All her Christmas cards are sent on December 6th; she books her Christmas Eve hair appointment in November to make sure she gets the right time. The turkey, ham and spiced beef are ordered weeks in advance and the shopping list, the Christmas countdown and two stuffing recipes are photocopied and pasted to the back of a cupboard door by the beginning of the month.

She knows a place where you can get a non-shedding tree, and bought it long before the rush so that she could get the right shape. The lights have been tested, a candle bought for the window, a holly wreath for the door.

The fridge and the freezer are filled with things that can be brought out instantly for unexpected guests, though there seems to be fewer of those than there once were.

Still, it's good to be prepared.

The children have all left home now, so you would think it would be less pressurised than it used to be. But Mrs Perfect laughs at this notion. It's worse than ever, she says:

you have to remember all their in-laws — a tin of mince pies here, a potted plant there. Not that in-laws is the right word, more like common-law in-laws. None of them married, all in what people call 'relationships' and not a sign of a grandchild from anyone.

Mrs Perfect says it doesn't look at all good at the bridge club, where she has no pictures to show. You can't show snaps of your gorgeous home — only grubby faces of little toddlers are acceptable, followed by screeches from the others saying that you don't look old enough to be a granny.

No brownie points for having made the cakes and the puddings in November, tippexed-out the changes of address in the Christmas card list book, polished the brasses and decorated the house within an inch of its life.

They have a drinks party about two weeks before Christmas and Mrs Perfect used to love the way people oohed and aahed over the way the house was already festive and decorated.

People groaned and said they hadn't even begun their shopping yet and everything was so rushed and there was so much to do and the Christmas season started earlier and earlier, preventing them from doing anything at all. She used to think this was just a way of going on, a style of speaking, until she noticed that it was quite possibly true. She saw neighbours dragging home a tree on Christmas Eve, and she would get the same, guilty poinsettia from apologetic friends who said it was so hard to think of anything but at least this would be colour-ful.

Mrs Perfect had been thinking of their presents for at least six months. Wasn't it odd that other people didn't do the same?

It's hard to know who to talk to about it. Mrs Perfect's considerably less than perfect husband isn't around all that much. He seems very delighted with his comfortable, well-run home. Well, she thinks he is. But honestly, it's hard to know. Things have changed, probably, from the way they were in her own mother's day when you were judged by how you ran a house.

Nowadays, people possibly had different goals, but it was complicated trying to work out what they were.

Mrs Perfect's husband told her to stop fussing round like an old hen when she said something totally innocent like how they need to get up at six o'clock on Christmas morning to have everything ready.

She had actually said it so that he wouldn't

come home at all hours from a do like he did last Christmas Eve.

That's when he snapped at her and called her an old hen. He said the children were in headlong flight from her because she made such an almighty fuss over everything. All people wanted to do at Christmas was get on with it, for heaven's sake. Why couldn't she take that on board?

He had apologised, of course, for his outburst, and said it was harsh of him, particularly when she went to so much trouble and wore herself out for everyone else. All he had been trying to say was that a tin of soup would do people fine rather than weeks of boiling bones. He hadn't meant to sound bad-tempered.

And of course Mrs Perfect had forgiven him, her mother always said that men hate a woman who sulks.

But it is worrying her.

None of her four children and their 'partners', as they call them, is going to be with her for Christmas Day this year. Is this pure chance, or the way things happen, or is it more sinister? Does she fuss them all to death?

At the Christmas drinks party this week she wondered were people annoyed with her and even slightly pitying rather than impressed with her perfect home.

Who moved the goalposts?

And when were they moved?

Mrs Perfect thinks we should have been told.

DEATH IN KILBURN

19 December 1997
The response to 'Death in Kilburn' was such that Maeve made it the basis of a play, Deeply Regretted By. *First produced as a television drama by RTÉ, the play won a Jacob's Award that year, the award for best script at the Prague TV Festival, and was chosen to represent Ireland at the Prix Italia and the New York TV Festival.*

Patrick went into hospital on December 1st. He was sure he would be well home for Christmas, because it was only a light form of pneumonia, they told him. Modern drugs cured that kind of thing easily.

They didn't cure Patrick. He died on Wednesday, 7th, without very much pain.

Stella was negotiating about the Christmas turkey when the news came from the hospital. She couldn't believe it, she kept thinking that it was a huge hospital and they must have made a mistake.

She asked the priest to come with her to the hospital. He was a nice new priest who had come to the area a couple of years before, he wasn't attached to the parish church, he worked in welfare.

Father O'Brien went to the hospital with Stella and he asked all the right questions. It was a viral pneumonia, it hadn't responded to antibiotics. Nothing could have been done, his coming into hospital had just meant that he died with less discomfort and he had aids to his breathing up to the very end. They were very sorry and they gave Father O'Brien and Stella cups of coffee out of a machine without asking them to pay for them. They told them to sit there as long as they liked.

Stella said they had better send telegrams to his mother and his brothers in the west of Ireland, and Father O'Brien brought her back to his office to do this. They gave his office number as somewhere to ring, because Stella and Patrick didn't have a phone.

She went home by herself to tell the children when they got back from school. They had four children, and they all came home around four p.m. She bought a cake for tea because she thought it would cheer them up, and then she decided that it was too festive, the children would think they were celebrating or something, so she brought it back to the shop and they gave her the 65p back.

On Thursday December 8th, the feast of the Immaculate Conception, the children were off school anyway. They sat around in the house while a neighbour made cups of tea for Stella and told her that she should thank her maker every hour of the day that Patrick hadn't been on The Lump like so many other men, and that there would be something to feed his wife and children now that he was gone.

Stella agreed mechanically, felt a sense of cold all through her stomach. She still thought that Father O'Brien might run in the door with his face all smiles, saying that it was a mistake, that it was another Patrick who had died of this thing that drugs couldn't cure.

But Father O'Brien was having a very different kind of conversation. Two men had arrived in his little office. They were Patrick's brothers, they had got the night boat over and come up on the train to Euston. It was their first time in London.

They hoped Father O'Brien would understand why they had come and appreciate

494

the urgency of what they were doing. They were bringing Patrick's body back with them to the west. They had been given the name of an Irish undertaker who arranged funerals across the channel and they were going to see him now.

'But he's lived all his life here,' said Father O'Brien. 'Won't he want to be buried here where his wife and children can visit his grave?'

'No,' said the older brother. 'He'd want to be buried in the parish church at home, where his wife and seven children can visit the grave.'

Oh dear God, thought Father O'Brien to himself. Here we go. 'Well I think you'll have to discuss this with Stella,' he began.

'We don't know anything about Stella,' said the brothers.

'I'll take you to Stella's house,' said Father O'Brien firmly.

The brothers agreed reluctantly that if it would avoid trouble they supposed they'd better go.

Father O'Brien got someone to look after his telephone and they walked off past the shops that were all lit up with Christmas lights and plastic holly sprigs. Father O'Brien got rid of the children and the neighbours and sat through the worst conversation of his 15 years as a priest.

Somehow anything he had to take before was easier than watching a woman realise she had been deceived for years, seeing the peeling back of layer after layer, realising that on five occasions when Patrick had gone home alone to see his old mother he had managed to conceive another child.

He could barely look at Stella's face when the halting, inarticulate sentences came out of the brothers, each one filling in a dossier of deceit and weakness and double dealing.

'What's she like . . . your sister-in-law?' Stella said eventually.

' "Like"?' Well she's a grand girl, Maureen. I mean she's had a hard life what with Patrick having to work over here and all, and not being able to get home except the once every summer.'

'But we were married in a church,' said poor Stella. 'We must be really married, mustn't we, Father?'

There was a throat-clearing silence and Father O'Brien started to talk about God understanding, and Stella being truly married in the sight of God, and nobody being able to make hard and fast judgments about anything, and his voice petered out a bit.

The brothers were even more restless than Father O'Brien. With some kind of instinct that he still doesn't know how he discovered, he suggested that he take them for a pint because the pubs had just opened, and that he would come back and talk to Stella later.

He settled them in the corner and listened. The story was simple, Patrick's funeral had to be at home, otherwise it was not a funeral. Otherwise his whole life cycle would have no meaning. It would be like being lost at sea not to be brought home to rest.

And that Englishwoman couldn't possibly come home with him and behave as a wife. They had nothing against the poor creature, it was obvious there had been some misunderstanding, but Father could see, couldn't he, how much scandal there would be if she came the whole way over in black and brought her children with her, it would be flying in the eyes of God.

Father O'Brien's pint tasted awful.

And then there was the mother to think of, she had worked her fingers to the bone for the family, she was 83 now, they couldn't have a common-law Englishwoman turning up at the Mass, now surely that was reasonable enough, wasn't it?

Stella was sitting where he had left her.

She couldn't have moved from the table, and the door was on the latch the way he had left.

'Maybe there's a case for what they want to do?' he began.

'Sure,' said Stella.

'It has nothing to do with the rules or laws or what the neighbours think, maybe there's just a case for letting him go back there to rest. It will give a lot of other people a lot of peace. . . .'

'Oh yes, that's true,' said Stella.

'And we can have a proper Mass for him here, too, you know,' said Father O'Brien desperately.

'That would be lovely,' said Stella.

'I've got to go back and tell them if you agree,' he said glumly.

'What do you think is best?' she asked sadly.

'Well, I don't think anything is best, it all looks terrible and bitter, and I feel hopeless, but if you ask me what I want, I want Patrick to be buried here with you and his family all there to say goodbye.

'If you ask me what would bring the greatest happiness to the greater number then I think that you should let him be buried in Ireland.'

'It's a bit hypocritical, isn't it, Father? Up

to this morning you regarded us as a good Catholic family, part of your flock. Now suddenly I am an "outsider", a woman living in sin, someone who can't go to a funeral in Holy Catholic Ireland in case I give scandal.

'I suppose the children are bastards as well. Everything that went before is all written off.'

'There's nobody who could say one word against you, Stella,' he began.

'Except that my husband was really my fancy man, and I can't go to his funeral, myself and the four love children stay here while the wailing and the drinking and the praising and the caterwauling goes on in the west of Ireland, isn't that right?'

'It's not like that.'

'It is like that. And someone would say what a great man he was and how hard it is that emigration causes the break-up of families for so many people. . . . I'm not English, Father, I was born here but my parents were Irish, and know about funerals, I've heard them talk about them.'

'No one said life was fair,' he said. 'It's been very cruel to you this Christmas.'

'Tell them they can have him,' she said. She didn't come to the door, she wanted no Mass in Kilburn.

The brothers arranged with the under-taker and the body was taken to London Airport and flown to Shannon and driven up the west coast and two weeks before Christmas on a cold Sunday afternoon Patrick was buried in a churchyard a mile from the house where he was born.

SAVED BY THE WILES OF CUPID

14 February 1998

Of course their names are not Sean and Maire, but they *are* from the south-west of Ireland and they are out in Cape Town on a holiday.

And when they arrived at their hotel they were asked did they want to make a book-ing for St Valentine's Day. Special dinner.

'Ah, we'll sort that out later,' said Sean.

After all, it was January 24th — three full weeks before the saint's feast day. This was serious advance planning that was being called for.

'Touting for extra business, looking for a quick buck,' Sean said to Maire on that first night. 'That'll be it, believe me.'

And Maire said 'fine', and that's all she said.

The hotel didn't tout for business in any other way. It let them bring wine into their room, it pointed out a cheap laundromat, it let them make sandwiches out of the breakfast buffet.

But the following Saturday it asked them again, 'Made your plans for St Valentine's Day?' And Sean, who by this stage had got a suntan and was thinking in rands, not punts, thanked them politely but said there was no real rush.

And then they began to read the papers.

Page after page showed the restaurants that are completely booked up for February 14th. They watched the talk shows at night on television, heated debates . . . is it all too much this Valentine fuss, or is it wonderful and symbolic?

Does it mean that 364 days a year your loved one does *not* think about you, but that's OK if there's one day that the loved one *does* made a fuss?

The flower shops all over town have had huge warning notices up urging people not to leave it until the last minute. The South African phone service, Telekom, has huge ads showing empty flower buckets outside florists, and giving the grim reminder 'Phone First'.

Everything seemed to be referring to the day. Slimming machines were offered at 10 per cent off if you ordered them before The

Day. Building societies were offering 16 per cent Home Loans on any love nest where the paperwork was done in time for St Valentine. There were so many heart-shaped Valentine balloons, paper flowers, teddy bears, gold-wrapped chocolates, satin and sequinned offerings in the newsagent's that Sean and Maire could barely find a picture of Table Mountain to send to annoy the folks back home in the rain.

Saturday night would be their last night. Sean did not want to be wandering the streets of Cape Town, his nose pressed against windows where lovers or pretend-lovers were toasting each other in sparkling wine at £2 a bottle and them unable to get anywhere to sit down.

He booked.

'All right, yes, a Valentine special,' he said awkwardly. He had never sent a Valentine to Maire. Not in 39 years of marriage. It wasn't the way for them, or their kind. They were people who worked hard and got on with it.

Not fancy words and poems and flowers.

Irishmen of his class, his age, didn't go in for that sort of thing. That was for romantic-novelists, card manufacturers, flower sellers, confectioners, restaurant owners. They were the people who made the money out of it.

Didn't Maire *know* he was fond of her? They had been married nearly 40 years, raised a family. You don't have to say these things with lots of red and white decorations for them to become real, Sean believes. And had Maire ever sent him a Valentine's Day card, did he think?

Well, in the past when the children were at a silly age she might have thrown an old Valentine on the table and they all had a laugh and wondered who it might be from. . . .

And I asked Maire on her own would she have liked Valentines at all over the years, and she said she would of course — like any human. But Sean wasn't made that way and it would be like asking for people to do something completely against their nature. He was a good man to her. He'd give her money to buy one for herself if he thought she was fussing over it.

But oddly, for the first time he was looking around him out there where waitresses and shopkeepers and barbers and deck-chair attendants were all talking about the feast day. He had actually said to her that maybe sending a card was a cultural thing — like wearing shamrock on St Patrick's Day. So she wouldn't be surprised if the man she fell in love with in 1958 when Mick

Delahunty's band was playing might well buy her a card this year. It wouldn't continue at home, but it was different in the southern hemisphere.

And love is in the air all over the place, not only for the Feast Day. This week Nelson Mandela's handsome face smiles out of every paper as he clasps the hand of Graça Machel, widow of the Mozambican President. He has now spoken publicly of his love for her, how they talk every day on the telephone and how she has changed his life. Commentators on all sides seem to be full of indulgence and delight about it all, even though weddings have not actually been mentioned. Even Archbishop Desmond Tutu harrumphs only mildly about it and though he has to point out to the President about being a role model for young people, there has not as yet been any serious thundering from pulpits.

And then there's the other marvellous love story that's all over the papers. The tale of David and Caroline Dickie. He is 80, she is 70. They only met recently at a party in England and confided to each other that their children were plotting to put them into old people's homes against their wills. So they came out on a holiday to South Africa and got married.

According to the way it's told here, their children *still* don't know. David is English and used to work in Kenya. Caroline is originally Irish, a teacher, and used to work in Zambia. They both look radiant, barefoot on a sandy beach under a caption saying 'Saved By The Wedding Bells'.

They are going back to England to face the music today, and if I had the energy and the time I'd find them and go with them myself just to see the St Valentine's Day surprise a lot of people are going to get when they find out.

JUST DON'T ASK

14 March 1998

When we were young teachers a wise woman told us that we should never ask the children to tell the class what they did for Easter or Christmas or Confirmation or St Patrick's Day.

Don't ask, she said, because it will turn out that some of them did nothing at all or — worse still — had a really awful time. Nothing points up the inequality of people's lives more starkly than asking innocent children to tell you how they spent what was meant to be a festival.

But once I forgot this and asked them what they did for the National Day.

There was the usual chorus of visiting granny and going to watch the parade and having lunch in a hotel from the lucky ones.

And then there was a child who said they spent the whole day looking for a vet's that might be open because their dog had got hurted.

And I asked what had happened to hurt the dog.

Later you get a sense of what not to ask, but you don't have it when you're 22 and eager to be nice to the children and encourage them to tell stories.

It was a tale of a brother who had been away at sea coming home unexpectedly and his not liking the fact that Mammy's friend was living in the house and breaking a chair, and the dog got frightened and ran under the table whining.

And there had been a fight between the girl's brother and her Mammy's friend, and the dog hadn't understood so he jumped at the brother not realising who he was and to save himself her brother had picked up a bread knife and the dog was badly hurted.

And we all sat in that classroom as the horror of someone else's St Patrick's Day came through to us.

And I remember her voice going on about it not being too bad in the end because eventually she and her sister brought the dog to a hospital — a hospital for people — and someone there knew a vet nearby, so they carried the dog to his house and he stitched the cut in the shoulder and the dog would limp always on his front left paw and he had a bit of a cough but he was not going to die which they thought he might when they saw all the blood.

I wonder do any of the other pupils remember her telling that story? She is dead now, so I can tell it without hurting her.

She left school without any real education or exams, nothing much at home to encourage her, and she married when she was 19 — to a very nice fellow apparently, and they had a grand marriage until she died at the age of 38, some complications after a routine operation.

I'm sure that during the years of her happy marriage she didn't keep thinking back to that terrible St Patrick's Day in 1962 when she and her little sister carried a big dog covered in blood all around Dublin and eventually going to a hospital for people.

Maybe even the sadness and fright of the Domestic Incident had long died down in her mind.

Not in mine.

I think of it every St Patrick's Day when I see the Special Menus advertised in hotels, when I hear the oompah-oompah of a band. Not because I want to superimpose on everyone else's happiness the image of those two frightened little girls whose dog always coughed and walked with a limp as a result of the day's events.

I suppose it's just to remind us not to assume.

It certainly cemented the lesson that the wise old teacher had taught us, and now that I'm not in the classroom any more it hasn't lost its relevance. I strongly believe that you don't do thoughtless, cheerful vox pops to people about feast days.

In spite of the greeting cards, the streamers, the cheerleaders and the festivities, a startling number of people may have remarkably little to celebrate.

And all this came to mind because I met a glowing young girl with a tape recorder who was doing a series of ad-lib recordings in a shopping mall for a radio programme.

She thrust her microphone at passers-by and with a huge infectious grin she asked every one of them, 'What will *YOU* be doing on St Patrick's Day?' Her tone expected a reaction of riotous excitement, fun, happy families and carnival time.

In my earshot she met a man who would be going to see his wife up in the hospital as usual.

She met a woman who said she was going to stay in bed all day with the sheet up to her chin because she was demented with all the demands her children were making.

She met an elderly woman who said she wouldn't be doing much because she had been broken into and robbed.

In one way I wished the gorgeous girl with the microphone might realise that not everybody on this windy day was gearing up to a party-party spirit. That she was unearthing more despair than hope.

But then as a co-worker I was sort of sorry for her. I know what it's like when people won't say what you want them to, when they refuse to behave like a crowd sent down by Central Casting who are mouthing exactly what you want to hear.

But finally she met another gorgeous young girl like herself.

'I'm a *SINBAD,* I'll be cruising Temple Bar,' said the interviewee, which seemed to satisfy the girl with the microphone perfectly.

But not me.

'Excuse me,' I said, coming out of hiding from my lurking position. 'What's a *SINBAD*?'

Apparently it's a Single Income No Boyfriend, Absolutely Desperate.

But then everyone knew that, didn't they?

BLEACH SNIFFERS
ON MY DESK

18 April 1998

It had been a good day and when I saw a little ant run across my desk I thought to myself, in a rare fit of Buddhist kindness, that the poor little fellow hadn't much of a life, really. The desk must have seemed endless to him and he didn't know what awful dangers, such as myself, were lurking nearby. So I picked him up on a postcard and carried him out to the garden and put him in a big pot that contains a fuchsia. There, now he would have grand things to eat — old fuchsia leaves, earth grubs, much nicer than a dull old desk.

Feeling very proud of myself and full of virtue, I went back to work and discovered 12 more ants crawling up the screen of the word processor.

Suddenly we had a distinct change of policy.

No more mercy dashes to the potted fuchsia.

The ants were too many and too insistent and in the wrong place. I went for the Parozone and a J-cloth, and having nearly asphyxiated myself I looked at the surface to see had I dealt with them as quickly and efficiently as I believed.

The ants loved the Parozone. They reeled a bit at first — as we all might with a first, strong gin and tonic — but they obviously took to it greatly, and sent out a message for their friends to come and join them. The other ants heard somehow that the good times were rolling on my desk and they arrived eager to share the delicious taste of bleach.

The day looked a lot less good somehow and I withdrew a bit to consider my position. Now, I don't like them. We're not meant to like things with six legs and antennae. Nobody enjoys seeing things much smaller than us scuttling around the place, particularly around our place.

And it was actually a question of numbers. One ant was all right but this amount was not. And I had the feeling the ant which had been carried outside had long said farewell to the fuchsia leaves and had come back to join the bleach sniffers. And of course there's the huge guilt feeling: this must mean I have a filthy house. Why else were crawling insects marching towards it? Quite obviously it's a place that any infestation would love to settle in.

This was doubly distressing because I was expecting a colleague to arrive from London and we were going to be spending some six hours at this desk going through a manuscript page by page.

The thought of having to beat the ants off with a ruler before we could even read the thing was not something I wanted to contemplate. Nor did I fancy what might be reported about the standards of hygiene in modern Dalkey.

Sitting well back from the desk full of reeling, happy ants, I reached cautiously for the telephone to ring Éanna Ní Lamhna, of RTÉ's nature-programme fame, who would be the right person. She would know what was politically correct about ants without being foolishly sentimental and asking me to give them muesli for their breakfast or anything. But there was only her answering machine. In times of stress nowadays I have a big mug of tea and turn on the radio. So, having examined the mug very carefully for fear of drinking a dozen ants accidentally, I turned on RTÉ.

A huge ant discussion was taking place. I looked at the radio beadily for a bit. People are always imagining they hear voices on the radio talking to them: it's a fairly common paranoia apparently. But I listened very carefully and they really were talking about ants.

And wonderful, healing words came out of the little radio: 'It doesn't mean your house is dirty.' The man said it twice. I could have leaped into the radio and hugged him. Apparently it's just that people have patios near their houses more nowadays, and grouting between tiles. Yes, yes, I was saying, looking out at the roof garden with its tiles, all this is true. The ants are just looking for food, that's why they come indoors, the calming voice said. Yes, well. That's as may be. But you'd wonder why can't they eat the grouting and the things outside where nature intended them to be? This point was not properly dealt with, I felt.

Anyway, they moved on to a pest person, and the pest person said that there were indeed far more inquiries about ants at the moment, a lot of people had been inquiring. Anxious even.

Well, that makes you feel better. Up to a point. At least the house isn't dirty. It has been said on the radio, so it must be true. And there's somehow comfort in knowing that they've got into other people's places.

But not huge comfort.

Remember the Hitchcock film *The Birds*? It wasn't that much help to know that they were in everyone else's house pecking their eyes out, too.

There's always a really good, kind person on these programmes and he came on and said that ants were fantastic little creatures and hugely helpful in the ecosystem. They ate dead insects and they aerated the soil.

Yes, well. I looked at them marching up and down the screen of the laptop and forced myself to think well of them. Even if I could carry them all out, would I be able to motivate them to eat dead insects and aerate the soil?

The kind man was saying that possibly the best thing to do was to make sure they didn't get in in the first place and more or less ignore them if they did.

But then I thought of the six hours of work at this desk that lay ahead, and I took a magnifying glass and looked at an ant carefully and whipped myself up with hatred for their species. And I went out and bought ant-killer. The ant-killer was full of warnings. First it said, 'Use only as an insecticide,' which was a staggering instruction. What did they expect people to use it as? A deodorant? To ice a cake?

Then it said that you should wear rubber gloves and keep it miles from any electrical equipment and never let any of it get into the air, only on to skirting boards and window frames.

They'd obviously never come across an infested desk because there were further warnings about not putting it near furniture or matt surfaces. And that it would be detrimental to pond life and must be kept far, far from anywhere animals might feed.

And just at that point the two cats came in, knowing that all was not well, and that *The Little Book of Calm* was badly needed. And the moment I thought of them licking this murderously poisonous stuff and lying dead beside the ants, all eight paws rigid in the air, my decision was made. I carried the ant-killer to the garden shed and all the pages that had to be gone through downstairs to the dining-room table. At the moment, an ant-free zone.

Talking to Various Ships Passing in the Night

18 July 1998

It's a crime to be lonely. Nobody might ever have discovered, it could have gone on for years, this harmless little scheme of Nora going out to the airport two or three times a week.

She went there because she was lonely, because it's easy to talk to people at airports, there's an atmosphere of excitement and energy and people going to places, and coming home.

Much better anyway than sitting looking at the four walls of your house.

And it's not all just looking at the people going off to their different flights, you can browse in the bookshop there, have a snack, get your hair done even.

Sometimes she would get talking to families with children.

Nora liked that, she'd ask them where they were going and what they thought it was going to be like.

One little boy said he'd send her a postcard, but Nora didn't mind when he didn't. There was too much to do in Disneyland.

There's a kind of system about striking up

conversations, she says. Like there's no point at all trying to talk to anyone who has a mobile phone, they're only dying to use it to make a call or else waiting for it to ring.

People on their own with briefcases are not likely to want to chat. And anyone rooting in a bag looking for tickets or passport is a bad starter, they're too fussed to concentrate on a nice conversation with a stranger.

Nora has had some of her best chats with people going on package tours, especially bus tours. Women wearing badges with the name of the coach tour company were particularly approachable.

Some of them had never travelled abroad before and were a little anxious. Nora would reassure them and say that these companies were great, they looked after everyone and nobody would get lost.

She has patted down a lot of those who were nervous about a trip to Lourdes or a Five Capitals in Seven Days tour.

Nora, who has been abroad only rarely herself, is well able to head their anxieties off at the pass. Oh yes, the buses do stop several times and indeed everyone in these hotels speaks English and there's great shopping where they'll give you the price in pounds as well as in foreign currency.

She waves them off, feeling that in a way

they almost are friends.

No, they don't ask her too much about where she's going herself; it's odd that, but people aren't all that interested. She doesn't tell them packs of lies and make up mythical journeys. She doesn't need to.

If they do press her, she says she's just on a little hop across the water this time, and they let it go.

Nora is a mine of information for travellers. She's nearly as good as the personnel in uniform.

She can tell you which gate your flight leaves from, where the letter box is, the nearest ladies' cloakroom.

She often carries paper clips which are a good way of constructing a makeshift lock on a suitcase. Someone showed her once, and it was too good a hint not to pass on. It would delay a thief anyway and that's what matters, Nora would explain sagely — and people were always very grateful.

She often talked to Americans who had been here on a holiday and they told her about their trip. One of them had even given Nora an address in case she was ever in Seattle.

Then she might take the escalator down from Departures and go to sit in Arrivals for a while.

It's very easy to talk to people there, particularly when flights have been delayed. That's a great opportunity.

She got talking to a woman once who was waiting to meet a cousin from America. A very nice person, they had a lot in common, Nora said. The woman liked the same television programmes, and was about the same age. She didn't live far away either.

She would have been a fine friend. But Nora didn't like to push things.

It was so easy for people to reject you, keep you out of their lives. It was hurtful when it happened.

Nora didn't see any point in going out of her way to attract it. This woman had a life of her own, a cousin from America, plans for the summer.

The woman had asked who Nora was meeting and Nora had been vague.

Oh, the flight wasn't due until much later, she said, and somehow that covered it. No need to say who was coming or who wasn't.

The woman had said that she too was a compulsively early person. They really could have become friends.

But then she might have found out that Nora was a person who went out to Dublin Airport not to meet anyone but just for something to do, and once this was revealed she would be seen in a different light.

Odd is what people called it. Odd and sad. The people who knew.

And they were many now because two people had said casually to Nora's niece that they had seen her aunt at the airport. Her niece was always saying Auntie Nora should develop some hobbies, get out more, meet people.

The niece, a busybody of the highest order, had interrogated Nora.

Nora was never good at lying, she couldn't think up a story that would sound convincing. So she told the truth.

And now they are all frowning and tutting.

Her sister, who lives in the country, came up to see her and tried to persuade her to go to the doctor so that he could give her a little something for her nerves. She said there was no shame in it these days.

But Nora says there's nothing wrong with her nerves.

And her nephew, who is in social work, says he can get her accepted for one morning a week in a day centre. Even though, strictly speaking, she's too young, not quite 70. A lot of the people will be quite frail and in wheelchairs but still it would be company and something to look forward to.

Wouldn't it?

Her brother's wife, always one for the tart word, apparently said that Nora was lucky to have so much time on her hands. If she had raised a family and had to look after a man, a house, a brood of children, she wouldn't have these problems.

Nora would love to have had a man, a house and a brood of children, but things didn't work out that way.

The bossy niece said that surely she must have some friends, neighbours, people she knew?

And it's very hard to explain to the young and confident that other people have their own lives and they close their front doors on you when they go back to them.

And Nora has only her little flat, which sort of chokes her if she's in it too long on her own.

She wasn't complaining about being lonely, she says. Nora never mentioned it to anyone really.

It was a thing people didn't understand, it seemed that you must be some horrible person if you didn't get on like a house on fire with your neighbours and have 100 people you used to know at work rushing in and out of your house.

It's as if everyone is afraid of lonely

people, if they reach out to the lonely who knows where it would end?

So she didn't tell anyone, she just went to a busy, exciting place and talked to a variety of ships that were passing in the night. That's how she saw it.

Not doing anyone any harm, filling her days nicely.

But now it seems this is odd and sad, normal people don't do things like that.

From now on Nora must be watched. Carefully.

SWEET DREAMS

25 July 1998

There's this good-tempered man called John, whose boss insulted him deeply at the end of May. His boss said, quite casually and without malice, that poor old John was way beyond being computer literate and though not exactly a dinosaur in the quill-pen league couldn't be expected to know a spreadsheet from a search engine.

John has August off and he has plans. He is a 51-year-old married man with two children. Normally they take a house by the seaside but the children were getting bored with it, so this year they are not packing the buckets and spades. His wife is going to take in three foreign students for the month. His sons, mollified by the fact that there are going to be drop-dead gorgeous Mediterranean girls, are going to hang around and help them integrate.

John is going to do an intensive, four-week computer course. It will cost exactly the same as renting the holiday home. John will eat less, drink less, spend far less than if he were in a resort. Ahead of him lies that glorious day in the first week in September when he will be so much on top of things that the man who called him Poor Old John will wilt in his soft Gucci shoes and be henceforth riddled with great self-doubt about his powers of judgment. It's a vision that will sustain John throughout concentrated hours of taskbars, title bars and toolbars instead of the kind of bars he was normally used to in August.

It will be the most satisfying summer ever.

Maria is 26 and this summer she is going to spend her summer holiday finding a husband. She knows how it's done. You just turn up looking well where there are loads of fellows. Not in a pub when they're all drunk. Not in a disco or a club when it would be dead easy to get a fellow for the night but not at all easy to get a husband. It had to be planned scientifically.

You don't want to waste time on tourists, visitors, handsome fellows passing through looking for one-night stands. You go where there will be a glut of marriageable men. She has studied lists of conferences, golf classics, race meetings, yachting events. She knows where they will be and she will be there. With a cover story.

She is here on a short vacation with her mother and she has come to the hotel. Mother will be distracted elsewhere with friends but will be constantly expected on the scene. This way Maria doesn't look like she's there to pick people up. She won't be taken for a Working Girl cruising the provincial hotels sending out wrong, if exciting, signals to professional men in their late thirties. Her quarry.

Her mother will turn up full of apologies later on in the evening when friendships have been made but before they can be expected to be cemented in bed or anything.

But could this possibly work and why would her mother go along with it? Maria shrugs. How else do you think her mother ever found Maria's father all those years ago? And it was much harder back in the 1960s than it is nowadays.

■ ■ ■ ■

Ronnie, who is 12, got third prize in a local photography competition. The prize was a book token for £10. But more important, he got a certificate and he has had this certificate laminated and wears it around his neck on a cord.

He lives near a well-known beauty spot in an area very much visited by tourists. Ronnie noticed that people coming to see the sights always wanted their whole family to be included in the shot. They would offer strangers their camera with detailed and complicated instructions of what to press.

How much better to have a semi-professional like himself involved. He stands nearby, hovering silently, ready for the opportunity.

'I'm in the business of photography myself,' he will say to a group as if they had actually asked a 12-year-old boy his line of work. He will indicate the certificate hanging around his neck like a press pass as proof of his great skills.

People usually nod gravely at this, there's not much else they can do.

'So if you'd like me to include you all in a snap I know the best place for you to stand

and I charge £1 per session.'

He will produce for inspection a pound coin of his own in case any of them might be confused about the currency. They normally enquire about the nature and extent of a session. Ronnie says that it would include up to half a dozen shots with any of the cameras of the group in question. Much more often than not, they agree. They admire his enterprise, his sheer gall.

And it is a help to have someone who doesn't keep bleating about what should they look through and what should they press.

He has been watched beadily since mid-June by a woman who runs a nearby craft shop. She still can't make up her mind about Ronnie. He's certainly putting in the hours and making the most of his summer. It's just that with no overheads at all, he can take in £50 on a good day. That's rather a lot for a 12-year-old boy, she thinks. In fact, it's astronomical.

But she has no proof that he'll spend it foolishly or that earning this fortune in a wet summer will somehow lead him into organised crime, so she still can't blow the whistle on him.

And what about myself, off on sort-of

holidays until the start of September —
what will I do? I know what I think I'll do,
of course, walk my legs off, read the 36
books listed in a spiral-bound notebook,
master the internet, deal with all the letters
in the in-basket, learn to cook with yeast,
visit at least six parts of Ireland I've never
been to, identify and plant a yellow flower
that has been driving me mad in other
peoples' gardens for years, write postcards
of praise to people I admire, teach the cats
some kind of trick, any trick, so that people
will think they are brighter than they are,
label the videos, learn to park in something
smaller than a football pitch.

But then maybe I won't do any of those
things.

The whole essence of anyone's summer
holiday is that it is always based on some
kind of dream.

STAVING OFF THE
SENIOR MOMENTS

17 October 1998

There was a time when I used to give
advice, serious advice, on travel pages,
about what to take with you on a trip. I
never took any notice of the advice myself
in those days, since as long as you had the

bottle of gin, the 200 ciggies and the portable typewriter everything else was only icing on the cake.

I used to look with scorn at all the people in airports fussing about their matching luggage, their eyes scanning the carousel in case one piece had gone missing. I was always half hoping mine would go missing and I might get the compensation. It did once, in New York, and instead of buying a nightdress and a change of underwear I bought a desperately expensive bubble bath and a bottle of champagne and even now, 35 years later, I remember it all with pure pleasure.

No such freedoms these days. If I should lose the case that has all my work in it, I may as well give up on the future.

If I lost the case with the garments, it would be serious. Being a large person, I can't easily get things in shops that will fit me. I have to speak at various functions and they might not take too well to my wearing the same outfit for six weeks. So I have joined the ranks of those who look anxiously until the two brightly coloured, glaring suitcases come out of the innards of a plane.

Tomorrow night I will be unpacking them in a hotel that looks out on the Pacific Ocean.

In the old days I used to pack in 10 minutes. The old days are gone. I'm ashamed to say it has taken a week to pack.

I got a clipboard — not just a piece of paper but a serious clipboard — and I listed all the items. I felt somehow powerful and in control as I wrote down things such as: Sellotape; torch; Velcro rollers; corkscrew; good black dress.

There was a time when I used to think only the insane would make lists like this, but alas I have travelled to too many places and found myself disappointed with the contents of the two glaring cases when I arrived. Like the time I took six pairs of shoes, six T-shirts and no skirts whatsoever to South Africa.

So I realised it was time for the clipboard. It's not that anyone is getting old or forgetful or anything. Lord, no. What people like myself have nowadays is what the Americans call a 'senior moment'. It's a wonderful phrase and one I have taken up enthusiastically. It takes the whole harm out of being bewildered.

Tomorrow night, when I am unpacking the glaring suitcases in a faraway place, I don't want any surprises. But if it were only a matter of what you took with you for six weeks it would be reasonable enough; sadly, it's also a matter of what you leave behind you.

There will be other people staying in the house here while we are gone, so it's not a matter of ramming awful things into a cupboard and saying that it can all be dealt with in December. It means a visit to the dump, which always frightens me because I assume everyone there is getting rid of dismembered bodies and that they think I am doing the same. And a visit in what might, hopefully, be off-peak hour to the bottle bank and the paper bank — rain forests of newspapers and magazines unread going back to be pulped somewhere. And taking out all the things from the press where the table napkins are, in case I might have hidden some cheese there to stop me eating it.

And one of the things I love to do, in what a psychiatrist friend calls my pathetically over-documented life, is stick my snaps in an album. I don't feel right until I'm up to date with this. So it involves getting out all the pictures since summer, and oohing and aahing over a trip to the Isle of Man, and to Schull, and to the Merriman Summer School, and to get an honorary degree in Queen's, and to visit Dickson's Nurseries in Newtownards, and a party in London, and a magical day at the National Ploughing Championships which I think I enjoyed more than anything else this year.

Sorting out all that takes time.

And there are the letters to write which I will not take with me and carry around the world as I have done so often: instead, I will stay up late and write them before I go.

And I won't worry that the cats will miss us because cats have their own agenda and they will think whoever is here is us really, just as long as the bowl of food is put out and someone tells them they are wonderful.

And it doesn't really matter that we will be in some places where it is snowing and others where the sun will be splitting the stones.

And as usual, Gordon is calm and has his own clipboard to humour me and tries to head off too many 'senior moments' by reminding me to take my laptop computer, which I nearly forgot.

I read once in an etiquette book that if you are about to travel, you should take out an advertisement in a quality paper and tell society of your plans. So in a way, that's what I am doing.

■ ■ ■ ■

2000s

■ ■ ■ ■

MR GAGEBY . . .

3 July 2004
There is a dangerous tendency of thinking your own time was the best, and there were no days like your days. Journalists fall into this trap more easily than anyone else.

It's as if we want people to know what stirring times we lived through, what dramas our newsroom saw and what near-misses we had, and what amazing never-to-be-equalled camaraderie we all shared.

All over Ireland this week there will be people telling such tales of Douglas Gageby's time.

And even as I write his name I feel forward.

I never called him anything except Mr Gageby.

I met him when I was a 27-year-old schoolteacher in Dublin, sharing a dream with half the country that maybe I could write if someone would let me.

Even when I nearly caught up with him in age and we were friends, when he asked me to call him Douglas, I could never do it. He was too important.

At the job interview where he asked what I would do if I were to run the Woman's Page, I suggested that we relegate Fashion to one day, Cookery to another, and then get on with what people would be interested in on the other four days.

He asked mildly what I thought people might be interested in, and I blinded him with my views.

'Of course, she's never worked a day in her life in a newspaper,' he said to Donal Foley, the news editor.

'She has to learn somewhere,' Donal said, and Mr Gageby nodded and said that was fair enough.

So who wouldn't love someone who took such a mad risk?

My memory of those days was that he seemed to be forever in his office.

Day and night.

That wasn't possible because we knew he had a great family life, he often talked about his children, and he always talked about his wife, Dorothy.

He was invited everywhere, but he was never a great one for going to receptions or dinners, except the Military History Society of Ireland which he was very keen on.

He was handsome, he was confident at work, he was happy in his home life, he was courageous and he was dragging the paper into modern times.

No wonder so many of us were mad about him.

He had, of course, a short fuse.

There is nobody who doesn't have a Mr Gageby experience of some kind. Like when he would bellow his annoyance at something that appeared in Yesterday's paper.

There was never such a thing as Today's paper, there was the one we had written Yesterday which, according to him, was full of faults and mistakes and unbelievable oversights, or Tomorrow's, which was going to be spectacular and we would stick everyone else to the ground with our stories, insights and backgrounds.

I have seen Mr Gageby incandescent with rage about a sports writer who said that a match was a nip-and-tuck affair and gave no further detail, and a financial journalist who said the AGM of some company was predictable, but hadn't explained what had been predicted.

He has been white-faced over someone who missed the one big row that week in the Senate, or called the ceremony that happens in England the Trooping OF the Colour when there should be no OF in it, apparently. And somebody invariably got it wrong, and somebody else invariably let it past.

I have been at the receiving end when the Woman's Page had a series of apologies in it.

We regret that when we said 11 1/2 pounds of split peas, we actually meant 1 to 1 1/2 pounds of split peas.

We regret that when we said this dress in Richard Alan's cost £20, we actually meant it cost £200.

We regret we have given the wrong number of the Gay Switchboard, the wrong score in the All-Ireland.

His eyes were narrow. I wondered how I had ever thought he was handsome.

'Your page is a laughing stock,' he said. 'With the possible exception of the *Straits Times* in Malaysia, I have never seen a worse Features page.'

My face was scarlet for 48 hours. I contemplated emigrating.

Next week it was forgotten and we could breathe again.

But, by God, how he stood up for us, all of us.

He never gossiped about one to another, and he fought our enemies and people who said we were less than great.

He said that we reported what we saw.

Even when his back was against the wall over what we had reported or misreported.

We knew we would not be sold down the river.

And I know he had hard times in Stephen's Green clubs when some of us were a bit light-hearted about the British royal family.

And though I lived my whole life slightly in awe of him, it was not of his doing. He was warm and friendly and interested in the lives of all his workforce.

When I took all my courage in hand and invited him to lunch with us, he said he would come if we had one course, and that he really liked sardines with lemon juice. He may, of course, have been protecting himself and Dorothy against botulism, since they knew only too well some of my limitations through the cookery page and my misunderstandings of presenting food.

If you were going to lunch with someone who had used a picture of open-heart surgery to illustrate veal casseroles, perhaps you, too, might have asked for sardines.

But we lunched happily summer after

summer, alternately in their house and ours.

And it was wonderful to be in the presence of a couple who loved each other and never felt they had to hide this from anyone else.

I would have liked them to live forever as part of all of our lives.

But they didn't, and I hope their family will always know how many of us got a great and exciting start in our writing lives under his editorship.

And how proud we were to be part of the time when he took our newspaper out of the shadows and into the light.

Every time I think of Mr Gageby, I straighten myself up a little and hope to try and do him some kind of credit somewhere along the line.

ANOTHER WORLD FOR THE PRICE OF A CUP OF COFFEE

30 October 2004
You would get the smell half a street away, coffee like it never smelled at home. And the fresh-from-the-oven cakes and buns, six of them on a plate ready and waiting for you on the table.

Long before the days of self-service, the waitresses would come and serve you,

540

always with a few words about the world we lived in. Like the rain maybe, or the sales, or Peggy Dell playing the piano in a furniture shop across the road, or the marriage of Princess Grace, or the hardy souls who swam all the year round in our cold seas.

And then they would leave you to your own chat, going off to talk on other topics at other tables.

Bewley's was filled with characters and we would talk about them for a bit before settling down to our own chat. There used to be a woman with a handsome, ravaged face and wild and curly hair, wearing a matted fur coat with not much underneath it. There was a rumour that she was a wealthy person and that someone had left Bewley's a sum of money to make sure she was fed every day, which she always was, with great kindness and charm.

There was an old man whose coat was tied with a rope, who always complained that the tea was cold. The thin, slightly stooped waitress would feel the side of the teapot and assure him that it would roast the hand off you, so then he would grudgingly drink it.

There were men with sheaves of papers covered in figures, adding and subtracting; there were well-known poets and writers and actors. Real celebrities were there, such as Maureen Potter at one table or Eamonn Andrews at another, and everyone would just nod at them, delighted to be sharing the same aromatic air — but we would never go up and disturb them.

When I was a student we could make one cup of coffee last an hour and a half and, like everyone else, we felt a slight guilt in case this sowed the seeds of the eventual decline of Bewley's fortunes. But we had to make it last because nobody wanted to leave the warm, happy coffee and sugar-flavoured fug and go out into the cold, rain-filled streets. And nobody had the price of another cup of coffee.

I look back on hours and hours of conversation then, about communism, about how to starch petticoats, about who would be on the committee of the L & H debating society. And about how, when we were old and rich, we would come back from overseas and buy a whole plate of cakes and have three coffees each. It was the 1950s then, and we all assumed we would have to go away to get a job, and a lot of us did.

Then, when I was a young teacher, I would bring the pupils' exercise books and correct them in Bewley's. History essay after history essay, more coffee, more cigarettes to keep me going, and the waitresses would be most sympathetic.

'You lot earn your money,' one of them said to me. I thought she earned hers much harder, clearing up marble table after marble table of slopped coffee and crumbs, but there was never a complaint.

Sometimes, when I didn't even have time to go in, I would stand and watch the windows and wallow in the smell. The amazing sight of beans jumping, being ground just for our pleasure — it was very heady. And then we all bought our first coffee-makers there and were surprised that it didn't taste quite as good at home.

When I joined *The Irish Times* there was Bewley's right opposite us at a time when it was slightly easier to cross the road than it is now. And there were many long discussions there too. Things that were too private to be discussed in the Pearl bar or in Bowes but which needed the solidarity of the marble table and the almond bun.

Like what? I don't know. Love, hope, disappointment, press freedom, whether we had better coverage of something than the other papers, elections, sports, and what readers really wanted and whether or not we should try to give it to them.

In those days the budget extended to more

than one promised cup of coffee. But when the bill was being totted up the waitress would ask, 'How many almond buns?'

The number would be admitted.

'And did you have butter with them?' she would inquire, in the kindly but firm way that a priest might have asked you, 'did you take pleasure in it?' a long time ago.

Oh yes, we always had butter with the almond buns. Like we always loved going in to sink down and forget the outside world in Bewley's, and like we sang carols outside it for many Christmases, and like we always felt safe there and at home.

It was all things to all people and we are allowed to be sentimental and sad that a little bit of everybody's past has gone and that we can't conjure it up any more just for the price of a cup of coffee.

'ONE UP FOR THE CARDIGANS'

12 February 2005

The news programme announces the engagement in the little minimarket where people are doing their morning shopping. The younger people ignore it, as they continue to root around looking for extra complimentary CDs among the magazines or to lick bits of frozen yoghurt from the outside of the cartons. . . .

The older people are more interested.

'That will be a relief to Her Majesty,' says the woman with a basket full of lentils for herself and choice cuts for her cat. 'Her poor Majesty was exhausted trying to turn the other way; now it will all be above board.'

'A lot of bloody nonsense,' says the man in the cloth cap with the north of England accent, who buys tins of pilchards and oven chips and nothing else. 'Pair of them were perfectly all right living over the brush like half the country; he's only marrying her because they're asking questions about how much of our money he spends on her anyway.'

And the large, comfortable woman who sits like a wise old bird at the checkout is very pleased.

'It's one up for the cardigans,' she says. 'I knew the day would come when a woman as shabby as myself would marry a prince.'

I lived here in these London streets in 1981 when Charles was getting married for the first time, and the atmosphere was electric. The playboy prince was going to settle down, and he had found a nice virgin girl to marry. Yet, at his engagement press conference, when asked was he in love, he had said rather ominously, 'Yes, whatever that means.'

But the country had gone mad with an innocent pleasure. It was July 1981, and there was a huge fireworks display in Hyde Park the night before the wedding. There were street parties, and I was almost afraid to tell people I was talking to on the tube to St Paul's that I had an invitation to the do in my handbag. They might have killed for it. And I say 'the people that I talked to' because for a day or two London forgot its introversion and everyone spoke to everyone else. It was like the day the Pope had come to Dublin two years previously.

It was something that was of its time and will never happen in the same way again. There's no excitement about Charles and Camilla in the streets of west London this time around. No spontaneous flags and bunting, no lump in the throat empathising with the happy event.

The past 24 years have seen too much murky water flow under too many bridges. The little virgin bride shed all her shyness and puppy fat and became one of the world's most beautiful women, and Charles, who had never loved her remotely, behaved as badly as any pantomime villain. The disastrous royal marriage was lived out in public, with other parties briefing the media about the rights and wrongs of the situation. The couple's two little boys struggled on, surrounded by butlers, nannies and nonspeaking relatives.

Princess Diana, who at one stage held all the cards because she was *nice* to people and full of charm, lost out in the end in every possible way. Charles, who became more arrogant and mutinous with every passing year, made little attempt to hide his relationship and now seems, oddly, to have won. It looks now as if he is being rewarded: he is getting the marriage he should have had 35 years ago when Camilla was certainly up for it but when he dithered and couldn't make a decision.

It's not a love story that immediately sets the bells ringing or promises to get to the heart of the nation. But never underestimate the power of the media. About 20 minutes after the usual messed-up announcement from Clarence House, a statement that left so many questions unanswered and showed a complete lack of planning and preparation, all the television channels had wheeled in the ageing royal-watchers. They were brought out of mothballs and dusted down and wound up to go. I know what I'm talking about; I was one of them.

■ ■ ■ ■

Queen Elizabeth II has four children. I was at three of their weddings and I didn't bring any of them much luck. Only Prince Edward's first marriage has survived, and Princess Anne's second marriage.

I am sure Charles and Camilla, who have had each other out on approval for some time, will make a go of it. And truly, most people of goodwill will wish them happiness, as you would to anyone who has had a troubled journey in romance.

But it's such a different scene this time around. I wonder whether Charles, in his very narrow world, knows this. It's hard for any of us to know what other people think and how they live and what their values are. But it must be harder for the Prince of Wales, surrounded as he is by sycophants and by people who grew up in the same strange enclosed world as himself, where journalists are called 'reptiles' and where there are the People Who Matter and then the rest of the world, which doesn't matter a bit. He must think he is a scream, because I have seen the awful, fawning, servile press, really worse than reptiles, laughing hysterically if he makes a stupid joke. Why would he *not* think that his forthcoming wedding should be on the same scale as the last one? He has no loving family to lean on.

His parents never went to visit him when he was at that terrible school, Gordonstoun. Do you know anyone who was *never* visited at boarding school by their parents? He was completely out of touch with the life his first bride wanted to live, and there was nobody to advise him, except in the ways of protocol, history and tradition, which could be summed up as 'wives must learn'. He was singularly unlucky in that his wife never did.

His polo-playing friends told him that Diana was a loony tune and that his best bet was to invite Camilla to their house parties. Then, somewhere along the line, somebody taped his intimate conversation with Camilla years ago and broadcast it to the world. That was the only day I felt really sorry for Charles. I could have wept for his sheer embarrassment as I saw him on television straightening his cuffs and going to see his mother, who was after all the queen of the country that was rocking to his bizarre sexual fantasies. Strange as they were, they *were* his and Camilla's own business.

So the man who will presumably one day be king may not have a clue how his future subjects think of him and his wedding.

For a start, most of the broadcasts and breaking news and interviews focused on the issue of what poor Camilla would be called. She would not *dare* to call herself Princess of Wales, would she? She couldn't ever be queen, could she? And eventually, two hours later, Charles's expensive spin doctors and PR people issued a statement defining what the woman would or would not be called.

Then there were hours of debate about whether a civil ceremony would be a proper marriage for a head of the Church, or whether a church wedding would be worse. Then they debated whether Charles was only marrying Camilla now because the House of Commons Public Accounts Committee might uncover something too damaging about what he had spent on the lady. Or because the results of the second inquest into Princess Diana's death were to be published, possibly throwing up even more bad publicity about the royal family. Or because the Archbishop of Canterbury said that they should regularise their situation.

And as if all this wasn't bad enough for a couple planning their wedding, it was said that the Labour party was incandescent with rage because Charles and Camilla's plans were messing up the timing of the next election.

I am basically a big custard heart. I don't know these people at all. I've watched them for three decades, notebook in hand, but I don't know them or know anybody who knows them. But I am interested in their love story. I think Charles is arrogant and selfish, but the roots of that lie in his upbringing. I think Camilla is basically a decent and horsey cardigan who loves Charles and is prepared to go through all this (like she has gone through so much already) from the sheer accident of falling in love with him. And really, I don't think she cares *what* she is called. She isn't even trying to be 'queen of hearts', and it must be painful and hurtful when she is compared to her beautiful, warm, but deeply unhappy predecessor.

The young have no interest in the affairs and doings of such elderly people. The Diana activists may feel that somehow Camilla triumphed in the end, and perhaps they will dislike her for that. I can't be the only person in the world who doesn't think hereditary monarchy is a good idea but who still does genuinely wish these two confused middle-aged people a great wedding day and a good time together.

My Part in the Movies

17 September 2005

They say that handing over your story to film-makers is like sending your first child to school. The book, like the child, still belongs to you in a sort of a way, but it's not the same way. Now there's a different life, with a lot of other people involved. But a child can't stay at home forever, and a book is better when it gets a further life, so I am always delighted when someone thinks that one of my stories is good enough to make into a movie.

I know, of course, that not everything will fit in. *Tara Road* is a long story, with many characters, so some have to go if we are to make sense of it in an hour and a half of cinema. I don't write the scripts myself; I have tried, but I'm not good at it. I prefer to tell a story in big, swooping terms, pausing to tell you what someone's thinking about, worrying over, hoping for. You can't do that in a screenplay. It's very brief, with lots of short sentences and plenty of white space on the page. That's not my scene at all.

You have to suggest things in a screenplay, so the director and actors can take it up and make sense of it. I find it much easier to tell things. So I have great respect for those who can write a script and then for the others who can turn a short screenplay, of about 100 pages, into a whole film.

The author has no say in casting, finding locations or choosing music. So you wait with an eager face to see what they will do. It's as much a surprise for the writer as it is for the audience.

Sometimes people have very unhappy times watching their beloved book transfer to the movies, but I enjoyed it all so much and had such good times on the set that I thought I would share it with you.

I have been lucky before. I enjoyed so much the filming of *Circle of Friends,* with Minnie Driver and Chris O'Donnell, the television version of *Echoes,* with Geraldine James, and the TV movie of *The Lilac Bus.* But *Tara Road* has long been one of my favourite stories. It's about two women who exchange homes and, in doing so, find more than a place to spend two months and lick their wounds: they discover redemption.

Many years ago we exchanged our London property for a house in Sydney, and it was a great experience. *Tara Road* is not our story, because nothing would be duller than reading about two happily married, settled couples, which is what we and they were. Still, it was fascinating living in their home, knowing their secrets and realising that they knew ours. They had no corkscrew; we had no cereal bowls. By the time I left their house, with its wonderful bottlebrush trees and exotic birds on the garden fence, I felt I knew them more than I knew neighbours of 20 years at home. And so I wrote the story.

I can't remember what I thought my characters Ria and Marilyn looked like, because all I can see are the beautiful, strong, sensitive faces of Olivia Williams and Andie MacDowell registering hope and grief and triumph when it is called for. I don't think I ever saw in my mind's eye all the other characters, either. I just had a feeling for them, and now they are brought to life for me: the strong-willed Mona, played by Brenda Fricker; the elegant and faithless Rosemary, played by Maria Doyle Kennedy; the sexy, feckless Danny, played by Iain Glen; the handsome Stephen Rea, playing Colm, the restaurant owner; and the children, who behave just like Ria's children would have behaved. I will never see any of them in any other way.

As for the house, I had a road in mind in Dublin for which I made up the name Tara Road. The film company asked where I was thinking of, and I told them. It wouldn't work, they said, as it was much too narrow. They would hold up traffic with their huge generators and all the crew. So the location people went out and found another house to film it in, which is perfect. It's almost as if it had been built for it, exactly the kind of road I had in mind, with those big, high-ceilinged rooms where Ria had been once so happy, then so lonely; where Marilyn tried to look for peace and found half of Dublin passing through to interrupt her.

So I approached the filming with great optimism. I have always known that film-makers hate the author around the place. They always fear that he or she is going to say that it wasn't at all like that. We are looked at with fear and mistrust. Yet it isn't human to expect us to stay away, especially when it's being filmed down the road. So I asked politely if my husband, Gordon, and I could come along and watch. Quietly. I stressed the word.

And that's what we did. We peeped in at the huge Tara Road house, the apartment where Bernadette lived; we watched astounded while our marvellous local fish-monger's was changed into a US delicatessen over a bank holiday weekend. We were very polite to Gillies MacKinnon, the director, and to his camera and sound people; we admired all the actors and told them they were just the part.

Eventually they realised we were just ageing groupies, loving everything and therefore no trouble. And they sensed that Gordon and I were dying for little walk-on parts. So it was arranged that we were going to play Martini drinkers in Colm's restaurant.

I wish I could tell you how excited we were. We went to bed early the night before, because the limo came for us at seven a.m. Then we went to make-up. We didn't have to go to costume, because they asked us to wear anything of our own that was not black or navy. For some reason now forgotten, I wore lilac. Then it was time for our scene. We would be sitting on high chairs at the bar in Colm's restaurant. Stephen Rea was to serve us with two triangular Martini glasses, each with an olive in it. We were to say nothing aloud but to mouth thank-you words at him.

Just before they said 'Lights, camera, action' I said to Gordon that I could murder this Martini. I felt we had been up for hours. He said he wouldn't hold his breath about its being a real Martini, but I am an eternal optimist. I said we should look at the way there was condensation on the glass; they wouldn't have gone to all that trouble to chill a glass of water.

'It's twenty past nine in the morning,' Gordon said.

He was right. It was water.

I ate the olive resentfully. Each time during the three takes. Then the camera moves inexplicably from us to the stars. But we are there. You wouldn't want to blink or look down to choose a sweet or anything, or you would miss us, but we are part of it.

In the last cut I saw of the film we are still there, sipping delicately, mouthing our thanks and, in my case, wondering why on earth I wore lilac, which is the most enlarging colour in the spectrum.

It's a terrific, moving and touching film. We have all had losses in our lives, we have all loved foolishly and been lonely. The film tells very clearly, as the book tried to do, that the solution is in our own hands, that we have to make ourselves better. There is no cavalry waiting on a cliff to rescue us. We have to do it for ourselves.

Marilyn and Ria do that on the screen as much as they did in the book, played by two wonderful actors who, with the rest of my cast, told this story as well as I could have hoped and better. I was lonely when the film crew packed up and went away, as they do. But at least we have the book, and the movie is out there to be seen as well.

STRIKING A POSE
FOR MY COUNTRY

25 October 2005
When the National Gallery of Ireland first suggested it, I had the very real fear that it might be some terrible practical joke. That it could be a *Candid Camera* style television programme watching people making fools of themselves by accepting huge honours like that and then having to bluster their way out of it.

But they seemed serious. So I was utterly delighted and waited for the artist to arrive.

She was Maeve McCarthy and had been at the same school as I had, though admittedly a quarter of a century later. We talked animatedly about loved figures and less-than-loved figures in the place, and had a great bond.

I had looked her up and seen how successful she was, as well as all the competitions she had won. She had painted a self-portrait which everyone had said was very good, but in real life she was good-looking, and the self-portrait had made her look a lot less attractive than she was. If she's so tough on herself, I thought, what is she going to do to a subject? And I sort of hinted that.

But she explained that there were various conventions about a self-portrait, which I thought was all very well in theory but going to be a bit tough on me if she was into too much gritty realism. Still, we were into it now.

She told me the bad news was that she couldn't paint from photographs, but the good news was that I didn't have to sit still. I could move about and talk and drink mugs of tea and everything.

So I was busy then trying to look for nice bits of our house to be painted in — near the one good piece of furniture maybe, with some tasteful glass arranged on it?

She said she would like to prowl about the place looking for a setting and could I just get on with my life so that she could observe me?

So I chose a day when Gordon would be out and I got on with life, trying to ignore her. For a whole morning I yacked away on the phone, typed with my four-finger typing, looked things up in the dictionary, stroked the cat who had settled in the 'Action This Day' basket, and had a script conference about a project with Jean Pasley where McCarthy was most helpful and came up with some good ideas.

After a day of prowling she had chosen the location. It was to be upstairs in our study where you can see Dalkey Castle in the background over the roof. And she wanted Gordon to sit in on the roof terrace — sort of out of sight but with his legs in the picture. His legs? Yes, just his presence around the place apparently, and he would be reading *The Irish Times.* What? Product placement? No, you would only get a hint that it was *The Irish Times.* Right. Right.

So we had the first sitting; there was some discussion about the colour I would wear, and eventually I settled on blue. Maeve McCarthy set up her easel and I sat down nervously and waited for it to begin.

We talked about everything under the sun — life, death, hopes, disappointments, friends, family, travel. And then the sitting was over.

I had heard you must not look at your own portrait until it is finished. But she shrugged. Of course I could look at it, she said.

Interestingly, there was no face.

Lots of Dalkey Castle, and the roof, and the desk I was sitting at, and big, blue shoulders, but no face.

I managed to say nothing. After the fourth sitting, when there was still no face — only pixelation like they put in a newspaper to hide the face of the Accused or the Suspect — I thought I would mention it.

'Oh I won't do your face,' she said, at which I felt dizzy and wondered had I entirely misunderstood the whole thing.

'Not until much later,' she added to my relief, and the blood returned slowly to my veins.

After the sixth sitting, still no face as such. She asked me if I liked the picture. We were such friends now, I had to be honest. 'I spend over €20 each time you come getting my hair done and it doesn't really show. I wonder does the hair look a bit flattened in the portrait?' I said nervously.

'You're very lucky you didn't have Gwen John painting you — she made subjects put Vaseline all over their heads so that she could see the shape of the skull,' Maeve McCarthy said unsympathetically.

And then the pixelation went and I saw my face, and the lovely picture of our cats, and a picture of our friends on the wall, and a mug of tea with Nighthawks on it. And best of all the reassuring presence of Gordon outside the window, reading a paper, which could be *The Irish Times*. And then it was all over.

Maeve McCarthy packed up her easel and her brushes and her little jars of whatever it was and left.

And I missed her like mad.

She made it all very painless, she was great company and I am as pleased as anything that it was done.

It is a huge honour to be chosen by the national gallery of your own land to hang in its halls, and to be lent a talented portrait painter for a summer of friendship and insights.

I will of course be hovering a lot about the gallery for some time pretending I have come to see something else, or that I am taking some overseas visitors for a tour. But really I will be there to make sure they don't take it down.

TEN THINGS YOU MUST NEVER SAY TO ANYONE WITH ARTHRITIS

30 January 2009

1. 'Cheer up, nobody ever died of arthritis.' This statement is, oddly, not cheering at all. We have dark,

broody feelings that if people did die of arthritis there might have been huge, well-funded research projects over the last few decades, which could have come up with a cure.

2. 'It's just a sign of old age, it will come to us all.' No, it's not a sign of old age. Even toddlers can get arthritis, and some old people never get a twinge of it. The very worst phrase you can use is 'Haven't you had a good innings?'

3. Remember that marvellous radio series about disabilities called *Does He Take Sugar?* The message of that title means you should never ask, in the hearing of someone with arthritis, 'Do you think she'll be able to manage the stairs?' Arthritis can make us many things, but it certainly doesn't make us deaf.

4. Avoid mentioning magic cures, as anyone with arthritis will already have heard of vinegars, honey, mussels, berry teas, and so on. We will probably have tried them too. It is

dispiriting to be told of someone else who was once bent double but now climbs mountains before breakfast.

5. Don't ever say, 'That walking stick is very ageing — I wouldn't use it if I were you.' Did you think we thought of the stick as a fashion accessory? Of course we know it's hardly rejuvenating to be seen bent over a stick, but when the alternative is a knee or a hip that could let us down, or pitch us into the traffic, then the stick is a great help. It is sad when people give us the impression that it makes us look 100 years old. At least we are getting out there, and that should be praised and encouraged.

6. Never let the phrase 'a touch of arthritis' pass your lips. You don't say someone has a touch of diabetes or a touch of asthma. It is denying sympathy and concern for people who have a painful and ever-present condition to minimise it to just 'a touch'.

7. Don't suggest a healthy walk to blow away the cobwebs. People whose joints are unreliable don't want to get further proof of this when they are halfway down the pier. Unless you are a physiotherapist, don't impose exercise on others.

8. Don't tell arthritis sufferers to go and live in a hot, dry climate like Arizona. We know it might be easier on the joints, but some of us are very happy here with family and friends, and we don't want to be packed off like remittance men.

9. One time you shouldn't stay silent is when your favourite restaurants, theatres or galleries are difficult to access for a friend with arthritis. Before you turn your back on them, be sure to tell the owners or proprietors exactly why you will not be making a booking. You can be very polite and praising ('I hear such good things about your place'), but after the flattery should come the reason for regret ('Can I just confirm that there isn't a lift and that

the cloakrooms are up or down a flight of stairs?'). If enough people were to do this, it would not take long to improve facilities. If we don't tell the offenders, how will they know there's a problem?

10. Don't ever say, sadly, how tragic it is that nothing has been done for poor arthritis sufferers. Plenty is being done. Just contact Arthritis Ireland, or phone its new helpline. Then you will have an idea of how much is happening and you can be a true and informed friend rather than a false and frightening one.

WHAT'S IT LIKE TO HAVE A HOUSE FULL OF FILM CREW? LET ME TELL YOU ALL ABOUT IT

24 December 2010

Well, I did say from the very start that there was a problem. There was no extreme poverty in the tale, no family discord, no feuds, no emigration. Nothing to hang a good story on. But they said they knew all that and they still wanted to go ahead.

So Gordon and I had a working party on it and listed the arguments for and against. Against doing the whole thing were the fact that the story was too tame to hold people's interest and the fact that I love talking so much that once I get started I can't be stopped. And in favour of it was that it would be good to have something that would confound my enemies, but we couldn't think of any enemies we wanted to confound, so that one didn't really work. But also in favour of it was that we know Noel Pearson, whose company would be making it, and we knew it wouldn't be a dull and glum sort of thing.

I checked with my sister and brother to see whether they would be horrified by it all, and they said nonsense and I should go ahead. So I said yes, because I'm as easily flattered as the next person, and I thought it would be great to be made much of and for people to arrange flattering lighting and tell me they were ready for my close-up. And of course this was all at the end of the summer, when autumn seemed miles away.

But, the way things do, the day arrived. I met the director, Sinéad O'Brien; I actually knew her mother and her father and her grandmother. I wondered mildly was she old enough to be directing documentaries, but she assured me she was, so we got that out of the way early on.

And then, bit by bit, I met everyone else, the cameramen and the sound recordists, all of them cheerful, charming and hugely apologetic about the amount of gear they had to bring into the house. We were apologising equally for the smallness of the house, as we would reverse into the bathroom, climb over what seemed like gigantic metal trunks, and negotiate floors covered with thick cables.

The lights were so bright you could see everybody's nose hair and any other imperfection in the skin; but there was Make-Up to deal with that. There were never fewer than 12 people around, each one knowing exactly their role. Archives would be taking out my papers, borrowed on a daily basis from UCD library, and getting out old scrapbooks that I had totally forgotten. Continuity was making sure I was wearing the same dress to continue a conversation as I had been wearing to begin it the day before — people with clipboards who knew far more about me than I knew about myself. When I would say vaguely that something happened back in the 1960s or 1970s, they would actually know the date.

A gloom-ridden acquaintance told me I

would be demented from making them all tea. I want to put on record that no cup of tea was ever brewed in this house for the crew.

Magically, trays of sandwiches or little cakes appeared from Dalkey's cafés and food shops; cartons of good coffee were always available.

If they had been doing a documentary with a more able-bodied person there could have been great shots of me striding along the beach at White Rock or climbing Killiney Hill. I could have been down at Dalkey Island, talking to the porpoises and the seals.

But this wasn't on.

I find moving about very hard these days, so it all had to be done at home. I caught sight of myself on a monitor one day and almost forgot to talk, because I was in a kind of torpor, wondering why I hadn't gone on that diet I thought I was going to try, a diet that apparently puts hollows in your cheeks and makes your neck long and thin. I had even cut it out of a newspaper and filed it away carefully in a yellow file called 'Action This Day' last August and forgotten about it totally.

But otherwise I just talked and talked until I felt there wasn't one more word to say.

Any question I was asked I answered at immense length. I exhausted myself and them.

They reassured me and said that once the editor had got at it these monologues would look much more acceptable.

I dearly hope this is so.

Then I would hear tales of the days they interviewed other people: family, friends and colleagues. It wasn't that I was worried would these people tell any Awful Secrets, because, honestly, there aren't any Awful Secrets, but I hated them having to say nice things on order.

I wasn't allowed anywhere near all this filming, quite rightly, and I even had to leave the house when Gordon, my husband, was being interviewed, because they didn't want me staring at him beadily, willing him to say how wonderful I was and am.

And it all became a pleasant and entirely unreal routine.

Even the cats got used to the film people being here and came out of hiding to take part once they realised that there was no threat to their existence and that these people left every evening having tidied up the house to a much better degree than they had found it in.

And then it was over, from our point of

view anyway, and I sort of missed the huge vans drawing up outside the door, disgorging crates of equipment, and cheerful young people fitting things together and making cameras and lighting out of them as if they were children with building bricks. We used to look around our room that used to have 12 people in it, each one at some task, and now there was only us finishing breakfast, and the cats looking faintly bored that no cabaret was being put on for them today.

And then there came the whole dread feeling of self-doubt. Why had I brought this on us? We were fine as we were. What if people who had been interviewed were on the cutting-room floor? How could I ever meet their eye again? Nothing is any help. One man who tried to calm me down said that nobody will watch it anyway, because they'll all be asleep or drunk at that time on Christmas Day. Somehow that was not as reassuring as he had intended it to be.

Another friend said that it would be undemanding and that was the key word I must remember. Once people had got through a family meal and had all eaten far too much to digest, then something totally bland and undemanding was what they were looking for. And somehow that didn't entirely cheer me up either.

So what *did* I want? I suppose I wanted to acknowledge how lucky I had been in my life and that I had been dealt a great hand of cards. I didn't want it to sound smug or self-satisfied. That's not the way it feels inside, and I hope it doesn't come over like that. I suppose I wanted to thank my family and friends and all the great people I've met along the way — tell them how much I love them.

I didn't say it like that when I was faced with the lights and the cameras. But that's what I meant.

Will and Kate Show Is Testament to Abiding Allure of the Royals

30 April 2011

Well, everyone mellows a bit in 40 years. The edges blur. You see more innocence and hope and harmless lunacy than arrogance and triumphalism. It was a day when two people got married and two billion other people watched them. It was a day when millions dressed up, got over-excited and partied to celebrate young love.

And it wasn't all in England. A man from Eircom who came to sort out the broken-down broadband said that every house he had visited was glued to a television. It was on in the bank and the customers dawdled so that they could see more.

The streets and shops in Dalkey were emptier than on any other Friday. There were many households where ladies gathered, each wearing a hat and carrying a bottle. And why not? It was not a question of wanting to be English, nothing to do with losing our identity, changing our allegiance. It was all about watching a big, glittery show. A well-choreographed parade. With fine horses and gold carriages and flags and marching bands. If that's how you look at it then it's a morning well spent.

The best bit is that we know the cast. The Duke of Edinburgh, who always looks irritated and as if he's on the verge of imploding, looked just the same. But he is going to be 90 next birthday. He has a silly sort of sword, which would be handy to lean on, but he never uses it even though it's hanging from his waist. He walks upright on his own. Queen Elizabeth is 85 and well able to climb into a glass coach and leap out of it without assistance. These are sturdy people; Ruritania doesn't seem to have affected their stamina.

It was so different watching a royal wedding from my own home. For years, I have been going to Westminster Abbey or St Paul's Cathedral and climbing almighty scaffolding to get to a seat on the top of a specially constructed press section. I was at Prince William's parents' wedding and his aunt Anne's and his uncle Andrew's. Not a good fairy at the feast, I fear I brought them no luck. All three marriages ended in divorce.

In a way I wish I had been in London. I miss the magic of the English losing all their reserve, their fear of having a conversation with you in case you might go home with them. Street parties are so much the opposite of the British way of life, which is based on people keeping themselves to themselves. And yet when they did sit down they loved the chance to get to know their neighbours. I remember with great affection those parties at trestle tables with beer and cider and something roasted on a spit.

But hey, what do I know really? Everything's changed since I started being a royal wedding watcher in 1973. For William and Kate's wedding the guests arrived in buses as if they were going to a football match. Years back it was a long line of Bentleys. There was constant reference to the fact that the couple had lived together already for some years. At the time of Diana's wedding her uncle had to tell the world that she was a virgin. At those long-ago marriages Elton John and his partner David would not have been ushered politely into the Abbey. Nor would there have been a rake of red hats — one token Catholic would have covered it.

Of course it's not perfect. Hereditary power is never a good thing. But it's a lot better in a few decades than it used to be. Yes, they still made her change her name to Catherine. They didn't invite poor Fergie, who would have loved a day out. They left Tony Blair off the list. Tony who saved their bacon when Diana died.

But in the end, the bride was beautiful, the groom was handsome, the little pages and flower girls were adorable. It all went like clockwork. The somewhat tarnished image of royalty was forgotten for a day anyway.

Woody Allen always has a useful phrase. And when asked in a movie whether he was mellow, he replied, 'I'm so mellow I'm almost rotten.'

I know what he means. It's not a bad place to be.

■ ■ ■ ■

POSTSCRIPT

■ ■ ■ ■

'I Don't Have Any Regrets About Any Roads I Didn't Take . . .'

In conversation with Joanne Hunt,
3 July 2012

The great thing about getting older is that you become more mellow. Things aren't as black and white and you become much more tolerant. You can see the good in things much more easily, rather than getting enraged as you used to do when you were young.

I am much more understanding of people than I used to be when I was young — people were either villainous or wonderful. They were painted in very bright colours. The bad side of it, and there is a corollary to everything, is that when we get older, we fuss more. I used to despise people who fussed.

If I was going on a holiday, I'd just fling a few things into a suitcase and race out to the airport and not talk about it. Nowadays, if I'm going anywhere, the smallest journey, it has to be planned like the Normandy landing.

The relaxing bit is that you don't get as het up and annoyed and take offence as much as you used to.

Another good thing is that you value your friends more as you get older: you're not in any kind of competitive relationship with them any more, wishing to succeed or show off, or impress others.

You value people just for themselves. Unfortunately, as you get older, your friends die. It's that cliché of being afraid to look at the Christmas card list each year because of the people that have gone from it — that is a very sad and depressing thing.

I'm almost afraid to look at photos of my wedding now because so many people have died who were at it. You can't believe they are not all there in some part of the forest, still enjoying themselves.

I have more time certainly . . . and I'm more interested in everything. I'm interested in what other people are interested in, much more. However, you don't have enough energy to do things. It would be lovely to have the energy to do all the things I'm interested in now.

I think it's a balance: nobody has everything at the same time. When you are young, you have time and energy but you don't have any money.

When you get a job, you have energy and money but you don't have time.

And when you are older, you have time and you have money but you don't have enough energy. Nobody has all three together.

I think, as you get older, you do fewer unexpected things. You wouldn't head off somewhere not knowing how you were going to come back again. It's like going out to the middle of a frozen lake: you're always plotting your journey home before you set out somewhere.

I've found growing older most extraordinary. I thought inside you'd change and you'd start thinking like an old person, but I don't think inside I've changed at all. I've just become slightly more tolerant of everybody, which has to be good.

The best is Brenda Fricker's remark that when people of her age meet now they have something called 'the organ recital' where they go through all the organs that are not working. I think that's so funny.

So health is a nuisance and I was talking to a friend of mine and she said, 'Do you remember when we used to have conversations that didn't begin "When I was at the doctor . . ."?'

What did we do with our time when we weren't at the doctor? It does take up a disproportionate amount of your time, just the business of maintenance and keeping yourself together.

There are lots of things I wish I had done more of — studied harder, read more and been nicer and all those things — but I don't have any regrets about any roads I didn't take. Everything went well and I think that's been a help because I can look back, and I do get great pleasure out of looking back.

I get just as much of a laugh out of thinking of funny things from the old days as if they were last week.

I've been very lucky and I have a happy old age with good family and friends still around.

EDITOR'S ACKNOWLEDGMENTS

What struck me when I began trawling through the archives was the fact that Maeve arrived at *The Irish Times* in 1964 with a fully evolved writing voice. Whether writing about royalty or reporting from a warzone, her incomparable style was there from the beginning — intelligent, incisive, warm, conversational and witty. She was a one-off in the newspaper world which made selecting the pieces for *Maeve's Times* a real joy.

I was given invaluable help on this project by Maeve's great friend and colleague Mary Maher, who acted as Editorial Consultant. I'm also grateful for the help of Maeve's agent and friend Christine Green and Maeve's husband, Gordon Snell. Thanks to all of you.

At *The Irish Times,* thanks to deputy editor Denis Staunton who gave me this lovely job and to Irene Stevenson, librarian and

Maeve fan, who was a constant support. Thanks for putting up with my endless requests, Irene.

The unflappable Ciara Considine at Hachette Books Ireland pulled it all together beautifully — thanks a million, Ciara. Love and gratitude are also due to my mother, Ann Ingle, she knows why.

Finally, thanks to my journalistic hero Maeve Binchy for five decades of stunning service to *The Irish Times.* What a woman.

Róisín Ingle, The Irish Times

ABOUT THE AUTHOR

Maeve Binchy is the author of numerous best-selling books, including her most recent novels, *A Week in Winter, Minding Frankie, Heart and Soul* and *Whitethorn Woods,* in addition to *Night of Rain and Stars, Quentins, Scarlet Feather, Circle of Friends,* and *Tara Road,* which was an Oprah's Book Club selection. She has written for *Gourmet; O, The Oprah Magazine; Modern Maturity;* and *Good Housekeeping,* among other publications. She died in July 2012 at the age of seventy-two.